D0262403

A NIGHT AT THE MAJESTIC

A Night at the Majestic

*Proust and
the Great Modernist Dinner Party
of 1922*

RICHARD DAVENPORT-HINES

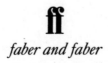

faber and faber

First published in 2006
by Faber and Faber Limited
3 Queen Square London WC1N 3AU

Photoset by Faber and Faber Ltd
Printed in England by Mackays of Chatham, plc

A CIP record for this book
is available from the British Library

ISBN 0–571–22008–8

2 4 6 8 10 9 7 5 3 1

Contents

For David Gelber and Peter Parker

So great a man he seems to me that thinking of him is like
thinking of a great empire falling.

THACKERAY ON SWIFT

People are always shouting that they want to create a better
future. It's not true. The future is an apathetic void of no interest to anyone. The past is full of life, eager to irritate us, provoke us and insult us, tempt us to destroy or repaint it. The
only reason people want to be masters of the future is to
change the past.

MILAN KUNDERA

There is only one thing that matters: to set a chime of words
tinkling in the minds of a few fastidious people.

LOGAN PEARSALL SMITH

Living? The servants will do that for us.

PHILIPPE-AUGUSTE VILLIERS DE L'ISLE-ADAM

Torn between the homosexual's terrible love
for forms, and his anarchic love of man.

ROBERT LOWELL

CHAPTER I

18 May 1922

It is a May evening in Paris in 1922. After several dismal, wet weeks the weather has turned warm and sunny. 'All the signs of real spring are here,' according to an Englishman in Paris. 'The café terraces are crowded, the fountains of La Place de la Concorde are spurting their columns of scintillating water exuberantly into the air, and the taxi-men have become more than usually reckless and even more profane to one another when they just miss a collision by inches.'

A supper party is being held in a private dining room at the Majestic, an *hôtel de luxe* in Avenue Kléber, one of the twelve avenues named after Napoleon's generals which radiate out from the Arc de Triomphe. A similar hotel to the Majestic had been described in a recent novel that was the talk of Paris at the time: its guests likened to the audience in a theatre, who find themselves enlisted as a cast of extras, adding colour and diversity to the spectacle in which they are caught up, 'as if the spectator's own life were unfolding amidst the sumptuousness of a stage-set'. Certainly, three years earlier, the Hôtel Majestic had been the stage for an international spectacle when it was taken over by the British delegation to the Versailles Peace Conference. There had been a perpetual stir of journalists hustling after stories and of secretaries scurrying about with papers. Diplomats from a score of countries had loitered in its spacious lobby. Vigilant-looking businessmen had tried to pull strings or jockey for advantages. So intense were the intrigues that British servants had temporarily replaced the regular hotel staff so as to reduce the risk of leaks and espionage. Augustus John and Sir William Orpen, the official painters to the British delegation during the Conference, stayed at the Majestic, and recorded the sumptuous scenes there. 'The Hôtel Majestic is a very lively place,' Sir Maurice Hankey, the Secretary of the British delegation, told his wife. 'All the most beautiful and well-dressed society ladies appear to have been brought over by the various Departments. I do not know how they do their work but in the evening they dance and sing and play bridge!' The ostentation of the evening parties shocked some British officials. 'The dance at the Majestic last night was an amazing affair – a most cosmopolitan crowd – the last touch was put on it when Lord Wimborne arrived with a crowd of wonderful ladies,' one member of the British delegation noted in 1919. 'People rather resent this invasion of the Majestic on Saturday nights, & steps are being taken to put a stop to it, otherwise the thing will become a scandal.'

This seething diplomatic intrigue was a phase of the Majestic's history which passed as quickly as French enthusiasm for President Woodrow Wilson, whose arrival in Paris in 1919 – a messenger of peace, supported by all the wealth of America – caused the greatest excitement since the state visit of Tsar Nicholas of Russia in 1896. The over-worked, high-minded British civil servants had to endure the Majestic's shocking pleasures for only six months before the hotel was restored to its usual guests to whom display, luxury and wonderful ladies never seemed scandalous.

The hosts of this supper party on 18 May 1922 are just such guests: a rich, cultivated and cosmopolitan English couple, Violet and Sydney Schiff. They have chosen to hold their party in the Majestic because the management of the Ritz would not permit music to be played after 12.30 at night: the Majestic, they know, vies in its splendours, comforts and cuisine with the Ritz. A vivid description of the Schiffs has been left by the novelist Stella Benson. 'Pretty elderly,' she wrote of Sydney Schiff in 1925, 'a jew [*sic*], with twisted yellow white moustache like an ex-colonel – very deaf but not irritable – very very attentive to everything that he hears – rather argumentative for the sake of arguing – too logical to hold a human view in argument. He has a wife, a placid and possibly stupid creature.' Later, in 1928, when Benson was entertained with Aldous Huxley by the Schiffs at the Gargoyle Club in London, Schiff seemed 'very human and eager, as ever – he makes almost a parade of being anti-art and pro-man in all things, and he loves youth and all modern symptoms.' Wyndham Lewis, who was first a protégé and then a tormentor of Sydney Schiff, showed less generosity a year or two later. He depicted Schiff as presenting the 'earnest mask of a beardless, but military-moustachioed, spectacled Dr Freud', walking with 'an alert dandified energetic shuffle', and behaving towards others with 'solemn, loyal-and-affectionate unction.' Violet Schiff, so Stella Benson found, was 'rather frosty to women, but she is evidently attractive to men since her husband so volubly adores her that she herself, without embarrassment or false humility, embroiders on his theme – herself.' Others were more affectionate about Violet Schiff. 'Her Jewish origins showed in her Biblical profile. The line of her hair rolled back from her brow, the high cheekbones and straight, strongly-bridged nose, and the sensitive modelling of the lips and chin suggested the feminine equivalent of some beautiful statue of Moses,' according to one of her younger admirers, Julian Fane. 'She liked,' he recalled, 'to discuss character and motive by the hour. The point of her talk was not only her relish in it, her wit, imagination, subtlety, the clarity of her analyses, and the aptness of her instances, but also its intimacy. She could draw references to herself and whoever she was with, and to general laws and truths, from the strangest anecdote.'

The 'great point in the Schiffs' favour,' according to their friend T. S. Eliot, was their capacity when entertaining 'of bringing very diverse people together and making them combine well'. Sydney Schiff prided himself on being a 'resourceful, dextrous and untiring host' who 'ordered and arranged everything in a handsome and convenient way'. His hospitality always seemed effortless and polished because he had the money to pay for the staff to proffer expert advice, anticipate his needs and deflect stressful worries. This Majestic evening was particularly unforgettable because Schiff had proposed to the impresario Serge Diaghilev to pay for a party at which some forty guests were invited to celebrate the first public performance of Stravinsky's burlesque ballet *Le Renard*, performed by Diaghilev's company, the Ballets Russes, and had then delegated its arrangements to the Russian. Diaghilev could muster for his productions all the greatest talents (both émigré and French) available in Paris, and had spared no pains to promote the success of the Paris Opéra evening. He had even arranged for *Le Figaro* to publish on its front page that morning 'Une lettre de Stravinski à Tchaïkovski', in which the composer offered a creative manifesto for Russian music. He was equally meticulous about the sequel: the supper-party was matchless, Schiff acknowledged, precisely because Diaghilev stage-managed the proceedings as if he was directing one of his own ballets.

Le Renard lasted twenty minutes, required four dancers, four singers and fourteen musicians, and was premièred that evening as the culmination of a programme of Schumann's *The Carnival*, Tchaikovsky's *Caisse-Noisette* (*The Nutcracker*) and *Le Mariage de la Belle au Bois Dormant* (*The Sleeping Beauty*), and Borodin's *Les Danses de Prince Igor*. The playfulness of *Le Renard* – with its mischievous, acrobatic dancing and simple yet challenging music – puzzled and even displeased those members of the audience who took their pleasures seriously, or wanted their Arts easily docketed and categorised. 'The first performance of the Ballets Russes in the season just opened at the Paris Opéra was of peculiar interest, because it will certainly give rise to polemics,' reported the Paris edition of the *New York Herald*. Although 'the greater part of its program was splendid', Stravinsky's quest for musical innovation was not judged enjoyable. 'He is going through a process of evolution which, however, is not likely to be followed easily by the public. For music must not be turned away from its real purpose, which is to please and charm the ear, and the ear is offended by a medley of tonalities, which form what is termed polytonal music. It seems like the noises in cadence made by negroes and not a work inspired by the heart to appeal to the heart. This first experiment by a musician of M. Stravinsky's rank was received politely. It was just as well, however, that the applause of his friends was not enthusiastic enough to provoke a counter-demonstration.' The distinguished composer and conductor André Messager had a similar reaction. He praised the earlier parts of the Ballets Russes programme on 18 May but felt 'truly embarrassed to speak of Stravinsky's *Renard* after a single audition'. It seemed to Messager 'a piece of buffoonery' with 'extremely odd' orchestral effects. 'Unfortunately, just as it's impossible to hear the singers, it is equally difficult to follow a comic action that only lived in the detail. Nevertheless, the ensemble is amusing and the music has ingenious novelty.' These ambivalent notices were not published in time to irritate Stravinsky or disappoint Diaghilev at the Majestic.

The audience at the première of *Le Renard* were jolted and provoked by some of Stravinsky's surprise effects; but the Schiffs' first-night party afterwards was even more memorable with its glittering guest-list. 'Kind Mr Schiff gave a supper-party in honour of Diaghileff after the first night of some ballet or other,' recalled the art critic Clive Bell, one of the few Englishmen present at the Majestic party. 'He invited forty or fifty guests, members of the ballet and friends of the ballet, painters, writers, dress-makers and ladies of fashion; but that on which he had set his heart was to assemble at his hospitable board – in an upper room at the Majestic – the four living men he most admired: Picasso, Stravinsky, Joyce and Proust.' The Schiffs' creative heroes – the painter, the composer and the novelists who were the foremost leaders of the Modernist movement – were acutely conscious of each other, and full of mutual curiosity and respect; but they cared supremely for their own ideas and for the progress of their own work. Always susceptible to well-informed admiration, they enjoyed being fêted at parties where the other guests' prestige felt like an apt tribute to their own importance. Indeed in 1922 they were reckoned by intelligent Parisians to be more important than politicians or manufacturers. Diaghilev's first productions of Stravinsky's ballets, the opening of Picasso's shows in Rue de la Boëtie, the week when *Ulysses* was published, the appearance of successive volumes of Proust's long novel, were dominant events in the city. This was despite the fact that the avant-garde movement's efforts were not directed at the unhappy majority whose lives were so strained by work and responsibilities that they only wanted Art to provide an anodyne, effortless form of escapist entertainment. Instead, Modernism's audience was the privileged minority whose circumstances enabled them to approach Art with an intelligent concentrated consciousness.

The work of the Schiffs' guests of honour impedes, confuses and distorts the readers' or viewers' perceptions: they set out to bewilder, challenge and enhance. It was for this reason that they were often reckoned as revolutionaries: the uproar which greeted the first performance by the Ballets Russes of Stravinsky's *Le sacre du printemps* (*The Rite of Spring*) in 1913 was a furious, fearful reaction against a perceived New Terror in the arts and politics. Yet in truth the consecrated leaders of Modernism entertained by the Schiffs were neither Decadents nor Nihilists: they detested the bogus feelings, specious opinions and general decrepitude of twentieth-century culture; they despised mediocre writers and artists who depended for their effects on conjuring tricks and cheap magic; they did not work in a state of self-induced or self-admiring delirium. Diaghilev, Stravinsky, Picasso and their *confrères* were not hell-bent on demolition, but worked instead at the renovation and strengthening of the artistic glories of the distant past – without, however, the mawkish idealism that produced the pastiche medievalism of the Victorians. They developed new ways to exploit very old sources. Two of the chief inspirations for Picasso's first and greatest Cubist painting, *Les demoiselles d'Avignon*, were exhibitions in Paris of prehistoric Iberian sculpture and of primitive African masks. Stravinsky reworked the ancient rites and barbaric dances of old Russia when he composed *Le sacre du printemps*. Of the two most important English-language publications of 1922, Joyce reworked Homer's *Odyssey* to create *Ulysses*; and when T. S. Eliot wrote *The Waste Land* he drew on the anthropology of vegetation ceremonies, the Grail Legend, Ezekiel, Marvell, Dante, Ovid, St Augustine, Jacobean playwrights and the Cumæan Sibyl.

In the spring of 1922 Modernism was about fifteen years old, and at its apogee. It had, arguably, been inaugurated in 1906–7 when Picasso began painting *Les demoiselles d'Avignon*. It had entered a more established phase in 1910 with the triumphantly successful first performance of Stravinsky's 45-minute-long ballet *L'oiseau de feu* (*The Firebird*) by the Ballets Russes at the Paris Opéra, and with the opening in London of the Post-Impressionist art show at the Grafton Galleries. It was in 1910, too, that Marinetti began bombarding Europe with his loud, violent lectures on Futurism (one of which was delivered in the Schiffs' London drawing-room). There were other dates and incidents that defined the epoch: the riotous Paris première of Stravinsky's *Le sacre du printemps* in 1913; the publication that same year of the first volume of Proust's great sequence of novels collectively entitled *À la recherche du temps perdu*; the opening of the Armory art show in New York City later in 1913; the début of Eliot's J. Alfred Prufrock in 1915; and in 1922 the publication of *Ulysses* and of *The Waste Land*.

Diaghilev was both the guest of honour and the master of ceremonies during this night at the Majestic. He was always a dominant figure at the first-night celebrations after his productions.
'His linen was immaculate, but his evening clothes sometimes
showed signs of wear', his friend Cyril Beaumont recalled. 'He
had a suave address, not unlike the bedside manner of a fashionable physician. His voice had a soft, caressing tone, infinitely seductive. His "*mon cher ami*", accompanied by an
affectionate touch of his hand on your wrist or forearm, was
irresistible. On the other hand, when cross, he could be brutal-
ly hurtful and arrogant, and no one could snub with more bit-
ing sarcasm. He always dressed his hair with a brilliantine
perfumed with almond blossom.' Bronislava Nijinska, who had
choreographed *Le Renard*, has also given a vivid account of
Diaghilev's appearance. 'He was broad-chested and had a big,
almost square head, slightly flabby cheeks, and a full lower lip.
In his big black eyes there was always a look of sadness, even
when he smiled. The expression on his face was at once menac-
ing and attractive – like a bulldog's.' The Schiffs' friend Osbert
Sitwell, too, thought Diaghilev resembled a hybrid animal: as
tall and burly as a bear, but with a badger's stripe of white in his
black hair. When preoccupied, Sitwell continued, Diaghilev's
massive head had an 'air of solemn pathos and listless fatality;
but this was quickly banished by the intense energy of his eyes,
as they came to life again, and as he gave his very charming
smile.'

Although the period from 1919 to 1923 marked 'the most brilliant years of the Ballet Russes', according to its conductor,
Ernest Ansermet, 'truly an extremely important period', at the
time of the Schiffs' party Diaghilev was recovering from a finan-

cially disastrous London season which had threatened even his resilience. He was keener than ever to ingratiate himself with rich patrons, and had recently been forced into a reconciliation with an American-born heiress whom he had previously spurned but whose support he now needed. Once Diaghilev had been netted by the Schiffs, there was little difficulty for them in catching Stravinsky and Picasso. Stravinsky had been composing for Diaghilev since 1909; Picasso had begun designing stage sets for the Ballets Russes in 1917, and had married one of its ballerinas. In Diaghilev's mind the two men were conjoined: reporting that Stravinsky had instructed that *Le Renard* should be 'performed by "clowns, acrobats, or dancers",' he commented, 'Stravinsky is often a musical acrobat, just as Picasso is a pictorial one.'

In May 1922 Igor Stravinsky was a few weeks short of his fortieth birthday. His three early ballets, *L'oiseau de feu* (1910), *Pétrouchka* (*Petrushka*) (1911) and *Le sacre du printemps* (1913), had all been commissioned by Diaghilev, and premièred by the Ballets Russes in Paris. Their exuberant novelty, violence and sophistication had proved his inventive genius. These early works were more indebted to Russian music and cultural traditions than he cared to acknowledge, but *Le Renard* (composed during his war-time exile in Switzerland) gave explicit homage to the traditions of old Russia. Cyril Beaumont has pictured him in the 1920s with his 'slender, stooping shoulders, egg-shaped head, big nose, straggling moustache, and globular eyes peering owlishly through horn-rimmed spectacles: he reminded one of a harassed headmaster.' Stravinsky's wife, weakened by years of tuberculosis, had acquiesced in his post-war affair with the Paris *couturier* Coco Chanel. This foundered after Chanel met Grand Duke Dmitri Pavlovich, Rasputin's murderer: the bad news was broken to Stravinsky by Diaghilev's closest woman friend, Misia Sert, who sneered that Chanel had only the mentality of a shop-girl who prefers grand dukes to artists. By May 1922 Stravinsky had reached an intense phase of his affair with Vera Sudeykin, the wife of a theatrical designer sometimes employed by Diaghilev. Their involvement was open and acknowledged; and when, shortly after the Majestic party, the Sudeykins parted, Stravinsky was free to enter his devoted, lifelong partnership with Vera. The late spring of 1922 was a liberating moment in Stravinsky's emotional life.

The physical presence of the Schiffs' third guest genius, Picasso, was always intense and commanding. He was short, stocky and tanned; in the 1920s his smooth dark hair, with a strand falling over his brow, added to his air of Napoleonic energy and ambition. At the Majestic party, Picasso is said to have 'exhibited his secret dandy soul by wearing a Catalan faixa wound above his eyes to upstage those dressed in white tie'. Picasso, who was abstemious and even faddish about food and drink, had long ceased to be a penniless Spaniard living in a Montmartre tenement. Apollinaire had in 1907 introduced him to Georges Braque, and during the next three years the two painters together invented the greatest visual innovation of the early twentieth century, Cubism. The ideas that resulted in Picasso's *Les demoiselles d'Avignon* and Braque's *Houses at L'Estaque* provided a new means of depicting space, volume and mass, and developed a new pictorial language, which synthesised multiple views of the same object. The commercial success of Cubism transformed Picasso from the leader of a small, obscure artistic faction into a public figure with extensive influence. A rich cast of rivals, sycophants, self-publicists, models, mistresses, dealers, collectors and critics had collected around him.

After Picasso was recruited by Diaghilev to design stage sets for the Ballets Russes, his creative ideas began to move from Cubism to natural form. Diaghilev's circle, moreover, had far more luxurious habits and veneered manners than the studios of Montmartre. Picasso settled into an elegant apartment, and became a lion to be captured by smart hostesses (such as Violet Schiff) and art-collecting *hommes du monde*. Artists and collectors alike recognised his worth. Ezra Pound extolled his genius: 'not merely knowledge of technique, or skill, it is intelligence and knowledge of life, of the whole of it, beauty, heaven, hell, sarcasm, every kind of whirlwind of force and emotion'. The Duchesse de Clermont-Tonnerre was 'not certain if Picasso is the greatest, but he is certainly the most astonishing and the most disconcerting of all the painters'. He seemed such a wonder that she used to tell herself, 'On the seventh day, God created Picasso.'

Madame Picasso was at the Majestic too. Picasso had met Olga Koklova, one of the lithe and beautiful Ballets Russes dancers working under Massine, in Rome in 1917. She was a colonel's daughter, who had been better educated than most of the troupe, and had preserved a decorous, even conventional, outlook. She withstood Picasso's attempted seduction, which is why, said Ernest Ansermet (who was staying in the same Rome hotel), 'Picasso finished by marrying her.' Their marriage, in August 1918, was a 'frivolous stunt', according to Picasso's confidential friend Max Jacob, the 'result of roguish twaddle'. In her dancing days Koklova had been supple and dark-haired, with a demure or even insipid expression, but after her pregnancy she became plump and almost dowdy. 'The first time I saw her,' said Alice Derain, 'I took her for a chambermaid; she was a plain little woman with freckles all over her face'. As the Picassos' marriage deteriorated after the birth of their son Paolo in 1921, Koklova became tetchy and sullen. Picasso reacted to her pressure to conform to bourgeois conventions by hanging a sign on his studio door announcing, '*Je ne suis pas un gentleman.*' Paolo's birth coincided with, or perhaps contributed to, a period of uncharacteristic creative quietude, but in May 1922 Picasso was again resurgent. Picasso, said his friend Cocteau, 'has eyes only for Picasso. I think he's a devil.'

It is impossible to name everyone at supper with the Schiffs, who did not send a guest-list for publication in *Le Figaro* or *Le Gaulois*, but leading members of the ballet company were certainly there. Foremost among these was Bronislava Nijinska, who had danced the title role in *Le Renard* and was responsible for its choreography, which pleased Stravinsky more than any other Ballets Russes production of his work in the 1920s except Balanchine's *Apollo*. A Russian of Polish ancestry, Nijinska was a dancer of exceptional gifts who, after the Russian Revolution, had become the first successful woman choreographer. She was the sister of the Russian dancer Vaslav Nijinsky, who had astounded pre-war audiences with his daring performances at the Ballets Russes premières of Stravinsky's innovative ballets *Pétrouchka* and *Le sacre du printemps*. Nijinska had fled from Soviet Russia in 1921 when she had received confirmation that her brother had succumbed to schizophrenia, and went to join him in the West. After a long, gruelling, clandestine journey from Kiev (accompanied by her elderly mother and two small children), she re-joined Diaghilev's company in Paris and was its sole choreographer until 1925. Nijinska's career was complicated by invidious comparisons to her brother (Diaghilev had been Nijinsky's infatuated lover before the war) and by a disagreeable prejudice about her looks. The balletomane Arnold Haskell's compliments were typical: 'she has much of the strength and elevation of her brother, his own particular attack. She is also the only ugly dancer to find fame, ugly but never in any sense plain.' Although Nijinska's choreography ultimately attained an outstanding influence on twentieth-century ballet, her successes with the Ballets Russes were achieved despite Diaghilev's ambivalence towards her. 'Poor Bronia' and her brother had been unsurpassable dancing together, Stravinsky thought; but after Nijinsky forsook Diaghilev and the Ballets Russes to marry Romola de Pulszky in 1913, the older man could not restrain his animosity against the remaining sister. 'She looked like Nijinsky, was shaped like him bodily, with the same big shoulders, and was a constant reminder of him,' Stravinsky recalled. 'It pained Diaghilev doubly that this person who dared to look like Nijinsky was a woman.' Nijinska's choreography for *Le Renard* was influenced by the circus acrobatics that she had seen as a child. Her Ballets Russes colleague Alexandre Benois reckoned her choreography was that of 'an artist of rare talent and wonderful critic'.

There were two conductors at the Paris Opéra that night. The Polish composer Grzegorz (Gregor) Fitelberg had conducted the opening pieces of the Ballets Russes evening. Fitelberg was an energetic organiser and impresario who enabled many young Polish composers to have their works performed, and later founded the National Polish Radio Symphony Orchestra.

He had been a mentor to the young pianist Artur Rubinstein, acting as his second in a duel fought in Warsaw, but was nevertheless mistrusted and disliked by his protégé. 'He put on grand, superior airs', according to Rubinstein. 'He was a broad-shouldered, strong man, though only of middle height, and he had thick, wavy black hair, a round, shaven face, and behind his eyeglasses a stern expression . . . Fitelberg was, without doubt, a good musician and a talented composer; but a ruthless character. Nothing was sacred to him; he would walk over dead bodies to reach his goal.' Very different in type was Ernest Ansermet, the Swiss who conducted *Le Renard* on 18 May, 'like an accomplished musician,' according to *Le Gaulois*. In Cyril Beaumont's words, 'tall and spare, with a pale face, high brow, luxuriant tapering beard, and magnetic eyes, he had a Svengali-like air. He was a dominating, energetic personality.' Ansermet was a former schoolmaster who taught himself conducting at concerts for English ladies taking afternoon tea in Montreux. He first met Stravinsky in 1911, and for many years the two men were intimate friends: once, in Paris, after drinking a whole bottle of Framboise together, Ansermet began barking like a dog under Stravinsky's piano. After their friendship chilled, Ansermet still valued his early memories of the Russian: 'always very lively, full of spirit, temperament, and working very hard'. Ansermet was committed to his art, and contemptuous of gossip. Asked by a New York journalist for a quotable anecdote on his career, he replied forcibly: 'Write in your article: this artist doesn't have any anecdotes, and it's that which typifies him.' Accordingly he left no account of the Schiffs' supper-party.

The Ballets Russes entourage also included the painter Michel Larionov, one of Diaghilev's most entrenched artistic collaborators, who had undertaken the décor and costumes for *Le Renard*. Larionov had a big head, with plump cheeks, which he had an aggressive way of pushing in other people's faces when he was arguing to gain a point. Stravinsky was delighted with Larionov's work on his burlesque ballet, and recalled him as 'a huge blond *muzhik* of a man, even bigger than Diaghilev – Larionov had an uncontrollable temper and once knocked Diaghilev down.' Alexandre Benois, a rival stage designer, who had worked with Diaghilev in the past, regarded Larionov as 'a very gifted artist, but one in whom a strange sterility is combined with a remarkable eagerness to show himself in the foreground'. Larionov was so lazy that it was suspected that his talented wife, Natalia Gontcharova, completed his work for him.

The four dancers in this first production of *Le Renard* were Nijinska as the Fox, Stanislas Iszikovsky as the Cock, Jean Jaswinsky as the Goat and Michel Feodorov as the Cat. All were guests of the Schiffs. The Pole Stanislas Idzikovsky was 'the greatest jumper', Stravinsky thought, 'after Nijinsky . . . and the greatest Petrushka.' Cyril Beaumont equally admired the strength and versatility of his dancing – and perhaps rather more than his dancing. 'Idzikowsky's thin, sallow features, short stature, and slight build gave an illusion of under-development. Only when he sat down did the ripple of muscles under his close-fitting trousers suggest that he might be stronger than he looked. When he was stripped he revealed an extraordinary muscular development.' The two other male dancers in *Le Renard* were less celebrated. Michel Feodorov, who remained loyal to the Ballets Russes until Diaghilev's death in 1929, subsequently hanged himself in Paris after his savings were stolen.

Jean Jaswinsky died in even deeper obscurity.

Other prominent Russian Ballet dancers, who had performed in the earlier parts of the 18 May programme, went on from the Opéra to the Majestic supper party – with especial gratitude for the food as they would not have eaten before performing. Pre-eminent among these were Vera Trefilova and Lubov Tcher-nicheva. Trefilova was a wonderful dancer who had been appointed ballerina on the same day as her school friend Anna Pavlova. She left the stage as a young woman, when she mar-ried; but was obliged by financial hardship to return to her old work on being widowed. The resumption of her dancing career proved difficult; but she was resolute and tenacious in re-estab-lishing herself. Small, slender yet muscular, with dark eyes and hair, but a pallid face, Trefilova was middle-aged by 1922 but still danced with perfect poise, lightness and timing. Everyone who knew her or saw her dance had similar admiration. 'Trefilova is quiet, deliberate, calm and infinitely methodical,' wrote Arnold Haskell, who was half in love with her. 'The sense of reserve power that is so great a feature of her dancing is there in life.'

The other ballerina Lubov Tchernicheva was, in Stravinsky's words, 'a beautiful Firebird Princess and a beautiful woman, too, who had infatuated Alfonso XIII and was the only woman who ever attracted Ravel.' The King of Spain, in other respects a philistine, was a fervent admirer of the Russian Ballet, and liked to attend rehearsals as well as every possible performance: he saved Diaghilev from financial disaster when their tour was caught up in the Portuguese Revolution of 1918. According to Ansermet, King Alfonso once teased Diaghilev: 'What is it then that you do in this troupe? You don't direct, you don't dance, you don't play the piano, what is it you do?' Diaghilev replied:

'Your Majesty, I am like you: I don't work, I don't do anything, but I am indispensable.' Tchernicheva, who was nicknamed Luba or Lubasha, was Nijinska's close friend. In 1909 she had married Sergei Leonidovitch Grigoriev, Diaghilev's formidable stage manager, and in 1911 she left the Imperial Theatre in St Petersburg to join Diaghilev's company. Her husband Grigoriev was doubtless at the Schiffs' party too. A tall, spectral figure, with terse speech and usually reticent manners, his responsibilities at the Ballets Russes were all-embracing: rehearsals, lighting, costumes, make-up, cues for the curtain to fall, understudies, artistic discipline, box-office arrangements and commercial business. He was methodical, punctual and carried everywhere a little notebook in which he recorded notes and aide-mémoires. When frustrated by other members of the ballet company, Grigoriev would yell, beat his brow with histrionic fury, and flourish his arms without ever intimidating anyone.

The brilliant young pianist Marcelle Meyer was another of the Schiffs' guests. She had enjoyed a prominent part in the musical avant-garde of Paris since 1917, when she had played the piano in some performances of Cocteau's *Parade*. At the end of that year, when, at the age of twenty, she married the physician, actor, singer and director Pierre Bertin, Cocteau and Picasso were among the wedding party. In the same year she met Erik Satie, who became a close friend, nicknamed her Dadame and dedicated his 'First Nocturne' to her. She was Satie's piano accompanist when he played his *Morceaux en forme de poire* at a Dadaist happening, the Soirée du Coeur à Barbe, organised by Tristan Tzara in 1923. It was at this event that André Breton slapped Jacques Baron's face and struck a young music critic with a walking-stick before being ejected by the police amidst

shouts of 'Murderer!' Meyer was a close friend of Max Jacob and
an active participant in the musical agenda of the Groupe des
Six. Le Groupe des Six was an epithet coined in 1920 to denote
six avant-garde young composers (Georges Auric, Darius Milhaud, Francis Poulenc, Germaine Tailleferre, Arthur Honegger
and Louis Durey) who were all influenced by Satie, hostile to
Debussy and opposed to Wagner. Their compositions – drawing on the music of circuses, music-halls, jazz clubs and fair-
grounds – were championed by Cocteau among others: several
of them collaborated with the Ballets Russes, and Poulenc's *Les
Biches* of 1924 was commissioned by Diaghilev. Marcelle Meyer
was at the heart of this network of creative originality and heartfelt friendship: indeed she was included at the centre of Jacques-
Émile Blanche's famous 1923 painting of the Groupe des Six
which is now in the Musée des Beaux-Arts at Rouen. Meyer was
trusted and admired by Ravel, Massine, Diaghilev, Stravinsky:
Poulenc called her a 'great pianist'. Her career, however, did not
develop as brilliantly at her gifts deserved, partly from an excess
of modesty, and partly from her preference for pieces by Satie
and Stravinsky rather than Liszt or Chopin.

Another pianist, Léon Delafosse, was also invited by the
Schiffs. Delafosse had been a protégé of Violet Schiff's mother
when he visited London to give piano recitals in 1904, and Violet was always assiduous in maintaining her family's cosmopolitan network of musical friendships. Delafosse had been born in
1874, the only child of elderly parents, and from infancy was
trained in music by his doting mother. He gave his first piano
recital at the age of seven, won first prize at the Conservatoire
aged thirteen and became a minor composer; but since his
death in the 1950s his name is only recalled for its literary asso-

ciations. In 1894 he was living with his mother in a gloomy apartment dominated by a rosewood grand piano resembling (said a visitor) 'a dolmen stained by the glistening, blackened blood of the victims of public concerts'. He was an ambitious blond, with piercing blue eyes, who desperately needed a rich patron to protect his career. A young man-about-town called Marcel Proust obligingly introduced Delafosse to a rich aesthete, Comte Robert de Montesquiou, who became the pianist's patron. When Delafosse played, the Count wrote, his 'little face, with its silly laugh, became transfigured by superhuman beauty and invaded by sublime power (until it assumed the pallor and expression of death)'; but their relationship was fraught, and eventually Montesquiou repudiated Delafosse: '*Arrivistes*,' he declared, 'not only do not arrive but they never get started.' Subsequently Delafosse strove to ingratiate himself with Diaghilev's pre-war patron, the Marchioness of Ripon: it was during one of his visits to Edwardian London that he was introduced to the musical salon of Violet Schiff's mother, Zillah Beddington.

Sir Charles Mendl, another guest at the Majestic, was also an old London friend of the Beddingtons. He had been trained (like Violet Schiff) by an expensive singing teacher, and sang French and English songs, as well as German lieder, in a velvety baritone voice; but his distinguished position in Paris society depended on his successes as an international fixer. Mendl had been an importer of Romanian grain before settling in Paris in 1912 as the financial representative of several South American railway companies. After proving his usefulness to British officials during the war, Mendl was appointed as special attaché at the British Embassy, handling international journalists during the Peace Conference in 1919. Afterwards he served five British ambassadors as press attaché in Paris. With wide contacts in the worlds of business, politics, journalism and the arts, he brought together apparently incompatible guests at small, sumptuous luncheon parties held at his apartment in Avenue Montaigne. A contented and comfortable bachelor, with all the tact, good-will and moderation of a man-about-town, in late middle age he married an elderly American interior decorator named Elsie de Wolfe. 'I must have someone to look after the cellar,' she said of him, though it was his title that was a stronger attraction. Elsie de Wolfe had been a professional actress, living with Bessie Marbury, a leading New York theatrical agent, before becoming the US's first professional woman interior decorator. She and Marbury acquired the Villa Trianon at Versailles in 1903, and thereafter spent much of their time in France. De Wolfe was one of the first women to accompany Wilbur Wright on a flight in 1908, befriended Diaghilev and Cole Porter, started the fashion among older women for blue-tinted hair and was celebrated for performing headstands at an advanced age. After escaping from France in 1940, Mendl lived with De Wolfe in Beverly Hills, where he appeared in several Hollywood films.

A second English guest was the art critic Clive Bell, who had in 1907 married Vanessa Stephen, the sister of Virginia Woolf, and subsequently became a central figure in the Bloomsbury Group. A regular visitor to Paris from his youth, it was there that he had amassed exhibits for the crucially influential Post-Impressionist exhibition held at the Grafton Gallery in London in 1910. When sober he could make shrewd and just appraisals of early twentieth-century Modernism, but in party mood he could be less discriminating. There was an evening at a fashionable night-club, Le Bœuf Sur Le Toit, when Bell, 'too far advanced in [his] cups, beflowered [Picasso] with sugary compliments', and as an onlooker described, was rewarded with a basilisk glare from the painter. He combined critical austerity with a taste for flirtation and frivolity. 'Clive has taken to high society,' Virginia Woolf gossiped to a friend in 1922. 'He's a raging success, and his *bon mots* are quoted by lovely but incredibly silly ladies.' His manners, she thought, had suddenly become 'loud, familiar and dashing'. This is too grudging about such a gregarious, grateful guest who seldom failed to gladden his companions with his infectious social glee.

Clive Bell, alas, never named the 'ladies of fashion' with whom he had supper at the Majestic, but their identities can be surmised. Princesse Edmond de Polignac had in 1916 commissioned Stravinsky to write an orchestral piece for performance by a small ensemble, which emerged as the burlesque, semi-acrobatic short ballet called *Le Renard*. The princess had also recently come to Diaghilev's financial aid after a period of coolness caused by his jealousy of her influence over Stravinsky. She had been born Winaretta Singer, in Yonkers, New York, in 1865, the daughter of the inventor of the Singer sewing machine. Her widowed mother's marriage to a Luxembourgeois duke had propelled the adolescent Winaretta into the higher altitudes of European nobility during the 1880s. Despite the annulment of her early marriage to Prince Louis de Scey-Montbéliard, apparently because as a lesbian she declined to consummate it, she was accepted in Paris society, where ultimately she was nicknamed Tante Winnie. Comte Robert de Montesquiou and Comtesse Greffulhe encouraged her in 1893 to contract a *mariage de convenance* with the elderly music-loving homosexual

Prince Edmond de Polignac. It proved the happiest of arrangements. Later, when their friend Marcel Proust sought her permission to dedicate *À l'ombre des jeunes filles en fleurs* to the
memory of her husband, she withheld her consent, acting with
the immovable composure, emotional caution and social discretion that always characterised her. Although the Princess had
some racy connections – Colette was a friend, and her brother
Paris Singer fathered Isadora Duncan's son, who was drowned
in 1913 – her lesbianism was never scandalous, although it titil-
lated gossip-mongers. 'She looked like Dante, and was very
masculine and imposing, rumoured to be fond of whipping
young women,' Stravinsky said ungenerously of his generous
patron. The Duchesse de Clermont-Tonnerre agreed about
Dante: the Princess's appearance, she wrote, 'combined the hard
skeletal boniness of Dante as painted by Giotto with that of an
Indian from Milwaukee. With her the dry Anglo-Saxon
humour reigned instead of French glibness.' Music was always
the Princess's consuming interest. She befriended Fauré, from
whom she commissioned musical compositions to Verlaine's
words, and was the patroness of Debussy, Satie and Stravinsky.
The preliminaries of Diaghilev's momentous Russian musical
season of 1909 were held in the large music room of her house
on Avenue Henri-Martin. Her generosity to composers and to
the Ballets Russes prompted Jean Marnold to call her a 'munificent Princess Maecenas'. Ravel dedicated to her *Pavane pour
une Infante défunte* (*Pavane for a Dead Infanta*), which was
played by Proust's wish during his funeral.

The Duchesse de Clermont-Tonnerre was possibly also invited to the Majestic at Diaghilev's instigation. Like Princesse
Edmond de Polignac, she was far from being an insipid, artifi-

cial Society woman. Avant-gardiste, epicurean, writer, traveller,
sculptor and librettist, she knew all the guests of honour, and
afterwards described the party with confident familiarity. Elisabeth de Gramont had been born in 1875, and at the age of twen-
ty-one married Philibert de Clermont-Tonnerre, a duke who
beat her so badly that she suffered two late miscarriages. They
were eventually divorced after her decision that her sexual preference was for women, and she underwent a form of marriage
ceremony with the American-writer-in-Paris Natalie Clifford
Barney. 'The Duchess is a delicious being, interested in everything; and how she does love life!' wrote the former courtesan
Liane de Pougy, with whom the Duchess was having an ardent
affair at the time of the Schiffs' party. 'Lily', as she was usually
called, was shrewd, honest and kind: she is memorable as one of
the earliest French admirers of *The Waste Land*, which was published a few months later in 1922. Her massive range of human
contacts and breadth of culture are exemplified by that passage
in her memoirs in which she authoritatively compared her
friend Marcel Proust's character Albertine with the Lady Chat-
terley of her acquaintance D. H. Lawrence. Altogether she was
a woman of conflicting propensities: a Communist sympathiser
who in 1922 visited Austria to buy platinum and jewels on the
cheap for profitable re-sale in Paris; an avant-gardiste who wrote
four poignant volumes of memoirs about late nineteenth- and
early twentieth-century Paris society. She translated Keats's
poetry into French, was an acknowledged expert on Mallarmé
and commissioned Honegger to compose his ballet *Rose de
métal* from an idea of Robert de Montesquiou's (about whose
friendship with Proust she wrote a perceptive book). Her ances-
tor Epicurus and her lover Natalie Barney shared the dedication

of her *Almanach des Bonnes Choses de France* (*The Almanac of the Good Things of France*) – 'a jewel of a book, sensual, enlightened, even erudite, and above all full of poetry', as one of her readers recorded.

The Polignacs, the Gramonts, the Beauvau-Craons and the Clermont-Tonnerres, the *ancien régime* dynasties to which these two women belonged, had little in common with the great bulk of French provincial nobility, who lived quietly on their estates, hunted, played sports and looked askance at Paris. For the backwoodsmen, in their scattered and sometimes remote demesnes, the capital of the Third Republic was a political bordello, full of venal politicians, scurrilous journalists and fraudulent financiers. Its social life was characterised by repulsive ostentation, they thought, and degraded by accommodating those upstart nobility whose titles had been created by Napoleon I or Napoleon III: accordingly it was a place to be hated like poison. The provincial nobility's one common point with those surviving families of the *ancien régime* who were still rich enough to maintain great houses in Faubourg Saint-Germain or Faubourg Saint-Honoré, and who entertained lavishly during the Paris season, was that after the failure of moves towards a royalist restoration in 1873–4 they spurned the sordid middle-class world of party politics. The provincial nobility and the prominent *ancien régime* survivors in Paris alike put their energies into army life, into hunting and racing, and into maintaining their local social prestige; but they disdained to chase after political power, or deal with republican politicos who seemed to them foxy, vain, vacillating, pompous and boring. In consequence they were – mainly by choice – the most disempowered nobility in Europe. Many of them were suspicious, ignorant and philistine; but equally, among the 'smart' women as well as 'smart' men who gravitated to Paris, there were conspicuous individuals like Princesse de Polignac, Comte Étienne de Beaumont, Comte Gabriel de la Rochefoucauld and the Duchesse de Clermont-Tonnerre who were well-informed about the arts, discerning and discriminating in their tastes, and receptive to contemporary trends. They used their privileges to share in the excitement of creative originality rather than participate in the turmoil of power politics. This choice was a matter of self-respect, of family pride and of good taste: the tarnished record of the inter-war period further entrenched their general determination to boycott the Third Republic.

The eclectic guest-list on the night of 18 May 1922 was typical of the Schiffs: they were eager and receptive artistic amateurs, with a real zest for creative novelty in all the arts. Both were intensely musical: they had first met in an opera house; the opera singer Paolo Tosti had been a witness at their wedding. Violet, indeed, had grown up in a house with a piano on every floor, and as an older woman made a record singing delightful French and Italian songs in her 'warm contralto' voice. In one of these private recordings she sang a setting by Diaghilev's sometime collaborator Reynaldo Hahn of Verlaine's poem 'Voici des Fruits'.

Violet Schiff seems to have invited the leader of the English Vorticist movement, Wyndham Lewis, or at least to have told him that she wished he had been among their guests. Lewis's magazine *The Tyro* had been subsidised by Sydney Schiff, who had also commissioned him to sketch Violet; so Lewis tried to reply politely from his London garret, though he could not wholly restrain his resentful rage against other artists. 'I should have enjoyed being there with you for your day, but that has not been possible,' he told her, before dismissing Diaghilev, Stravin-sky and the other Modernist leaders as 'not [a] pleasant group'. It was as well that so uncouth and irate a man as Lewis could not attend the Schiffs' party; for it was tense and confusing enough without his disruptive rancour.

Long after midnight the Schiffs' guests sat down to supper. The celebratory champagne continued to be served after the last plates had been cleared by a dozen or more discreet and punc-tilious waiters dressed in the hotel's livery: Schiff preferred champagne above all other wines, and drank it copiously. As befitted a late-night, after-theatre supper, the food was not heavy. Schiff and the chefs of the Majestic wanted to compli-ment the many Russian exiles who were among the guests by providing Russian hors d'oeuvres, caviar and other light delica-cies from their homeland. A light fish course, such as sole Waleska with its delicate sauce and almost imperceptible flavour of cheese, or a light meat course, such as noisettes of lamb with green beans, were requisite. But Schiff was so zealous an admir-er of Proust's *À la recherche du temps perdu*, which contains so many lingering evocations of taste and smell, that he tried to turn the details and nuances of Proust's narrative into actuality in his own life. As a result Schiff shared the novelist's *penchant* for asparagus – a vegetable which Proust had beautifully and playfully described in his book – which was in season at the time of the party. Suitable choices of meat for Proustians includ-ed a leg of mutton with *béarnaise* sauce (an egg and butter sauce flavoured with shallots, tarragon and chervil); *boeuf à la gelée* (spiced beef and carrots in aspic composed of best rump steak, shins of beef, calves' feet); and chicken *financière* (a tomato-based brown sauce flavoured with Madeira and garnished with seasoned meatballs, chicken kidneys, truffles, mushroom caps and green olives). Lobster *à l'américaine* (cooked with tomatoes, cognac and white wine) might be rather rich; but red mullet, or brill cooked in a white butter sauce, would surely please Proustians with a taste for fish. And for dessert there was no end of Proustian possibilities: pineapple and truffle salad; Nesselrode pudding (a creamy chestnut cake, coated with vanilla ice-cream and flavoured with kirsch); almond cake; coffee-and-pistachio ice cream; and strawberry mousse. As to the savouries, one of Proust's characters had a foible for *croque-monsieur* (cheese on toast) with a dish of creamed eggs.

About coffee time, after the food has been cleared, a shabby, confused, blundering man appeared amidst the elegantly dressed throng. 'He seemed far from well,' Clive Bell recalled. 'Certainly he was in no mood for supper. But a chair was set for him on our host's right, and there he remained speechless with his head in his hands and a glass of champagne in front of him. Between two or three o'clock appeared, to most people's surprise I imagine, a small dapper figure, not "dressed" to be sure, but clad in exquisite black with white kid gloves.' The previous guest had entered the room with anxious clumsiness: the new arrival was poised, and entered with an insinuating air. The seedy drunk was James Joyce; the dapper late-comer was Marcel Proust; and this was to be their only meeting. Bell enjoyed re-telling the story. 'At half-past two in the morning up popped Proust, white gloves and all, for all the world as though he had seen a light in a friend's window and had just come up on the chance of finding him awake. Physically he did not please me, being altogether too sleek and dank and plastered: his eyes were glorious however.'

Joyce, who had arrived late because he had no evening clothes and had got drunk to cover his nervousness, had first met the Schiffs while giving readings from the manuscript of *Ulysses* in Adrienne Monnier's Paris book-shop, the Maison des Amis des Livres, in 1920 or 1921. On several occasions he lunched at the Schiffs' London house, perhaps in August and September 1922, when he visited London to consult ophthalmologists about his deteriorating eyesight, or in the summer of the following year. Joyce had rather formal manners, Violet Schiff recalled, and seemed thoroughly civil. When he saw the piano in her Cambridge Square drawing room, he asked if he might sing, and to her accompaniment, sang several songs by Schubert in a pleasant, melodious voice: the effect, she thought, was charming.

Schiff had not issued a formal invitation to Proust because of the novelist's notorious reluctance to leave his bedroom, but a few days earlier, in a letter, he had delicately alluded to the party he was giving. It was Proust's first outing since the evening a fortnight earlier when he had scorched his throat by swallowing too much undiluted adrenalin to invigorate himself for an earlier rendezvous with the Schiffs. It was a great compliment to the English couple – and an eloquent affirmation of his devotion to them – that he appeared at their Ballets Russes party. In May 1922 Proust was at the height of his fame: his sequence of books entitled *À la recherche du temps perdu* was generally acknowledged as the apotheosis of the French novel. Although these volumes undeniably constituted a great work of literature, it seemed debatable whether they constituted a novel, a fictive autobiography, the history of a personal vocation served with selfless dedication, or a version of Saint-Simon's memoirs set in *la belle époque*. Proust, it was agreed, had evolved his own distinctive literary style: his prose, with its long, sinuous convolutions, was radiant, voluptuous and mesmerising – indeed the height of sophistication – yet no writer was more responsive to the taste and smell and sound and sight of everyday things: indeed his sequence hinged on a rapturous moment of involuntary recall provoked by its narrator dipping his *madeleine* in a cup of lime tea. This narrator was an oddity too: at times self-immured in a disassociated, hermetic vacuum; and at other times pitched into wild emotional turbulence, intolerable obsessions and hyper-sensitivity. Proust was half-Jewish, ferociously intelligent and above all things a moralist. The grandson of a provincial grocer, he had until middle age no reputation except as a pampered and futile Parisian social-climber: 'Proust of the Ritz, do you mean?' a well-informed man had asked incredulously when told in 1913 that a man called Proust had just published rather a good first novel. Ruthless in pursuing his creative destiny, desperate to perpetuate the memory of his name after his death, Proust used the people he met as ingredients for his great concoction: wooing them, flattering them, cajoling them and harassing them until they had served his purpose. Then he discarded them as a cook jettisons the dry rind of a squeezed lemon.

Joyce said that Proust entered the Schiffs' *salon privé*, still wearing his fur coat, looking 'like the hero of *The Sorrows of Satan*'. The Frenchman's arrival at musical parties was indeed always conspicuous. The Duchesse de Clermont-Tonnerre watched him at the entertainment given by the Marquise de Ludre-Frolois in 1918 (an event made memorable for Proust because he was afterwards caught in an air-raid): 'He entered blinking like a night-bird, he looked at the assembly with the

astonishment of a convalescent who resumes his life, he scrutinised the corners and recesses of the room, and after a few
moments sat near me. "I don't know anyone. Who is that
shrewish woman? And who's that one? And that one?"' Proust
sometimes made people feel squeamish when he was first introduced to them. Prince Antoine Bibesco recalled his first impression of Proust at their earliest meeting: 'an abundance of brown
hair, a very pale face, and eyes like Japanese lacquer. He offered
me his hand. There are many ways of shaking hands. It is not
too much to say that it is an art. He was not good at it. His hand
was soft and drooping . . . There was nothing pleasant about the
way he performed the action.' When Bibesco knew Proust better, he tried to teach him how one ought to shake hands firmly,
with a strong clasp. 'If I followed your example,' he objected,
'people would take me for an invert.'

Proust was drawn to the Majestic by his affection for the
Schiffs; but large, mixed events had been increasingly to his
taste since 1910. 'As I never go out,' he had written a decade earlier, 'I prefer to "intimate" re-unions great "slaughters", where in
the surging crowd one can glimpse a face that one can dream
about long afterwards.' He retained the same preference to the
end of his life in 1922: 'Nothing amuses me less than what was
called, twenty years ago, "select". What does amuse me are the
many parties and mêlées which are like fire-work displays.'
While he preferred the Ritz Hotel to the Majestic, he had
recently complained that its rooms were as 'horrible' in appearance as the 'hovel' in which he lived, a fifth-floor apartment at
44 Rue Hamelin, a street that runs south-east from Avenue
Kléber towards Place d'Iéna and the Seine: Proust's building
(now the Hôtel Élysée Union) was only one block away from

the Majestic (itself renamed the Hôtel Raphaël some seventy years after the Schiffs' party). Proust not only preferred large brawling parties, but often eluded efforts to lure him into attendance at select celebrity events. At about this time Cécile Sorel decided to introduce him to Max Jacob, and enlisted the help of Proust's close friend Lucien Daudet, who opened elaborate and protracted negotiations: eventually they agreed to congregate at a smart night-club called Le Jardin de ma Soeur. 'I can see our table,' Poulenc said thirty years later, 'with Sorel crowned with feathers and literally bound up in a string of pearls, Lucien phlegmatic and very spruce, Jacques Porel, Réjanne's witty son, the master of ceremonies on this occasion, Georges Auric and me, astonished and delighted, and Max wearing a frock coat with velvet collar that made him look like a provincial schoolmaster.' Despite Daudet's pertinacity, Proust telephoned from the Ritz to say he was too exhausted to join them as he had promised.

People with great dignity, or world-wide reputations, are often pitchforked into absurd or fraught situations. When Diaghilev in his youth had visited Tolstoy, the old novelist had shown his picture gallery by the light of a big lantern, and then asked his visitor if he played draughts. According to Stravinsky, Diaghilev knew nothing of the game, but said he did, and then humiliated himself by making all the wrong moves. Finally Tolstoy stopped the farce. 'Young man, you should have told the truth right away; now go upstairs and take tea.' On another occasion, Charlie Chaplin held a dinner party to which he invited Albert Einstein, Mary Pickford, Douglas Fairbanks, William Randolph Hearst and the newspaper tycoon's winsome mistress Marion Davies. As the evening progressed, there was a 'slow freeze-up' between Einstein and Hearst until neither would say a word. 'The dining-room became charged with an ominous silence,' Chaplin recalled, until Marion Davies decided to vamp Einstein. 'Hello!' she said, turning and twiddling her fingers through his white mane, 'Why don't you get your hair cut?'

Mismatched guests can, though, succeed in charming one another if they are not too competitive. Duncan Fallowell gave a famously successful lunch in Knightsbridge at which his three guests – Joan Collins, Quentin Crisp and Arnold Schwarzenegger – delighted each other; and twenty years before the Majestic supper, at the height of the ferocious disagreements surrounding the Dreyfus Affair, Proust had given a dinner to which he invited some of the most bitterly opposed partisans from both sides. One of the guests, Léon Daudet, expected 'every piece of china to be smashed', and was astonished at 'the currents of understanding and benevolence originating in Marcel that flowed about the guests and enveloped them in coils'. When Daudet complimented Proust as his host, the latter produced a deprecating explanation: 'Really, monsieur, it all depends on the first reaction to each other of the different characters.'

The first reaction to Proust's arrival in the Majestic supper room was inauspicious. One of the Schiffs' guests was a fashionable lady of economical habits who underpaid her footmen and discharged them at the end of every season to avoid paying them when her Paris house was closed up: she also suspected that Proust had based a parsimonious character in his novel on herself. Schiff, who had recently regaled Proust with servants' gossip that the Princesse Violette Murat was so strapped for cash that she could only manage to pay her lady's maid on a day-to-day basis, indicated that the fashionable lady darted a look like an armoury of daggers at Proust when he arrived and left the party swiftly.

From the outset Proust was watched by his fellow guests – notably by his keen and observant English admirer, Clive Bell. In 1919 a woman friend had given Bell a copy of *Du côté de chez Swann*. 'She had fallen in love with the book and through the book with the author – as ladies will; and I, instead of feeling grateful for having been brought acquainted with a masterpiece, felt jealous – as men will. I began reading *Swann*, not in the hope of a new experience, but with a view to picking holes in a rival.' His cantankerous mood was soon superseded by rapture. 'I went down before the revelation and wallowed,' Bell wrote. 'Here were the memoirs of my age.' Thereafter he was a dedicated Proustian. 'Each new volume became an emotional event and the vagaries of his creatures matter for conversation, letters, post-cards, telephonings, telegrams even. The book with its moods lived on through ours – gay, agitated, intense, cynical: not only did everything about it become of consequence, everything about the author became interesting.'

Proust was flustered by the snub delivered by the fashionable but departing lady – would have been especially upset if she was, indeed, a duchess, as Schiff hinted – and blundered when he first began to talk with Stravinsky. Stravinsky's recollection of their exchanges was substantially accurate, although he misremembered some details: he thought, for example, that the hostess of the party after the première of *Le Renard* had been Princesse Violette Murat. 'Most of the guests had come directly from my première at the Grand Opéra, but Marcel Proust arrived from his bed at the Ritz, getting up as usual late in the evening. Elegantly dressed, wearing gloves and a cane, he was as pale as a mid-afternoon moon. I remember that he spoke ecstatically about the late Beethoven quartets, an enthusiasm I would have shared if it had not been a commonplace among the *literati* of the time, not a musical judgement but a pose. James Joyce was there that night too, but in my ignorance I did not recognise him.' Clive Bell confirmed Stravinsky's account. Proust, who was given a chair between Sydney Schiff and Stravinsky, tried to be 'infinitely gracious', but unfortunately 'in paying Stravinsky a compliment he paid Beethoven a better'. In Bell's version, '"Doubtless you admire Beethoven", he began. "I detest Beethoven" was all he got for answer. "But, *cher maître*, surely those late sonatas and quartets . . .?" "Pires que les autres," growled Stravinsky. Ansermet intervened in an attempt to keep the peace; there was no row but the situation was tense.'

Proust's questioning of Stravinsky about the Beethoven quartets may have been tactless at a moment when the composer was still excited by the première of a new work of his own, but it was not fatuous. Stravinsky had been paid to write *Le Renard* by Princesse Edmond de Polignac, in whose house it had first been privately performed; it was in her musical salon, too, that the taste for playing Beethoven's late quartets had been revived. Proust (who had often attended the princess's musical evenings) associated her as much with the championing of these quartets as with the commissioning of *Le Renard*. His conversational gambit was therefore not inappropriate, although the princess's biographer suggests that she would have been horrified by Proust's remarks to Stravinsky, if she overheard them, for they gave the impression that he was a 'musical snob'. Proust's enthusiasm for the quartets was sincere: after hearing them played in the Salle Pleyel, he poured out his 'rich impressions and

thoughts' to the violinist Lucien Capet, who had been the conductor. 'Capet had never heard equal appreciation of
Beethoven's genius and soul', though he may have been less
pleased when Proust later telephoned at three in the morning to
discuss Debussy's quartets.

Proust, who in *Sodome et Gomorrhe* had recently extolled the
'prodigious efflorescence of the Ballets Russes' coupled with
Stravinsky's 'genius', had met the composer before. In 1913 he
had attended the notoriously rowdy première of Stravinsky's *Le
sacre du printemps*, and afterwards a supper party given by
Diaghilev's friend Misia Sert, the model for Princesse
Yourbeletieff in *Temps perdu*, where the other guests included
Stravinsky, Cocteau and Léon Yeatman. 'The Russian ballet,
supper at your house,' Proust wrote to his hostess, 'bring back
to life so many cherished memories and make one almost
believe in a recurrence of happiness.' In his novel he commemorated and transmuted Misia Sert's party into an 'exquisite supper' given by his repulsive character Madame Verdurin under
Princess Yourbeletieff's auspices. The guests of honour comprised the dancers, their director, Stravinsky and his fellow composer Richard Strauss. The assembled fashionable Paris ladies
and foreign royalties were 'enchanted to see close up the great
revivers of theatrical taste who in an art that is perhaps more
contrived than painting has created a revolution as profound as
Impressionism itself.'

In addition to Stravinsky, Proust already knew and admired
Diaghilev and Picasso. In 1910 Proust had twice attended
Diaghilev's productions, and later alluded in *Temps perdu* to this
season of 1910 as a 'charming invasion, against whose seductions
only the critics who were devoid of taste protested, [and which]

aroused Paris . . . with a fever of curiosity that was less bitter, more purely aesthetic, but perhaps quite as intense as the Dreyfus Affair.' In subsequent years Proust was regaled with news about Diaghilev's company and methods from his intimate friend Reynaldo Hahn. Though Proust appreciated Diaghilev's company, he proved indifferent to a production of *Pétroushka*, with decor by Benois, which he saw at the Théâtre du Châtelet in 1917. He also attended the Ballets Russes' première of Stravinsky's *Chant du rossignol* in 1920. There was a double-edged compliment to Diaghilev buried in the volume of *Sodome et Gomorrhe* that had been published just before the Schiffs' party. 'Imagine,' writes Proust, trying to convey the artistic virtuosity of his superb but grotesque character Baron de Charlus, and the baron's genius for enriching the creative potential of his musical young boyfriends, 'imagine a merely skilful performer in the Russian Ballet, formed, educated and developed in all directions by M. Diaghileff.' Diaghilev read and admired *Temps perdu*: he even corresponded, despite his hatred of letter-writing, with Proust.

As early as 1917 Proust had sent Picasso a message, through Cocteau, expressing his admiration of the costumes and stage set that the Spaniard had designed for Cocteau's burlesque ballet *Parade*. 'How *handsome* Picasso is,' the letter ended. (Proust was evidently attracted by the Spanish type and flirted more with the Catalan interior decorator José-Maria Sert than with his wife Misia.) The following year a rich young connoisseur, Comte Louis Gautier-Vignal, who was Sydney Schiff's stepnephew, took Proust to watch a crate-load of Picasso's sky-blue and white geometric pictures being unpacked in the apartment of Eugenia Errazuriz, a Chilean beauty and generous, perceptive early patron of Picasso and indeed of other Modernists, including Stravinsky. Proust later gracefully alluded to his experience of the Errazuriz Picassos in *Temps retrouvé*. A few months after the Majestic party in 1922 Schiff tried to obtain Proust's consent to Picasso coming for an hour to make a drawing of him. This excellent proposal was never fulfilled.

The Schiffs had also re-united Proust with Léon Delafosse, whose looks he had likened to an angel's when they had known one another in the 1890s. At the age of forty-eight Delafosse had lost the pallid beauty of his youth, and was disappointed by his artistic career, which never reached the altitude he had wanted: he had been reduced to paying for puffs in Swiss newspapers which he then circulated among his Paris friends. In later years, when Delafosse's former mentor Montesquiou was asked, 'whatever happened to Delafosse?', he replied, 'He fell down his own name' (*fosse* means hole or pit). It was no compliment to Delafosse that Proust used the pianist as one of the models for Proust's egregious character Charlie Morel, which is the only reason that the pianist's name is remembered at all. It was apt, though, that they converged for the final time in their lives at a great party. The earlier climax of their relationship had been a sumptuous fête held in 1894 by Comte Robert Montesquiou, with the primary intention of promoting Delafosse's musical reputation among the brilliant host esses of the Faubourg Saint-Germain. Proust's inclusion in Montesquiou's guest-list had inaugurated the phase of his life in which he became a frequent guest of the same great ladies.

Bell's account of the evening at the Majestic peters out after the contretemps between Proust and Stravinsky – and James Joyce is to blame. 'Joyce began to snore – I hope it was a snore. Marcelle Meyer, who sat next to me, suggested that the Avenue de Breteuil lay not so far out of my way, which was hardly true, but I jumped at the excuse. Of course I should be delighted to drop her home; Mr Schiff would understand; besides it was very late.' He had seen Proust plain, but still, the evening seemed to Bell only a partial success as a social event, although it provided a juicy paragraph for his letters home.

Soon after Marcelle Meyer and Bell had left, Joyce stopped snoring and began talking to Proust. The conversation between the two novelists has been cheerfully garbled in the stories recorded by Joyce's boon companions. It is clear, though, that their exchanges were dislocated, muddled and absurd. In one account Proust asked if Joyce liked truffles, and the Irishman replied 'Yes, I do'. According to another version (reported by the Duchesse de Clermont-Tonnerre, who knew both men) their exchanges were more retaliatory. 'A bad joker put Joyce and Proust together. "I have never read your works, Mr Joyce." "I have never read your works, Mr Proust".' Some of Joyce's admirers discounted this story: he would never have been so rude, they claim; even when drunk, they protested, Joyce was only insulting to his family. Other friends later explained, convincingly, that Joyce's eyesight was too weak for him to have read the hundreds of closely printed pages of *Temps perdu*. Even so, Joyce's denial to Proust that he had read *Temps perdu* was essentially untrue: 'I have read some pages,' he had told his crony Frank Budgen in 1920: 'I cannot see any special merit but I am a bad critic.' Joyce had resorted before to false denials that he had read any of a writer's *oeuvre* as a way of evading obligatory compliments. When Wyndham Lewis first met Joyce in Paris in 1920, Joyce pretended not to have read anything he had written, although he certainly had done. As a result, 'what should have been a momentous encounter,' according to Lewis, 'turned out to be as matter-of-fact a social clash as the . . . brusque *how do you do* of a couple of dogs out for a walk.'

Joyce complained that whereas he wanted to talk of chambermaids, Proust would speak only of duchesses. As he told Budgen, 'Our talk consisted solely of the word "No." Proust asked me if I knew the duc de so-and-so. I said, "No." Our hostess asked Proust if he had read such and such a piece of *Ulysses*. Proust said, "No." And so on. Of course the situation was impossible. Proust's day was just beginning. Mine was at an end.'

According to Padraic Colum, his friend Joyce resented Violet Schiff's somewhat contrived attempt to 'create a historic occasion by bringing the two celebrated authors together' and therefore determined 'to be taciturn in the presence of the featured great.' In the anecdote with which Joyce regaled Colum, he cut short all Proust's efforts at dialogue or to establish mutual acquaintances.

> *Proust*: Ah, Monsieur Joyce, you know the Princess . . .
> *Joyce*: No, Monsieur.
> *Proust*: Ah. You know the Countess . . .
> *Joyce*: No, Monsieur.
> *Proust*: Then you know Madame . . .
> *Joyce*: No, Monsieur.

The novelist and editor Ford Madox Ford, an unblushing embellisher of other people's stories, claimed in 1934 to have heard a similar version both from Joyce and from Violet Schiff:

> Two stiff chairs were obtained and placed, facing the one

the other, in the aperture of a folding doorway between two rooms. The faithful of Mr Joyce disposed themselves in a half-circle in one room; those of M. Proust completed the circle in the other. Mr Joyce and M. Proust sat upright, facing each other, and vertically parallel. They were invited to converse. They did.

Said M. Proust: 'Comme j'ai dit, Monsieur, dans *Du Côté de Chez Swann* que sans doute vous avez lu . . .'

Mr Joyce gave a tiny vertical jump on his chair seat and said: 'Non, Monsieur . . .'

Then Mr Joyce took up the conversation. He said: 'As Mr Blum [sic] says in my *Ulysses*, which, Monsieur, you have doubtless read . . .'

M. Proust gave a slightly higher vertical jump on *his* chair seat. He said: 'Mais non, monsieur.'

Service fell again to M. Proust. He apologised for the lateness of his arrival. He said it was due to a malady of the liver. He detailed clearly and with minuteness the symptoms of his illness.

' . . . Tiens, Monsieur,' Joyce interrupted. 'I have almost exactly the same symptoms. Only in my case the analysis . . .'

So, till eight next morning, in perfect amity and enthusiasm, surrounded by the awed faithful, they discussed their maladies.

The expatriate bohemian community in Paris was avid to know the exchanges between these two novelists who were destroying nineteenth-century literary certainties as surely as Einstein was revolutionising physics. It was a measure of their critical acclaim in 1922 that the embroidered stories were so abundant. Accord-

ing to a version heard by the American poet William Carlos
Williams during his visit to Paris in 1924, Joyce said to Proust,

> 'I've headaches every day. My eyes are terrible.'
> Proust replied, 'My poor stomach. What am I going to do?
> It's killing me. In
> fact, I must leave at once.'
> 'I'm in the same situation,' replied Joyce, 'if I can find some-
> one to take me
> by the arm. Goodbye.'

'Charmé', said Proust, 'oh, my stomach, my stomach.'
The flurry of stories was so confusing that even Richard Ellmann, Joyce's biographer, lapsed from his impeccable standards
of accuracy, and mis-dated the Schiffs' party by a year. Joyce
regretted that their remarks had been so mundane. 'If we had
been allowed to meet and have a talk somewhere . . .' he mused
to Samuel Beckett.

Conversation with Joyce was often difficult. When mutual
friends introduced Joyce to Le Corbusier, hoping to spark a brilliant dialogue about their work, the sole subject between them
was Pierre and Pepi, Joyce's two parakeets. It proved impossible
to draw Joyce into conversation when Aldous Huxley invited
him to a Paris dinner party. Joyce sulked because the Huxleys
served red wine, which he seldom drank, because he believed it
harmed his eyesight, and ignored the overtures of the novelist
Pierre Drieu la Rochelle. Maria Huxley, the hostess, in a paroxysm
of despair, finally made a commonplace remark about some
flowers decorating the table. 'I hate flowers,' Joyce snapped, and
resumed his silence. There were similar tensions when the
American critic Dwight MacDonald visited Joyce in 1932. 'The

next twenty minutes were hell. We thanked him for letting us
come, we hoped we weren't disturbing him, we said we greatly
admired his work. He said nothing. Every now and then he
passed a limp hand over his face, a gesture that became more
and more unnerving. We began to ask direct questions: he
would answer yes or no, and then relapse into silence . . . At one
point the subject of language came up – or, rather, we hauled it
up – and I observed, desperately, that Mr Joyce must know all
there was to know about words . . . The effect was frightening;
a look of pain came over Joyce's face, and he slowly raised his
hands, as if to ward off evil. We dropped the subject.'

   The difficulties with Joyce continued after the Majestic supper party broke up. Proust had rewarded the Schiffs with an
invitation back to his nearby apartment to continue their conversation. Otherwise, he explained, with the affectionate solicitude that he always showed to hotel employees, 'those poor
waiters would have to stay up and clean the room after we left
and would get no rest as they had to be on duty early in the
morning.' The Schiffs, as soon as their guests had dispersed, followed Proust down to the taxi driven by Odilon Albaret, the
husband of his housekeeper, which was waiting outside the
Majestic to take him back to Rue Hamelin. Paris cabs of the
1920s seemed built for a race of pygmies so Albaret's passengers
were huddled tightly together. The crowding was worse because
Joyce squeezed in too, as Schiff told a friend (who recounted the
story in a BBC Third Programme broadcast in 1949). Joyce
began smoking tobacco, and opened a window of the taxi. As
Proust feared fresh air, and his asthma could not stand smoke,
Schiff shut the window immediately after the cigarette was jettisoned or extinguished. Throughout the journey, which can

scarcely have lasted a minute, as Proust's apartment was in the immediate vicinity of the Majestic, he 'talked incessantly without addressing Joyce,' said Violet Schiff: Joyce watched him in silence. When Albaret's taxi reached Rue Hamelin, Joyce seemed to want to come up to the apartment, but Proust, whom the Schiffs believed had come to deplore Joyce's manner, as well as his manners, was resolute in being shot of him. 'Let my taxi take you home,' he insisted. Fearful of the cold, Proust hastened indoors with Violet Schiff while her husband remained outside coaxing a stubborn, almost troublesome Joyce into going home. Once Schiff had despatched him, he came up to the apartment, whereupon Proust ordered champagne, beer and coffee, and made Schiff, who was puffing and blowing in the great heat of the apartment, take off his jacket. The Schiffs, who stayed talking until broad daylight, believed Proust had not been 'so eager and full of life for months'.

Drunken obstinacy was responsible for Joyce's unwelcome persistence after the taxi ride; but perhaps he was curious to see the interior of Proust's apartment about which the expatriate community in Paris gossiped so much. He had never been there, and did not know how cold and dingy it could seem: instead he nursed his sense of deprivation by comparing Proust's 'comfortable place at the Étoile, floored with cork, and with cork on the walls to keep it quiet', with his own bustling apartment ('people coming in and out. I wonder how I can finish *Ulysses*'). He envied the prosperity of another of the Schiffs' guests too. 'Picasso is not a higher name than I have, I suppose, and he can get 20,000 to 30,000 francs for a few hours' work. I am not worth a penny a line and it seems I cannot even sell such a rare book as *Dubliners*.'

Joyce's belief that Proust's successes were just beginning, while his own career was declining, betrays his insecurity. Though the first volume of *Temps perdu* had a muted reception on its publication in 1913, Proust's reputation had soared both in France and England after publication of the second volume, *À l'ombre des jeunes filles en fleurs*, and the subsequent award of the Prix Goncourt in 1919. His novel's historic resonance, his narrative teeming with invented people who seem like historical characters, his veneration of European artistic genius, were increasingly acclaimed. 'It is one of the deepest, most elaborate, most complex novels that have ever appeared in France,' the historian Albert Thibaudet (then poised to emerge as France's foremost inter-war literary critic) explained in 1920. 'It is a picture of the world, of ordinary life, and of Society; it is a work of psychological analysis; and its style has remarkable originality.' Proust was seen not as retrograde or unintelligible – but as the chronicler of the apogee of the confidence, foolishness and grace of life before 1914. 'He is, as you say, the culmination of an epoch,' Middleton Murry wrote to Schiff in 1922. 'He is very precisely the culmination of the 19th Century . . . but the culmination of the 19th is also the beginning of the 20th.'

Joyce was acutely aware that he and Proust were being set up as rivals in literary Modernism: that critics were behaving like bookmakers laying the odds on Proust and Joyce in their race for fame. 'I observe,' he had written to Frank Budgen shortly after his arrival in Paris, 'a furtive attempt to run a certain Mr Marcel Proust of here against the signatory of this letter.' Comparisons between the two novelists were seldom in his favour. In their literary work, so Richard Aldington pronounced in 1920, 'M. Proust is more coherent than Mr Joyce, more urbane, less preoccupied with slops and viscera . . . [with] the fine manners Nature denied to Mr Joyce when she gave him genius.' The *Times Literary Supplement* had endorsed a similar ranking in 1921: 'The glory of M. Proust . . . still holds the position, in one field of fiction, of the most remarkable novelist of the last decade, a position which only the novels of Mr James Joyce makes a little insecure.' Even Joyce's champion Ezra Pound made the same invidious comparison in May 1922: 'One reads Proust and thinks him very accomplished; one reads H[enry] J[ames] and knows that he is very accomplished; one begins *Ulysses* and thinks, perhaps rightly, that Joyce is less so.' As a result of these recurrent slights, Joyce thought critics had been bamboozled by the novelty of Proust's prose, which never impressed him. 'The French are used to short, choppy sentences, they are not used to that way of writing.' For him *Temps perdu* was an 'analytic still life' in which readers finished the sentences before Proust.

The Schiffs' party was the social climax of the last year of Proust's life. He was at the height of his literary success: *Sodome et Gomorrhe II*, had gone on sale a few weeks earlier, on 29 April; and in May 1922, supremely, Proust was the talk of fashionable Paris. 'From the day it came out,' he told Schiff proudly, 'people were reading it in the Métro, in their carriages, in trains, oblivious of their neighbours, forgetting their stops.' Proust's name was suddenly universal and ubiquitous. It was invoked daily in every quality newspaper, notably in connection with the Nobel Prize (which was awarded in the autumn to the Spanish dramatist Jacinto Benavente y Martinez). An extract from *Sodome et Gomorrhe* was even published on the front page of *Le Figaro* together with an editorial tribute to the 'immense psychological panorama of the great writer and incomparable novelist who is M. Marcel Proust'. Typically, on the morning of the party, Louis Vauxcelles had written in *L'Éclair*: 'Proust is the author most in the limelight at the present hour; all the world is infatuated with the Duchesse de Guermantes, with Basin, with Mémé, with Cancan and with baron de Charlus . . . in this unforgettable novel.' Among English cognoscenti the excitement was just as high. 'Not being able to get the new volumes in London, I couldn't wait,' Arthur Walkley, the theatre critic of *The Times*, wrote on 17 May, 'but borrowed them from a luckier friend, who had got them, by special favour, from Paris.'

By contrast, Joyce felt thwarted, insulted and unpopular. The taste for his work was confined to a tiny exclusive minority. 1922 was the year in which to have read *Ulysses*, in its entirety or in part instalments, was a badge of culture for the expatriate English and Americans in Paris – but for almost no one else. On 2 February, Joyce's birthday, nearly three months before the publication of *Sodome et Gomorrhe II*, Sylvia Beach, the Paris bookseller who had undertaken to arrange the publication of *Ulysses* in book form, had gone alone to the Gare de Lyon to meet the 7 a.m. Dijon–Paris express. 'I was on the platform, my heart going like the locomotive, as the train from Dijon came slowly to a standstill, and I saw the guard getting off, holding a parcel and looking round for someone – me. In a few minutes, I was ringing the doorbell at the Joyces' and handing them Copy No. 1 of *Ulysses*.' Other copies (as bulky as a London telephone directory) were delivered from the printers in Dijon, and sold from Beach's Paris bookshop, Shakespeare & Company, at a high price. Because of the book's supposed obscenity, it was not published in Britain for another fourteen years: its black-market price in London, so Joyce claimed in October 1922, was £40. (The first English translation of Proust, *Swann's Way*, which first appeared in late September 1922, cost fifteen shillings: twenty shillings equalled £1).

In the spring of 1922 Joyce was championed by the avant garde, who were convinced that his linguistic exuberance was the work of a genius. 'All men should unite to give praise to *Ulysses*,' wrote Ezra Pound from Paris in May: 'those who will not, may content themselves with a place in the lower intellectual orders.' Yet many others regarded Joyce as a dirty-minded charlatan. The *Quarterly Review*, which hailed the 'secret fire' of Proust's sensibility, denounced the 'literary Bolshevism' of *Ulysses*: 'anti-Christian, chaotic, totally unmoral . . . a mad Shelleyan effort to extend the known confines of the English language . . . unreadable and unquotable.' Edith Wharton told Bernard Berenson that *Ulysses* was 'a turgid welter of pornography (the rudest schoolboy kind), and unformed and unimportant drivel.' Even the compliments seemed ambiguous. 'The intelligent literary aspirant, studying *Ulysses*, will find it more an encyclopaedia of what he is to avoid attempting, than of the things he may try for himself,' T. S. Eliot wrote in 1922. Wyndham Lewis received his copy of *Ulysses* in London a few days after the night at the Majestic. 'There is of course a rather pretentious vein in it, a scholarly bluff which is irritating,' he reported on 26 May to Schiff, who had probably sent it. 'After reading a definitely romantic book like *Ulysses*, you want to get out of this masturbatory, historico-political Irish fairy land as soon as possible.' He condemned the novel as 'altogether too long . . . from a stupid motive – the intention to "impress"'.

Joyce's single meeting with Proust would, on its own, have

ensured that the supper party at the Majestic was exceptional. But the presence of Diaghilev, Stravinsky and Picasso made the Schiffs' evening a unique event in the history of twentieth-century art: it was the sole occasion when the most magnificent exponents of early twentieth-century Modernism gathered in the same room. For the Schiffs it was an opportunity to share their famous hospitality but also to show off the celebrated names who would accept their hospitality. Though the evening was ostensibly in honour of Diaghilev, the great lion whom they most rejoiced to catch was Proust. They used the party as a way to keep him in their social clutches, and continued to send him unctuous compliments in the months that followed. '*La recherche*,' they told him in July, is 'the ultimate form of the novel. There's nothing further left to do; all that the novel is capable of, you have done or are going to do.' Other novelists, 'without exception, seem lacking in authority or finesse, individuality as well as intelligence, after you'. But the Schiffs' plans for a long intimacy with Proust were baffled by Time: exactly six months to the day after his night at the Majestic, Proust – wearied by his heroic creativity and working fanatically until his last hours – would be dead.

CHAPTER 2

It's the Little Proust

One evening in 1918 the Schiffs were in Paris, went to the theatre with a Frenchman and then called at the Ritz for a late supper. As Violet Schiff always remembered, 'an extraordinary man, impossible to ignore, with very black hair, looking very ill, and wearing evening dress, came in, surrounded by waiters. He chatted to the waiters and distributed tips left and right, sat at a table alone and ordered asparagus, which he picked up and ate without removing his white gloves.' They discovered that it was Proust, introduced themselves as admirers of *À la recherche du temps perdu* and began talking. 'He wasted a lot of time, I thought, reproving Sydney for leaving his friend so soon and for not bringing him to his table.' But this Frenchman, who figured among the literary cognoscenti, 'had just told us that Proust was no good as a writer, was only an amateur, a society man and a snob'. Eventually Proust took the Schiffs back to his apartment in an old Renault taxi-cab driven by Odilon Albaret. 'The entrance looked sordid, the staircase was in darkness and those not using the lift had to hurry from one floor to the next in order to reach the switch before the light went out.' They stayed until dawn while Albaret waited downstairs. 'The strange enchantment of the nights we passed with Marcel Proust made us believe that no day-time meeting could have equalled them,'

Violet Schiff said. 'Nothing he said was trivial or unimportant, not that he was by any means serious all the time. His astringent satire left one with no feeling of sadness or bitterness. He put himself into his conversation as he did into his books, but not by talking about himself.'

A conspicuous eccentric, Violet Schiff thought, but not merely a Society gadfly: a mordant satirist with a compelling, even magical, conversational style rather than a spurious chatterbox. At first glance he seemed outstanding, and more intimate knowledge of him intensified this impression. There is no mystery about the effect he had on his contemporaries in the years after 1918. His life was so exceptional, his manners and his work so distinctive, because of his sense of vocation. Proust's ardent, self-punitive commitment to his art – requiring also a masochistic renunciation of his life – was both ferocious and overwhelming. Although the force of his vocation surged confusedly inside him from adolescence onwards, its power only became evident in his thirties, when he began to master his doubts and fears.

Marcel-Valentin-Louis-Eugène-Georges Proust was a child of apprehension: he lived always at an unbearable pitch of anxiety and always saw the world with a piercing, discomfiting insight. His parents, Adrien Proust, an ambitious young physician from a Catholic provincial family, and Jeanne Weil, the daughter of a rich Jewish stockbroker, had married in Paris on 3 September 1870. It was an ominous day, during which the news reached the capital that the French Army of Emperor Napoleon III had been defeated at Sedan by Prussian troops. The day after the Prousts' marriage a Paris mob proclaimed the death of the Second Empire and the birth of the Third Republic. On 19

September the Prussians put the city under siege and bombardment. Although Parisians were starved of food and fuel, enduring a vile stench of death and decay, the Prousts remained in Paris throughout this dangerous period: Marcel Proust was conceived during these anxious months. 'People who lived through the war of 1870 say that war came to seem natural to them', he later wrote, 'because they could think of nothing else.' After the Prussians withdrew in January 1871, prolonged and bloody street warfare erupted in Paris. Again Dr Proust chose to remain so as to care for the wounded. When his wife was six months' pregnant, he was almost killed by a stray bullet; appalled, she retreated to her uncle's house in the devastated Paris suburb of Auteuil. It was there that Marcel Proust was born on 10 July 1871: a puny infant, almost too feeble to live, whose physique and temperament were affected by the worry and privation that his mother had recently survived. After his first asthma attack, at the age of nine, in the spring of 1881 his delicate health became the constant preoccupation of his mother and himself. Adrien Proust became a renowned physician whose research interests and powerful intellect made him conversant with the great scientific trends of his age. During the 1880s he became Inspector-General of Sanitary Services, and Professor of Public Health in the University of Paris's medical faculty. His high and honourable medical achievements, his professional contacts, his discussions of his work at home all contributed to the clinical element that pervades *Temps perdu*: Marcel Proust pathologised the human condition, and sometimes assumed a quasi-scientific tone, as in the initial section of *Sodome et Gomorrhe* in which he scrutinised sexuality in the terminology of a botanist. Indeed he was a rare combination of personal subjectivity and diagnostic objectivity. He studied his own introspective depths, and tested the workings of his own conscience – as he did those of his contemporaries – with the detachment of a zoologist or botanist observing natural phenomena. Proust's allusions, too, in *Temps perdu*, to Paris medical specialists and society physicians have a keen air of authenticity. His background resembled those of W. H. Auden, whose father was Professor of Public Health at Birmingham University, and Gustave Flaubert, whose father held comparable responsibilities at Rouen. Like Auden and Flaubert, Proust's sense of human psychology was informed by conversations overheard in childhood and adolescence in a medical household, although unlike Auden, Proust's prescriptive view of human choices was limited by his diagnosis that after childhood we can expect nothing except ageing and death. Dr Proust held strong views on the correct education needed to develop children into 'energetic, well-balanced characters able to resist afflictions and depression'. He recommended the power of suggestion 'as a means of moral education and as a powerful modifier of hereditary tendencies', especially for 'nervously predisposed, impressionable children'. He was, for his epoch, a progressive parent who rejected Christian notions of Original Sin and preferred the inculcation of virtue to harsh discipline. 'The young child is too unconscious to have a deliberately perverse intention; to ascribe to him the fixed determination, the resolution to do evil, is to judge him unjustly and often to develop in him an evil instinct, together with the notion that he can deliberately commit a wicked action.' Dr Proust disliked negative parenting: a 'child that needs chastisement is lacking in affection,' he wrote; 'to multiply reprimands and corrections is to deprive them of all reforming power over the child's mind.' His precepts had strong influence on both his sons, who proved to be resolute and tenacious in their life work. 'The child must be habituated to *will* and to accomplish what he has willed, to persevere in his efforts,' Dr Proust urged. 'To this end all about him must encourage him and react sympathetically to whatever he does or says, only giving him gently to understand, if necessary, that he might have done better.' Dr Proust's precepts constituted a model system for rearing middle-class high-achievers. They certainly instilled in his son Marcel an intense perseverance at fulfilling his creative vocation: 'the miracle with M. Proust was his will-power,' said Céleste Albaret, 'and his will-power was all directed towards his work.'

Proust's mother was a cultured and intelligent woman whose pleasure in reading to him enriched his fantasy life and instilled in him a discriminating love of literature. He loved her with extravagant ardour, and suffered high anxiety when separated from her care. Asthma, coupled with insomnia, increasingly disrupted his existence, and eventually led him to become a reclusive invalid. Whatever the cause of his asthma, he used his attacks as a way to control Madame Proust's time, engross her attention and perhaps even to punish her for imagined defects as a mother. Unlike his father, and later his younger brother Robert, who were robust and decisive medical men, studying, diagnosing and curing the illnesses of others, Marcel Proust became a committed, lifelong and incorrigible patient. He was perhaps the most notorious valetudinarian in literary history, constantly preoccupied with his physical powers, monitoring his health, assessing his strength, doctoring himself in stubborn and eccentric ways. Nervous and sickly, he was possessive of his mother, and relied on her strength, just as later he became unreasonably intense about other people whom he loved and whose strength he hoped to absorb by physical proximity or intuitive sympathy. Lucien Daudet, who was his lover in the mid-1890s, recalled that when 'Marcel Proust said goodnight to his mother, he embraced her with a fervour that was childish, lingering, passionate, as if he wanted every evening to recover again the protection of the arms which had once rocked him in the cradle.' His mother's response rewarded his hypochondria and aggravated his morbid anxiety about his strength; her pampering ensured that until the end of his life he resembled a fervent, capricious child. The woman who nursed Jeanne Proust on her deathbed in 1905 told him that he remained 'still a child of four years of age for her'.

Dr Proust's distinguished publications included a textbook on nervous disorders, *L'Hygiène du neurasthénique* (1897), written in collaboration with a colleague, and translated into English as *The Treatment of Neurasthenia* (1902). Its subject engrossed his elder son. 'I'm not astonished Proust is always tired,' wrote Marcel's devoted friend Léon Daudet (who was Lucien's brother). 'I never knew anyone so harassed by the mysterious psychology and somatic disorders of his contemporaries and his ancestors.' Proust's fancy that he had a deep intuitive medical understanding, and indeed a rebel expertise in diagnosis and prescription, was important to his development as a novelist, especially after his father's death in 1903. One of the engrossing themes of *Temps perdu* is the origins, symptoms and ultimate consequences of nervous disorders: indeed Marcel Proust told an interviewer in 1913 that 'my book might be seen as an attempt at a series of Novels of the Unconscious'.

Dr Proust averred that boarding-schools were 'especially evil for children who are weakly or who have inherited a neurotic dis-position. Everyone knows the dangers: an unhealthy, shut-up, sedentary life, overcrowding, narrow rules and rigid arrange-ments that too often break the child's initiative and will.' Both his sons were kept at day-schools: at the age of eleven, in 1882, Marcel began his high-powered education at the Lycée Con-dorcet in Paris. He remained a pupil there until 1889. Daniel Halévy, Marcel's contemporary there, recalled his 'great oriental eyes, his big white collar, his flowing cravat. There was some-thing about him which we found displeasing, and we rebuffed him brusquely, we made a feint of shoving him away . . . he was not enough of a boy for us, and his kindness, tender attentions, caresses (incapable as we were of understanding so wounded a heart) we labelled as mannerisms, poses, as we told him to his face. His eyes, then, grew even sadder.' Proust certainly felt that he had been 'detested by nearly all my class-mates': some could scarcely bring themselves to speak to him. In England such schoolboy aggression would have been the work of flannelled fools and muddied oafs who made a fetish of contact sports and despised the intellect; and would probably have enjoyed the complicity of their masters. At Lycée Condorcet, however, as in much of France, brain-power was respected by teachers and pupils alike. Proust was bullied because he was too effusive, demonstrative and sexually alarming – just one of the millions of schoolboys who have been shunned, hit or demeaned because they were thought to be betraying signs of homosexuality. It only increased his vulnerability that he had a lifelong habit 'when someone is nice to me of dissolving into thanks, affection, tears', as he later wrote. His behaviour seemed inappropriate because, perhaps, he still lacked self-knowledge. It is too glib to take

Proust's narrator for himself, but some passages in *Temps perdu* seem distinctly autobiographical. 'No one can tell at first that he is an invert or a poet or a snob or wicked. The boy who has been learning love poetry or looking at obscene pictures, who then presses his body against a school-friend's, imagines himself only to be sharing with him in the same desire for a woman.'

Proust, who cheerfully survived a year of military service, was in early manhood still a spirited social creature with robust appetites. Restored to Paris life, sitting his final examinations in law and philosophy, he went for 'excellent lunches . . . at Foyot's, a delightful place, a thousand times superior to the Ritz,' as he recalled to Sydney Schiff in 1922. Like other epicene youths, he was attracted to both sexes just as he had characteristics of both sexes. There is a beguiling photograph of him laughing and clowning by some tennis courts at Neuilly in 1892 with several girls, including Jeanne Pouquet, who was one of several young women on whom he had crushes. His undignified and embarrassing efforts to obtain a photograph of Jeanne Pouquet were rebuffed by her shocked mother: he tried to bribe the Pouquets' maid and inveigled invitations to visit obscure Pouquet relations in Périgord, in order to steal from their albums. These inappropriate attentions persisted after she became engaged to marry Gaston Arman de Caillavet, the son of a hostess (born Léontine Lippmann) whose salon of literary intellectuals Proust had regularly attended since 1889. Proust could seem so talkative, obsequious and affected that many of Gaston Arman de Caillavet's set disliked him irreconcilably, and would not speak to him, but the two young men had an affectionate and trusting, if improbable, friendship. It was at a regular Wednesday party *chez* the elder Madame Arman de Caillavet that

Proust first met her lover Anatole France and another fledgling novelist, Colette. 'He was a young man at the same time I was a young woman,' Colette recalled sixty years later. 'I had little taste for his exaggerated politeness, the excessive attention he paid to his interlocutors, especially if they were women'; but his youthful appearance was memorable: 'great eye sockets, swarthy and sad, a complexion sometimes rose and sometimes pale, anxious eyes, the mouth, when he held his tongue, tight and puckered as if anticipating a kiss.'

Proust began to attend the salon of Geneviève Straus, the daughter of the composer Jacques Fromental Halévy and widow of the composer Bizet, whose second husband was supposedly an illegitimate Rothschild. Her salon, like that of Madame Arman de Caillavet, attracted literary intellectuals and political writers but was less exclusively middle-class. Proust cut a memorable figure *chez* Straus. The Duchesse de Clermont-Tonnerre's memoir *Robert de Montesquiou et Marcel Proust* begins: 'Astonished, I asked who was this peculiar young man, draping himself so affectedly over the back of the gilded Belloir chair on which Madame Straus was sitting. "It's the little Proust," someone replied.' It was not only his abundant black hair that impressed her.

His wan and thin face, with its long, aquiline nose, gave him an Oriental air, which became frankly Assyrian when he let his big beard grow. Large black pupils, which never betrayed any personal feelings, but which seemed intensively receptive to everything visual, sparkled at the people to whom he was speaking, while from his mouth, often twisted by a sideways smile, came an extraordinary voice, a bit juvenile, caressing, gentle, charged with a thousand gracious inflexions, giving the impression of little soft paws, smeared with jam, all soft and sticky.

The Duchess felt both flattered and bored by this intense attentiveness and by the obsequious phrases with which Proust sugared his conversation.

Proust had long hankered after the romance of the nobility. 'The weather is so beautiful today', he had written to a schoolfriend at the age of seventeen, 'that I would like to indulge myself in the fantasies of a great nobleman. I would like to conjure up wonderful spectacles.' There seemed to him no better way of living fully, of experiencing life at its richest and most satisfying, than by entering the great houses and attending the parties of people with historic names. He put himself under the social auspices of a temperamental dandy, Comte Robert de Montesquiou, began to receive invitations from smart hostesses and developed a youthful pleasure in the company of haughty yet alluring noblewomen. Aristocratic glamour proved irresistibly seductive for a time. Among the earliest hostesses to receive him were two Rothschild sisters, Marguerite and Berthe, who had married respectively the Duc de Gramont and the Prince de Wagram. It was as a guest of the Princesse de Wagram in 1893 that he first saw the Comtesse de Greffulhe, with her mauve orchids and chestnut hair falling to the nape of her neck. He became desperate to obtain her photograph, but she declined to provide anything so intimate to a comparative stranger.

Although the Comtesse de Greffulhe remained aloof, he maintained the most affectionate life-long relations with the

Duchesse de Gramont's son, Armand, Duc de Guiche, and her stepdaughter Elisabeth de Clermont-Tonnerre. As to the Princesse de Wagram, he used her in the most grateful spirit as a model for the Princesse de Parme, the most amiable of the nobility in *Le côté de Guermantes*. Proust presents the Princesse de Parme as gracious and full of good deeds because, he says, the 'arrogantly humble precepts of an evangelical snobbery' had been inculcated in her as a child: 'God in His bounty,' she was insistently told,

> has decreed that you should hold almost all the shares in the Suez Canal and three times as many Royal Dutch shares as Edmond de Rothschild; your pedigree in a direct line has been traced by genealogists from the year 63 of the Christian era; you have two empresses as sisters-in-law. So never seem to speak as if you are mindful of these great privileges, not that they are precarious, for nothing can alter the antiquity of race and the world will always need petrol.

The princess follows this creed of gratitude and is redeemed from the pettiness and stupidity around her. Proust, who was ashamed of having been an ungrateful young man, came passionately to believe in the human duty to be grateful – even grateful for the opportunities for emotional growth brought by anguish or despair – and in the Princesse de Parme he created a character who was rewarded for her gratitude by developing an unassailable sweetness of character.

Many of the men and women whom he encountered were later transfigured and re-invented as characters in *À la recherche du temps perdu*. The Faubourg Saint-Germain nobility became indispensable to his creativity. He attended their salons, watched, listened and remembered. Dr Proust was puzzled by his son's social success – asking 'Why is he invited to so many places? Is he really so fascinating?' – and deplored high society on hygienic grounds. '"Society" men and women,' he wrote in 1897 (almost in reproach of his son, who was by then a Society darling), 'have their whole day consumed by the duties that convention and the vain care of their reputation impose upon them: visits, dinners, balls, evening parties make their life one of continual constraint and obligation.' Such an idle yet weari-some life 'leaves little time for the restful pleasure of one's own fireside, or the calm and cheering distractions of *home*. None are more busy than those who do nothing.' The doctor's disap-proval of Society people focused on their weakness in caring so much what others thought of them: they let their purpose in life be defined by the opinion of their set; the mainspring of their actions was their reputation; they were nothing more than cap-tives of their social instincts. Proust's ultimate contempt for the party-goers in his novel is based on a similar fury with people whose lives are acted out in eager, smug conformity with the expectations of their friends and family. It was, he realised after his father's death, the recipe for spiritual self-immolation, aes-thetic sterility and emotional torpor.

Dr Proust's working life was a busy, tightly organised sequence of constructive action – admittedly the indoor action of hospitals and committee rooms – and his son had a hanker-ing respect for active men. From the late 1890s Marcel cultivat-ed a strong romantic admiration for several strong, agile young male noblemen, who proved amiably tolerant of his effusions and flattery. He resembled *Temps perdu*'s highly-strung, emo-tionally demanding and physically passive narrator who charms the adamant young bloods in the military garrison of a fictional town called Doncières. Proust himself craved support and protection from stronger men, and repaid these noble officers with eager, lively affection. 'He had a stunning verbal gaiety, which amused without ever tiring,' as the Duchesse of Clermont-Tonnerre recalled. 'Young men remote from literary culture or artistic tastes loved him as a delightful comrade, a bit unusual, someone whom they had to protect, who evoked a finer and more vibrant life than that to which they were accustomed. These young men felt that Marcel Proust gave them, solely by his conversation and presence, a pleasure as keen as an evening out with a girl. He loved to dazzle the cadets under going their military service in the different towns of the Île-de-France and Normandy.' Young officers like Louis, marquis d'Albuféra, Armand, Duc de Guiche, Comte Bertrand de Fénelon and Prince Léon Radziwill 'adored to spend a night with Marcel as much as with a high-class tart'. These were odd friendships, which in some cases endured to the death precisely because they were so out of the ordinary.

Proust's ancestral influences, the intensity of his feelings, his incompetence at handling them were always distinctive, and never permitted him to meld inconspicuously into fashionable Society. Proust was too impressed by his father's productivity, and too obedient to his father's suggestive moral education, to waste all his life as a social creature who cared chiefly for the approval of his friends. The extremism of his dependence on his mother equally made a conventional emotional life impossible: his tight bond with her distorted his affections, social outlook and sensibility. As a concomitant of his maternal veneration,

Proust took a horrified interest in other men's repudiation of maternal love. When Lucien Daudet recounted how a school-friend had pretended that his frumpy mother was a family servant when she visited him at their school, Proust hid his face in his hands and wept copiously. 'What horror!' he exclaimed in 1907 when Henri van Blarenberghe shot dead his octogenarian mother before committing suicide. 'I received ten days ago the most sensitive, saddest, most touching letter from that unfortunate van Blarenberghe, who is more pitiable than Oedipus.' This personal obsession with the profanation of mothers surfaces in several passages of his novel.

Madame Proust was Jewish by birth and never converted to Catholicism: there were no religious rites at her funeral. The Prousts never alluded to the fact that, under Talmudic law, a child follows the religion of its mother, and that accordingly, in the eyes of Jews, Marcel Proust (like Montaigne) was one of the Chosen People. He was baptised as a Catholic, and took communion, but according to Louis Gautier-Vignal, who became one of his nocturnal companions after 1914, he had only a scanty knowledge of the Bible. Proust was singular, though, because unlike many of his contemporaries in a like situation, he would never deny his mixed ancestry. 'Despite being a Catholic like my father and brother, my mother is a Jewess', he explained to Montesquiou in 1896 after evading a question prompted by an article of Zola's about Jews and anti-Semitism. 'Since I am not free to have the ideas that I might otherwise have on this subject, you might unintentionally have wounded me in a discussion.' As a boy and probably as a young man he attended the weddings and funerals of his Jewish relations, at which he will have heard Hebrew spoken and seen Judaic rites.

He was, indeed, a page at the wedding of his cousin Henri Bergson, the philosopher, at a ceremony performed by Rabbi Zadoc Kahn in a synagogue in Rue de la Victoire. Later, when *La Libre Parole* listed 'a number of young Jews including M. Marcel Proust' who supposedly hated the anti-Dreyfusard Maurice Barrès, Proust was plunged into a quandary, as he explained to his Jewish friend Robert Dreyfus. 'To correct this one would have to say that one was not Jewish and that I don't wish to do.' He would not issue a public denial of his Judaism primarily because it would have upset his mother, and to a subordinate extent because he did not want to be thought a temporising or apostate Dreyfusard. As a parallel, Bergson was attracted by Catholicism, but was never received into the Catholic Church, as he did not wish to repudiate Judaism at a time of persecution.

Proust felt an affinity with certain Jews: early in life he was welcomed into the salons of Léontine Arman de Caillavet, Geneviève Straus, and the two Rothschild sisters, the Duchesse de Gramont and Princesse de Wagram; in the closing years of his life he took a close interest in three Englishmen, Sydney Schiff, Sir Philip Sassoon and (the only full gentile) the Duke of Marlborough. Part of the attraction between Schiff and Proust was their mutual recognition of the other's cultural ambivalence: Schiff had a Jewish father but Christian mother. Schiff understood Proust's interest in English Jewry, and fed him anecdotes about his own relations and former school-friends like Lord Ludlow, an English nobleman of Sephardic ancestry who visited Paris in 1922. A full Jew, according to the Talmud, but ostensibly a Catholic, Proust extolled as general traits of Jewry the virtues which he recognised in his mother. 'The Jews,' he wrote to his Jewish lover Reynaldo Hahn, possess 'a kind of charitable self-esteem, a cordiality without pride, which is so precious'. Proust honoured the power of the Jewish prophetic tradition and attributed it to his Jewish friends: he admired Robert Dreyfus as 'a Conscience, a Judge, a *moral* Sage', for example. Similarly, in *Sodome et Gomorrhe*, when Proust's Jewish hero, Charles Swann, in the grip of terminal illness, forces himself to attend a last evening party chez Guermantes, his courage is identified with the endurance of the Jews and the example of its prophets. 'Swann belonged to that strong Jewish race, in whose vital energy and resistance to death its individual members seem themselves to share. Stricken by their own particular diseases, as the race itself has been by persecution, they each struggle interminably in a terrible death agony ... until all that is left to see is a prophet's beard surmounted by a huge nose, dilated in order to draw its last breath, before the hour strikes for the ritual prayers.'

Many contemporaries were struck by the pronounced nose and luxuriant dark eyes that Proust inherited from his mother, and deduced his racial components. His appearance makes it all the more impressive that he was accepted by the anti-Semitic Daudet family and by some of the equally prejudiced Faubourg Saint-Germain nobility. He did not endure racial bigotry without resentment – while visiting Évian in 1899, for example, he was riled when a 'brutal fool' made a jibe about the number of Jews staying at the Hôtel Splendide – but it is unclear whether he tolerated the anti-Jewish sentiments of the Daudets and others in a submissive spirit or whether they moderated their language in deference to him. Proust's foreign admirers tended to detect a vein of prejudice in French attitudes to him. Henry 'Chips' Channon, a Red Cross worker from Chicago who befriended him during the last months of the war, maintained that 'the accusation hurled at the time against many of his race (he was half Jewish) that they were "internationalists" was untrue of Proust. He was passionately French, or perhaps, I should say, passionately Parisian.' In fact, the phrase 'passionately Parisian' was almost a synonym for Jewish. Proust's lifelong friend Geneviève Straus was once described as a 'Parisian Jewess, that's to say twice over a Parisian: she could scarcely breathe except in airless places, caught colds whenever she went to the Bois de Boulogne, but once the night lights came on, she started to revive.' The English diplomat Harold Nicolson, who first met Proust at a dinner party at the Ritz in 1919, fancied that his 'very Hebrew' air was held against him. In *Some People* (1927), Nicolson's Proustian study of real people in imaginary situations and of imaginary characters in real situations, he reports leaving a party, talking excitedly about Proust, until his companion, a French marquis who is a candidate at the Jockey Club, brings him up short: 'a remarkable man, evidently, a remarkable man: *mais juif, juif*'. For Paul Claudel, too, Proust represented 'concentrated Jewishness. Certain racial mixes . . . express themselves in an exasperating exaggeration of type.'

Some allusions to Proust's Semitism were flattering rather than hostile: the Duchesse de Clermont-Tonnerre, who adored her Rothschild stepmother, interpreted his mixed ancestry as a source of strength. 'A splash of Jewish blood added to the colossal intelligence of Proust that special quality, detached yet all-embracing, which distinguishes the Hebrew race, and augmented his rich intellect,' she wrote. 'He inherited from Israel his perseverance, so that nothing could deter him from attaining his ends.' Another shrewd friend, Edmond Jaloux, insisted that the fact that Proust's mother was '*une Israélite*' was crucial to 'the formation of his fine mind'. The recognition by Proust's early readers of the importance of his Judaic heritage has been blunted in an age that is chary of attributing personality traits to racial or religious causes. His early English-speaking readers, like his more perceptive French friends, often celebrated his Semitism. 'A certain Jewish family piety, intensity of idealism and implacable moral severity, which never left Proust's habits of self-indulgence and his worldly morality in peace, were among the fundamental elements of his nature,' Edmund Wilson declared in his great study of modernism, *Axel's Castle* (1931). 'For all his Parisian sophistication, there remains in him much of the capacity for apocalyptic moral indignation of the classical Jewish prophet. That tone of lamentation and complaint which resounds through his whole book . . . is really very un-French and rather akin to Jewish literature.' Although this approach to Proust's work can easily become silly – 'the difference between a page of Renan and a page of Proust was that Proust was Jewish,' the Irish-American critic William Troy claimed in 1933 – his mixed heritage gave him (in the opinion of some shrewd readers) the creative advantages of alienation. Another American critic, Robert Adams, some of whose relations were European noblemen and others Jewish, immediately responded to Proust as a fellow 'artificial Jew' when he read *Temps perdu* in the early 1930s. Adams felt an 'ambiguous and subtle bond with Proust['s] . . . Jewishness, an affinity all the more binding for not being explicit – one aspect of which was perhaps a secret sense of pride at having some access to "good" society but scorning to make use of it.' Adams disliked the emphasis on homosexuality in *Temps perdu*, and found nothing noble or exciting about being a sexual outlaw; but felt inspired by Proust's 'sense of a private and vital society of outcasts (private merely in the sense of dismissing external remarks and official distinctions with the wry outsiders' wit)'. It was, Adams felt, essentially Jewish.

Proust defended Judaism and homosexuality as general phenomena but deplored vulgarity or stupidity in either group. 'What a crowd!' he complained in 1908 of his fellow guests at the Grand Hôtel in Cabourg. 'Some Israelite dealers are the aristocracy of the place, and what's more, arrogant too.' Equally he disliked the campness of 'young madmen' who wore cosmetics or effeminate clothes 'in order to tease their friends or to shock their parents'. From Judaism and from male homosexuality alike, he learnt by intense scrutiny all the possible depths and varieties of self-contempt. He likened the inhabitants of Sodom to 'the Jews (save a few who will only associate with others of their race and are always mouthing ritual words and consecrated pleasantries), shunning one another, seeking out those who are the most unlike them, who want nothing to do with them, forgiving their rebuffs, elated by their condescension'. Although he sympathised with those, like himself, who dissembled their sexual preferences as a social expediency, he felt it was intolerable of people to repudiate their race. It was for this reason that he detested Arthur Meyer, the proprietor and chief editor of *Le Gaulois*, the organ of the Comte de Chambord and the Bourbon Royalist Party. Meyer went everywhere, and for half a century was always to be seen paying suave visits to the expensive boxes on first nights. His head garnished by his white muttonchop sideburns and crowned by an aureole of carefully curled white hair, he could be glimpsed stooping to kiss the hands of the fashionable ladies. His career, though, rested on self-repudiation. The son of a Jewish tailor from Le Havre, Meyer had converted to Catholicism, and became an ultra-Catholic, anti-Dreyfusard and anti-Semite before marrying at the age of sixty the young, aristocratic Mademoiselle du Turenne. Proust despised him as a phoney and a renegade. People who become untrue to their origins are deplored at the conclusion of *Temps perdu*: 'I had difficulty recognising my old school-friend Bloch,' the narrator reports of an unexpected meeting with the enthusiastic, gauche, vulgar playwright. 'He had now adopted the name of Jacques du Rozier, under which it would have needed my grandfather's flair to detect . . . the bonds of Israel which my friend seemed definitively to have broken. A gloss of English chic had completely changed his appearance and . . . his once curly hair was brushed flat, parted down the middle and glistened with unguents . . . thanks to the haircut, to the removal of his moustache, to his elegance and sheer will-power, his Jewish nose had disappeared rather as a hunchback can almost seem as if he is standing up straight.' But on further scrutiny he decides that Bloch looks like a nervous old actor waiting to go on stage in the part of Shylock. Bloch – a pretentious, tasteless sophist – is perhaps the most contemptible character in *Temps perdu* (as Madame Verdurin is the nastiest) because he makes such a shabby contrast with the integrity of one of its heroes, 'the loyal Semitism of Swann'.

In *Temps perdu* Proust recurred time and again to anti-Semitism. His greatest fictive creation, Baron de Charlus, was never more disagreeable than in his diatribe against avaricious, sadistic Jews. He is outraged when Bloch's family rents a country house, La Commanderie, originally built by Christian

Knights Templar. 'As soon as a Jew has enough money to buy a place in the country he always chooses one that is called the Priory, Abbey, Minister, Chantry,' he fulminates. Worse still, the Blochs' office lies in a Paris street named to commemorate an order of Christian mendicant brothers. 'The profanation is all the more diabolical as within a stone's throw of the Rue des Blancs-Manteaux there is a street whose name escapes me, which is entirely taken over by the Jews, with Hebrew lettering on the shops, bakeries for unleavened bread, kosher butcheries, positively the *Judengasse* of Paris. That is where M. Bloch belongs.'

Proust was sympathetic, even reverential, towards his mother's Judaism and hated anti-Semitism as a maternal profanation. His maternal veneration was such that the anti-Semitism aroused by the Dreyfus Affair seemed a hateful insult to her. In 1894 a Jewish officer in French military intelligence, Captain Alfred Dreyfus, was convicted on concocted evidence of spying for Germany and was condemned to life imprisonment on Devil's Island. There is no doubt that he was racially victimised. There was an outcry in 1897 when Colonel Georges Picquart produced irrefutable evidence that it was another – and Catholic – officer who was guilty of the espionage. This forced a re-trial of Dreyfus, who in 1899 was again convicted by a verdict intended to uphold French military honour (he was, however, immediately pardoned by President Loubet). Anti-Dreyfusards supported Catholic and military institutions, and regarded the Dreyfus imbroglio (as Proust described in *La Prisonnière*) as a 'foreign machination intended to destroy the Intelligence Service, to undermine discipline, to enfeeble the army, to divide the French people, to prepare the way for invasion'. The anti-

Dreyfusards' ferocious and protracted polemical battle with the captain's champions hugely politicised French literary life. Indeed, the epithet *intellectuel* was coined by the radical politician and journalist Georges Clemenceau to describe those 'men of ideas, scholarship and creativity' such as Anatole France who signed a manifesto supporting Émile Zola's celebrated Dreyfusard manifesto 'J'accuse' (1898). In *Temps perdu* the Duc de Guermantes is convinced that his nephew Robert de Saint-Loup converted to Dreyfusism so as to be classed as an *intellectuel*.

Proust felt intensely involved in the Affair: it was the defining public event of his life. 'I was the first Dreyfusard, since it was I who approached Anatole France for his signature,' Proust claimed in 1919. It intensified his identification with Judaism; once, at least, he used the word 'us' when discussing Jews. The ultimate outcome of this long, ugly controversy – Dreyfus's military re-instatement, Picquart's promotion to the rank of general – was the one story with a happy ending in Proust's lifetime. He wept at Dreyfus's public vindication in 1906. 'I shall become more and more ill, I shall more and more miss the ones I have lost, and all that I dreamed of in my life will recede ever further beyond reach. But for Dreyfus and Picquart it is not so; for them life has proved as "providential" as in fairy tales.'

Proust's commitment – ethical, political and racial – to the cause of liberating and exonerating Dreyfus never veered into monomania. His interest in aesthetics always remained intense and original. Proust had lively, brilliant discussions with his intimate friends about literature, poetry, European painters, Oriental arts, symbolism, *vers libre*, and much else. His non-

Society friends coined a word to describe the shrill emotional intensity, the effusive affection, the elaborate, over-sensitive social manner and the precious aestheticism of their friend: to Proustify. There was zest, lyricism and even high spirits in his early Proustifying, eagerness and optimism about future experiences, a sense that life might prove enchanting. Proustification was always evident during his regular forays to Weber's restaurant in Rue Royale. 'Around 7.30 there would arrive *chez* Weber a pale young man, with the eyes of a fawn, sucking or fidgeting with the ends of his drooping brown moustache,' as Léon Daudet recalled. 'Having ordered a bunch of grapes and a glass of water, he would declare that he had just risen from bed, had influenza, was going back to bed, that the noise was making him ill, and look around anxiously, then mockingly, finally dissolving into enchanting laughter, and staying after all. Soon there would fall from his lips, in hesitant bursts, extraordinarily original remarks and devilishly clever ideas.'

It was the intensity of his scrutiny, the earnestness and originality with which he looked at people and studied objects, that made him so distinctive. His enormous dark eyes, with their heavy, half-closed lids, followed everything. He put himself through an instinctual training for his vocation even before he understood what his vocation was. A novelist, he declared, learns to observe and memorise in distinctive ways: 'the writer, long before he knew he was going to be one, habitually avoided looking at all sorts of things other people noticed, and was, in consequence, accused by others of absent-mindedness and by himself of inattention, while all the time he was ordering his eyes and ears to retain forever what to others seemed puerile.' This might seem like fatuous affectation, but when the novelist finally comes to write his masterpiece, 'there is not a gesture of his characters, a mannerism, an accent, which has not impregnated his memory; there is not a single invented character to whom he could not give sixty names of people he has observed, of whom one poses for a grimace, another for an eyeglass, another for his temper.'

Many examples of Proust's youthful lyricism survived in *Temps perdu* though the mood died in his life. The shimmering accounts of childhood, his descriptions of the flat countryside south-west of Chartres and of holidays on the Normandy coast show the intensity and gratitude of his perceptions. In *Sodome et Gomorrhe* there is a passage of heightened yet disorientated sensibilities and a distorted sense of time that preserves his boyish sense of wonder. The narrator – Proust's fictional impersonator – is among a group of guests journeying from a small railway station in Normandy to a country house party held by the odious Madame Verdurin.

> Once we were in the carriages which had come to meet us, we no longer had any idea where we were; the roads were not lighted; we could tell by the louder sound of the wheels that we were passing through a village, we thought we had arrived, we found ourselves once more in open country, we heard bells in the distance, we forgot that we were in evening dress, and we were dozing when, at the end of this long darkness which, what with the distance we had travelled and the incidents characteristic of all rail journeys, seemed to have carried us on to a late hour of the night, and almost half way back to Paris, suddenly, after the crunching of the carriage wheels over a finer gravel had revealed to us that we had turned into the park, there burst forth, reintro-

ducing us into a social existence, the dazzling lights of the drawing-room, then of the dining-room where we were startled to hear eight o'clock strike, an hour that we supposed had long passed, while innumerable courses and fine wines circulated among the men in black and women with bare arms, at a dinner ablaze with light like a real metropolitan dinner-party.

This description of a journey by horse-drawn carriage through a darkened countryside is a distillation of Proustian memories: it is the synthesis and refinement of experience by a man who was alert, inquisitive and original but above all *intense* in all his observations. Léon Daudet has described an occasion near the turn of the century when he encountered Proust, who was visiting Fontainebleau as a health cure. 'He stayed shut in his room all day, then, in the evening, he consented to take a drive through the forest under the stars. He was the most charming, the most fanciful, the most surreal of companions, as if a will-o-the-wisp sat on the cushions of the victoria. Not seeing what other people see, he saw things that no one else saw.'

CHAPTER 3

An Ark of My Own

The little dilettante perched on the cushions of the victoria trundling through the forest of Fontainebleau seemed too fey to attain greatness. His concentration on amusing his friends and winning the approval of salon hostesses promised to bring only the most ephemeral success. His parents would have been incredulous, and probably at any time before 1913 his friends equally disbelieving, of any prediction of his ultimate achievements. His gifts, his originality, his crazy shrewdness were not evidently stronger than his exhausting nervous excitability and his excessive need of the good opinion of others. As a man in his thirties, he continued, like a pampered child, to live in his parents' Paris apartment where he became an increasingly querulous and disruptive malingerer. Dr Proust's description in the 1890s of a certain type of neurasthenic patient sounds like a case-study of his problem son. 'Their emotionalism is extreme; everything impresses them, and every emotion is especially distressing to them because they perceive with unusual vividness the diverse emotions produced . . . by all emotional states.' Such neurasthenics succumb to hypochondria, anxious obsessions, intense but random outbursts of enthusiasm, according to Dr Proust. 'Sufferers are conscious of their moral inferiority,' he continued. 'They try their hand at occupations and subjects of study that seem suited to excite their interest; but . . . they tire quickly, are seized with distaste for their undertaking, and soon abandon it.' Certainly Marcel Proust throughout his early manhood depressed his parents by shirking steady employment, exasperated them with his irritable weakness and baffled them with his unreliability. His exceptional perseverance was not yet evident: although his quirks always seemed distinctive, his true powers only became clear in his forties. 'There were in Marcel Proust,' Lucien Daudet judged with hindsight, 'all the elements of a spoilt child: he never actually became one, because his genius had the corrective effect of dissevering these elements – his genius, his dignity and also his humour.'

Proust made an insignificant literary debut in 1896 with his luxuriously produced collection of languishing reveries and short stories about love and titled people, *Les Plaisirs et le jours*. The book, like his newspaper articles, confirmed his reputation as a semi-professional diner-out: Gide confessed that until he read *Du côté de chez Swann* he had dismissed Proust contemptuously as 'a snob, a worldly amateur.' For four years, until 1899, Proust worked – initially with concentrated effort but after 1897 in only a desultory way – at his abortive novel *Jean Santeuil*. This tentative, limited and humourless preliminary effort at the novel that evolved into *Temps perdu* was discarded: one of the roots of its failure is that Sodom, which plays so prominent a part in *Temps perdu*, was a theme to which Proust could only allude in oblique terms while his parents lived. After 1900 he prepared his Ruskin translations and commentaries, though it is hard to say if he laboured over them or tinkered with them: overall his approach to work remained that of a youthful dilettante, although he was no longer quite young.

His parents' deaths were indispensable for his genius to mature: their deaths proved his personal and creative liberation. One day in November 1903 Dr Proust was carried home from work on a stretcher, stricken by a cerebral haemorrhage, and died at the age of sixty-nine without recovering consciousness: his death, like his elder son's, was arguably induced by over-work. 'How very sweet and simple he was,' Proust reflected at the time. 'I tried, if not exactly to fulfil his expectations – for I am well aware that I was always the black spot of his life – but to show him my affection.' Proust became more decisive and confident after his father's death: he enjoyed, too, an outburst of heterosexual curiosity. He had for some time been a confidential intermediary between his friend Louis, marquis d'Albufera and a young actress called Louisa de Mornand, who had been kept by another of Proust's noble companions, Bertrand de Fénelon, before she became Albufera's mistress. Proust flirted with her while he mourned. His interest became increasingly explicit, and when he visited her on a Sunday evening in April 1904 to collect two photographs, she received him while lying under the canopy of her four-poster bed. It seems likely that they had sex-ual relations that night, and perhaps intermittently for several months – possibly until December 1904. 'No child that has just been given its first doll was ever as happy as I am,' he trilled on the Monday morning after his first night with Mornand. 'Ours was an *amitié amoureuse*', she explained in 1928, 'in which there was no element of a banal flirtation nor of an exclusive liaison, but on Proust's side a strong passion tinged with affection and desire, and on mine an attachment that was more than com-radeship.'

Some of his happiness may have come from fulfilling a manly

role that his father had played – particularly as his inamorata made clandestine night visits to his bedroom in the parental apartment where his mother lay sleeping. But Proust's triangular entanglement with Louis d'Albufera and Louisa de Mornand satisfied other profound creative and personal needs. It bridged the two genders, confounded and confused the participants' sexual identities, and its physical pleasures depended on Proust's highly developed imaginary world of symbols and meanings. He was always thrilled by overlapping erotic entanglements, and loved to plot the development of complicated sympathies among both his acquaintances and his characters: his prodigious imagination used Mornand, and others, to devise intricate patterns of attraction. It surely brought exciting feelings of closer sexual intimacy with Fénelon and Albufera, two men who had long attracted him because of their apparently unassailable heterosexuality, men with whose bodies he could achieve a pleasurable fantasy confusion by going to bed with their young mistress. Léon Daudet 'never knew anyone . . . more adept at transforming himself, according to his desire, into a psychological state analogous' to those of people in whom he was keenly interested. Proust's motivation, at this time, is comparable to that of Roberto Prezioso, a Triestine newspaper editor who having received private English lessons from James Joyce, made physical advances and an overt declaration to Nora Joyce in 1913: Joyce suspected that he was the true object of Prezioso's longing, and that for Prezioso the only way that two men could approach carnal union was through the body of a woman they had shared. Louisa de Mornand, then, was less important to Proust for the pleasure she helped him to achieve than for the discoveries he achieved through her about what it felt like to be

Fénelon or Albufera. This was another side – imaginative and erotic – to proustifying.

His feelings at this time for Albufera were so strong that when, in 1904, he missed, as a result of his own dilatory fussing, a train that would take him to visit '*mon petit Albu*', he broke into uncontrollable tears, and had an asthma attack that lasted nineteen hours. 'My little Albu I am well and truly stupefied by so many consecutive hours of physical suffering and above all by all the drugs that I've had to take, without which I would have again experienced all that I met with so violently after missing the train.' The crisis, though, he assured Albufera from his sick-room, had ended with 'an intense paroxysm, an enormous enlargement of my friendship for you'. Such overwrought scenes would be despicable if it was not for Proust's creative vocation. The mutually intense and possessive relationship between Proust and his mother had reduced the likelihood that he would seek emotional fulfilment in conventional ways, and by the mid-1890s he was already an expert in the pains, longings and dreaminess of unreciprocated love. By the turn of the century (when he was twenty-eight) his amatory life was set in a pattern of intense crushes, which were often unrealistic and always transient, combined with an overpowering demand for affirmative attention and almost unbalanced cravings.

Once Proust had accepted his vocation (after his mother's death in 1905) to write his great novel, he seems to have ensured more than ever that he remained unfulfilled and even twisted in his emotions. 'Do not grumble,' he told Prince Antoine Bibesco, who had consulted him about some trouble with a woman; 'an unhappy love affair is an unequalled acquisition.' Proust, it seems, needed to be unhappy, although he retained a child's capacity for joy: certainly his memories of his *amitié amoureuse* with Mornand developed a rancid flavour by the time that he drew upon them to write *Temps perdu*. She contributed to the characterisation of both the narrator's deceitful mistress Albertine and of Rachel, a sly, unkind, mercenary prostitute of little beauty or charm. Proust's unforgiving, resentful literary versions of Mornand suggest the annoyance of a man against the woman who showed him uncomfortable truths about himself. Albufera did not read any of Proust's books until *Le côté de Guermantes I* was published in late 1920: the passages describing Saint-Loup's love affair with Rachel, which recycled Proust's memories of Albufera's relations with Mornand, made him indignant – especially as Saint-Loup's sexual preference is for men. 'It's a pity; we used to be very close friends,' Proust said to his housekeeper Céleste Albaret after reading aloud to her a long, angry letter from Albufera. 'He never saw the duke again, but he didn't miss him,' Céleste Albaret recalled. By 1921 Proust was no longer in a state to repine over a final rupture with someone whom he described as 'kind and generous . . . but not very bright'.

In July 1905 the Duchesse de Gramont (mother of Proust's friend Armand de Guiche and devoted stepmother of Elisabeth de Clermont-Tonnerre) died. Her last days were filled with distress, for she feared that as a Jewess who had converted to Catholicism on her marriage, she might be prevented from a reunion in Heaven with her children. Although neither Proust nor his mother believed in an afterlife, he was desolated when the gravity of the duchess's illness became unmistakable. His condolences to Guiche were heartfelt if discomfiting: 'To think that your Mother perhaps felt that she was going to leave you, perhaps knew that never, for *all of eternity never*, would she ever again see *you*, from whom she drew all her happiness, it's that thought which has agonised me.' It distressed him to realise how much the Gramonts mirrored the Prousts with the Jewish mother and baptised Catholic child who would be separated by death for Eternity. The duchess's death was 'intolerably sad', he told Elisabeth de Clermont-Tonnerre. 'I don't want to think of it – yet I think of it ceaselessly . . . I knew her, and understand what death meant to her by separating her from all her children whom she adored.'

Proust's distress at the duchess's death proved only a subdued rehearsal for the fear and grief that overpowered him two months later. In September his mother fell ill with uraemia (in which urinary constituents usually eliminated in the kidneys enter the bloodstream), and refused the tests and treatment, as well as food and medicine, that might have saved her life. Her doting son, still living in her apartment, was panic-stricken about her survival and his own. 'I am so incapable of living without her; so vulnerable in every way,' he wrote to Robert de Montesquiou as she lay *in extremis*. Even at the end she remained hyper-alert to his needs. While she lay dying, so a servant told Proust, 'Madame trembled like a leaf, although she was quite unconscious, whenever she heard your three rings on the bell, because however quietly you tried to ring that week you have a way that couldn't be confused for anyone else's.' Her death left him sundered. 'My life henceforth has lost its only purpose, its only sweetness, its only love, its only consolation,' he told Montesquiou. 'Because of my bad health I was the sorrow and worry of her life,' he wrote in plaintive remorse. 'She must have understood the wisdom of parents who, before dying, kill their little children.' After she died he could only lament 'my ravaged life, my ruined heart'; and later he characterised men like himself, the inhabitants of Sodom, as 'sons without a mother, to whom they are obliged to lie even up to the hour when they close her eyes.'

Following his mother's funeral, stunned and mangled by grief, he lay in bed for several days weeping and starving himself. He remained obsessed with her memory, anguished by her absence and only coped with the intensity of his emotions by erecting barriers against the world. For six weeks he secluded himself under supervision in a sanatorium, and when eventually he returned to Paris apartment life, continued to isolate himself under the pretext of poor health and strained nerves. This reaction was in absolute conformity with his father's precepts. Dr Proust's greatest service to French health had been to propose a *cordon sanitaire* to exclude cholera from Europe, and to negotiate its enforcement at a series of international conferences in the 1890s with British and Ottoman officials. It was in the same decade, too, that he urged parents and physicians to erect an emotional cordon to protect highly strung children from their excessive emotionalism. As 'nothing is more contagious than an emotional state', such children should be 'removed' from surroundings or situations that agitate them as well as being isolated from 'the life of those around them'. The doctor's belief that overwrought men, women and children could immunise themselves against the susceptibility of their feelings by secluding themselves had an overwhelming influence on his son's life choices and the plot of *Temps perdu*. 'In withdrawing from his habitual circles,' Dr Proust observed, 'the patient . . . breaks away from that atmosphere of solicitude and commiseration, and sometimes also of ironical indifference, by which his depression and irritability have been fostered.'

Seclusion had long tempted Proust as a state in which he might fulfil his vocation. 'When I was a child,' he had written in 1896, 'the fate of no holy figure seemed to me more miserable than that of Noah, who was confined to his Ark by the Flood for forty days. But, later, I was often ill, and condemned to remain for long periods in an Ark of my own. It was then that I understood what a wonderful view of the world Noah could command from his Ark, despite being shut in, and though darkness enveloped the earth.' From early manhood he had affected world-weariness: 'better dream your life than live it, even though to live it is still only a dream'; only the redemptive powers of art and intellect could console him. He had railed against 'this life in which every pleasure is paid for without having been enjoyed' and where everything ends in 'miserable repugnance'. More than ever, after his mother's death in 1905, this outlook (superficially so blasé and ungrateful) became entrenched. Proust sought (during the seventeen years of life that remained to him) to confine himself in a Noah's Ark of his own devising. He adapted his father's *cordon sanitaire* to encircle his invalid's darkened bedroom. His life in the Ark helped to preserve the immediacy of his vision of people, objects and sensations. His privileges as a neurasthenic removed him from the agitation and pressure of Paris, enabled him to preserve and revivify the immediacy and vitality of his childhood sense of wonder, and intensified his adult awareness. His self-sequestration saved him from being besmirched, compromised or depersonalised by the minor vices, reductive judgements, anodyne tendencies and anonymous routines of a twentieth-century city.

His 'reclusiveness', he told an interviewer in 1913, had proved 'profoundly helpful to my work. Darkness, silence and solitude, by throwing their heavy cloaks over my shoulders, have forced me to recreate all the light, all the music and all the joys of nature and society in myself. My spiritual being is no longer confounded by the barriers of the visible world.' In effect Proust made himself the slave of illness. Prince Antoine Bibesco, whom Proust once said understood him best, certainly regarded him as a 'neuropathic case' who indulged in 'voluntary ill-health'. Bibesco felt his friend's 'malady was not very serious, that he was inclined to exaggerate and instinctively take advantage of it, and that, from the beginning, it was a method of blackmail, a refuge from existence, a means of procuring all the indulgences he found necessary.'

His parents had tried to foil the more disruptive whims of their pampered child, and had countermanded his inordinate claims on their servants. But after 1905 he lived in his own establishment. He made the requisite arrangements, isolated himself according to his needs, and paid the cost to live with himself on the terms that he willed. Proust inherited enough money (over 1.3 million francs in 1906) to preserve his cushioned way of life. He respected men who made fortunes from Stock Exchange manipulations – Charles Swann, like Sydney Schiff, was a stockbroker who had inherited his seat on the Bourse – and became an incorrigible speculator. The economist Paul Einzig judged that the rentier Proust was 'guided by the classical principle of the Rothschilds – never ring the bell while the shares are rising': that is, to hold on in an upward market. The truth is, though, that Proust had mixed luck. 'Rubber stocks, oil shares and the rest always wait until the day after I buy for the bottom to drop out of the market', he complained in 1906. He was always trying to collect financial tips and stockbrokers' gossip, and always going astray ('Someone advised me not to sell Egyptian Refineries and immediately from 1600 they fell to 500'). He often appealed for advice to the so-called 'best sources', but seldom heeded his advisers' warnings. Although he would have been a richer speculator if he had been less optimistic, in *Temps retrouvé* he satirised the pessimistic credulity of Stock Exchange operators who always credit the gloomiest rumours. His influential Stock Exchange connections included Reynaldo Hahn's Belgian banker friend Baron Léon Lambert, and Walter Berry, Edith Wharton's lawyer friend who presided over the US Chamber of Commerce in Paris. Before the war, too, in a transparent and unsuccessful effort to revive his waning intimacy with Albufera, he pretended to think that the young nobleman was an adept financier and consulted him about his shareholdings in the De Beers and Rio Tinto mining companies. Especially, though, he consulted the cream of Parisian Jewish *haute finance*, pre-eminently Lionel Hauser (the Paris representative of the Warburgs), Gustave and Léon Neuberger of Rothschilds, the lawyer Émile Straus (who was reputedly an illegitimate Rothschild) and the economist Georges Lévy.

Proust's investment policy seems partly to have reflected his state of boredom, and partly his susceptibility to the euphonious and exotic. The 'aesthetic pleasure' of the soft place-names of France – the reverberating sounds and historic associations of Montfort-L'Amaury, Cossé-le-Vivien, Nanteuil-le-Haudoin, Cricquetot-L'Esneval and La Ferté-Vidame – 'ravished Proust,' his protégé Marcel Plantevignes recalled. Proust's susceptibility to what Plantevignes called 'artistic geography' proved expensive, though. His holdings in the United States Steel Corporation or New York City bonds might be lucrative but sounded prosaic: he was more attracted by mellifluously titled companies such as Pins des Landes, Malacca Rubber Plantations, Banco Español del Rio de la Plata, Oriental Carpet, Doubowaia Balka and North Caucasian Oilfields. Foreign railways, too, interested the housebound asthmatic: Mexico Tramways, United Railways of Havana, the Tanganyika Railway, or (much to be savoured) S. A. Chemin de Fer de Rosario à Puerto Belgrano. Overall, Proust was too credulous and remote to make a successful speculator: Hauser begged not to be involved in some of his investments.

During 1908 Proust strove to bolster the intensity of his friendship with Albufera. In May he wrote recalling the 'subtle, profound, tender' beginnings of their *amitié*. 'My affection hasn't changed,' he promised, adding with customary self-abnegation, 'you have done me immense services and (to my great chagrin) I have never done you any at all.' He asked to be loaned some of Albufera's family photograph albums – always his way of seeking intimacy – and then, as a confidential privilege, revealed that he was working on a new literary project, which was evidently *Temps perdu*. He listed its component themes: the French nobility, Paris, novel-writing, tombstones and stained-glass, and it would also include, he promised, 'an essay on pederasty (not easy to publish)'. Proust had settled, in fact, to write his masterpiece, which it would have been impossible to consider publishing if his parents had still been alive. Violet Schiff suspected that it was Proust's 'devotion to his mother that prevented him from beginning *À la recherche du temps perdu* until he was approaching forty, several years after her death.' Primarily he needed the 'detachment' – the sense of finally being emotionally alone – that her death provided, but he also 'probably didn't want to shock her with his suspect knowledge of perversion'. Violet Schiff used to invoke a Proustian rule that her husband translated in *Temps retrouvé*: 'One can only recreate what one loves by repudiating it.' She understood that the deaths of Proust's parents' were a creative liberation, though he might have recoiled from admitting it.

The structure of Proust's masterpiece was conceived and settled in 1908. Although he was revising and amplifying the text almost to the moment of his death, the entirety was meticulously planned, as he declared with justifiable pride in 1919: 'The final chapter of the final volume was written immediately after the first chapter of the first volume.' His achievement seems all the more remarkable because there are such a variety of moods in the book's many volumes. Comedies of manners, such as the parties *chez* Verdurin or Guermantes, and moments of intense personal tragedy encase long passages of internal reveries, digressive commentaries, tireless disquisitions on the disappointments and frustration of love, analyses of aesthetics, mordant pictures of human types, uncomfortable scrutiny of human motives and voyeuristic sexual revelations. Proust insisted that he had not written a *roman à clef*, and that his leading characters were each modelled on the traits or experiences of eight or ten people known in life. This claim was partly made to disarm the protesting acquaintances whom he had satirised, but in substance it is true.

Although Proust was dissatisfied by his book titles, the overarching title of his sequence resounds with significance. In 1906 he had read Alexandre Dumas's novel *Le Chevalier d'Harmental*, which features a family living at 5 Rue du Temps-Perdu. This detail evidently came to resonate in his imagination for the chosen title of his life work was *À la recherche du temps perdu*. This phrase denotes *making up for lost time* as much as *in search of lost time* (the Shakespearean title bestowed on the earliest English translation, *In remembrance of things past*, is gravely misleading). As Sydney Schiff told Proust when he was dying, there is a 'melancholy nuance' in the novel's title, 'a touch of poignancy, of suggestiveness – a double meaning to the word *perdu*' – evoking time that has been squandered and a personal history that is regretted for its waste. There is a sympathetic minor character in *Temps perdu* – a financially ruined nobleman, living in a derelict château, but with fine tastes and sensibility – whose ancestral motto is a pun on his surname, Saylor, but also a motif for the novel. The Saylors' motto 'Ne sçais l'heure' is a corruption of a Latin maxim, *Vides horam nescis horam*, which can be rendered in French as 'tu vois l'heure, tu ne sais l'heure' ('You see the hour but you don't know the hour'). The ruined nobleman is not an obtrusive figure in *Temps perdu* but he holds major significance. He exists to remind readers of an obsessive Proustian fear: that one never knows how much time one has left ('I am ill, very ill, and consequently in a hurry to be published,' Proust declared in 1912 with ten years of life ahead); that every year one passes in ignorance a date which seems unremarkable but which will eventually, in some unknown year, become the date of one's death. Proust fretted over the cruel reality that none of us (except suicides) can foretell the timing of our demise: although we know that death may strike at any moment, we persuade ourselves that it is a distant prospect rather than an imminent event. There is a poignant passage in *Le côté de Guermantes* describing someone who decides he needs fresh air, fusses over which coat to wear, which cab to hail, settles in the cab happily anticipating a friend's visit later in the afternoon, imagines tomorrow's fine weather, without realising that he is already in the thrall of death, and will die as the carriage enters the Champs-Élysées.

In *Sodome et Gomorrhe* the narrator becomes oppressed, while wandering in some country lanes, by his sense of wasted time, and his realisation that life's possibilities are fleeting and finite. 'Reflecting that their trees, pears, apples, tamarisks, would outlive me, I seemed to receive from them the advice to set myself to work at last, before the hour should strike of eternal rest.' Time is a precious sensual commodity in Proust's universe. 'An hour is not merely an hour; it is a vase filled with perfumes, with sounds, with projects, with climates.'

Proust's commitment to write his great novel was frustrated by his nervous and physical weakness. In 1910 he imposed even more austerely hermetic habits on himself under the intensified conviction that he had an urgent and important appointment to write his essential book. It seemed at times a process of self-embalmment. He became more than ever apprehensive, querulous and repetitive, hiding in his apartment, protecting himself from the tactless, peremptory and selfish demands of other people's friendliness, sending out interminable and often insipid letters in the tone (as Samuel Beckett said) of a fussy old dowager – and incessantly, obsessively, industriously he wrote his great novel. His character Octave – originally an elegant nullity nicknamed 'The Also-Ran' but later a renowned author – is ultimately represented in *Temps retrouvé* by a partial self-portrait in the last dozen years of his life: 'acquaintance with the husband of Andrée was neither very easy nor very agreeable, and the friendship one offered him was doomed to many disappointments. He was already very ill and spared himself fatigues other than those likely to give him pleasure. He only liked meetings with people he did not know, people who had a chance of seeming, in his ardent imagination, different from the rest. He knew his old friends too well, was aware of what could be expected of them, and they were no longer worth a dangerous and perhaps fatal fatigue.'

Proust's behaviour resembled that of another of the Schiffs' guests of honour at the Majestic, Diaghilev, 'a man of many, very many, friends, and a man of unique, irresistible charm', as Serge Lifar wrote. 'Diaghilev loved friends and mankind, and was faithful to that love; but individuals were purely *episodes* in his creative activity, *necessary* at one moment, but *nuisances* when new horizons opened before him. From that moment, they ceased to exist for him.' Proust judged that this is a sane and admirable attitude for anyone with creative work to finish. He increasingly insisted on the 'unreality' of other people, 'their inability to satisfy us, as for instance in social pleasures, which at best cause that discomfort which is provoked by unwelcome food,' as he wrote in a passage that must have troubled Schiff when he translated *Temps retrouvé*. Friendship was 'a pretence' for the true artist, Proust continued.

> The artist who gives up an hour of work to converse for that time with a friend knows that he is sacrificing reality to an illusion (friends being friends only in the sense of sweet madness which overcomes us in life and to which we yield, though at the back of our minds we know it to be the error of a lunatic who imagines the furniture to be alive and talks to it).

His hypochondria, pedantry, excessive sensibilities and touchiness became ever more pronounced. To discourage people from depleting his time and energy Proust used 'sham tiffs, faked complications, so-called wounded pride, to skirt the danger of excessive social attentiveness,' as one friend lamented. Proust shut himself into his Ark because he believed it was the only way he could discover the meaning beneath appearances: that is, to create great art. 'The work of our pride, our passion, our emulative spirit, our abstract intelligence, our habits, must be undone by art, which takes the opposite course and returns to the depths where the real has its unknown being . . . it means above all abrogating our most cherished illusions.'

In 1910 Proust withdrew deeper from the world in order more vividly to relive it. He turned his sickroom into a place of concentrated attentiveness and idiosyncratic perception. 'He never noticed things at all apart from some quality of interest or beauty he found in them,' thought an occasional visitor to his post-war apartment, Sydney Schiff.

> When, for instance, the sun, casting its rays into the corner of the room, illuminated it in some fashion that pleased him, or touched with fantastic colour an object – a jug or a coffee-cup or a half-emptied glass of beer – then his eyes, falling on whatever object it was, would remain fixed upon it, sometimes for an hour or more, and whether it was day or night, he would not allow it to be moved. Sometimes he insisted on it remaining indefinitely, because he wanted to renew the sensation it had given him, so it often happened that in different parts of the room there were articles left for days in unsuitable places in case the light or the atmosphere should again transmute them into something different.

Sometimes Proust hankered for an end to his peevish invalid seclusion, and occasionally he broke from its grip: there were outbursts of sociability in the later years of the World War and again in his final summer. 'Not having even seen my family for several years,' he explained to Schiff in 1921, 'being unable to read, write, eat, get up, except for a rare outing like the one I made to see you, I could not persevere in such a frightful existence except by cherishing the illusion, shattered daily but renewed again next day, that everything will change. I have lived for the last fifteen years, one day at a time, on such hopes.'

Proust still received a few visitors after he intensified his seclusion in 1910. Jean Cocteau recorded several visits to Proust's apartment in Boulevard Haussmann during that year: 'Proust received us on his bed, fully dressed, wearing his collar, tie and gloves, terrified of a whiff of perfume, a breath of air, a window half open or a ray of sunshine.' He teased Cocteau by claiming that he was so susceptible to asthma that a passage in Debussy's opera *Pelléas et Mélisande*, suggestive of the wind whistling over a sea-shore, would induce a respiratory crisis. At times he read aloud from the manuscript of the first volume of *Temps perdu* entitled *Du côté de chez Swann*. 'These séances added a chaos of perspective to the pestilential disorder of the room,' Cocteau recorded. 'Proust read from anywhere, missed pages, turned over several, began again, stopped to tell us that the raising of a hat in the first chapter would be explained in the final volume, burst out laughing behind his gloved hand.' Sometimes he would exclaim, repeatedly, 'It is too stupid', and refuse to read any more. On other occasions, running his hands through his long, inky hair that he cut himself, he would retreat to his dressing-room. Cocteau glimpsed him there 'standing in his shirtsleeves and a violet waistcoat, his torso looking like a mechanical toy holding a plate in one hand, a fork in the other, eating noodles.'

Proust adapted a maxim of La Bruyère's to say: 'Men often want to be loved and yet do not know how to be, they seek defeat and so are forced to remain free.' Though Proust often fell in love, or (more accurately) met people by whom he wanted to be cherished ardently, he always behaved with clumsy idiosyncrasy, and denounced love as flawed or futile. Charles Swann makes noble acts of renunciation after his marriage to the courtesan Odette de Crécy, yet spoils his bliss by his compulsion to browbeat her with questions about her previous lovers. His need to be reassured that she has never cared for anyone as much as for him makes him behave like an examining magistrate trying to cajole a suspect into confession. 'Perpetual vivisection,' wrote Prince Antoine Bibesco, 'that is Marcel's conception of love, a conception sinister enough, in which the rôle of Sherlock Holmes is doubled with that of Othello.' Each of us, Proust insisted, is irretrievably trapped in inviolable solitude. Love, he claimed, is a self-deluding excitement in which the lover invents an imaginary person, who is all too cruelly different from the person who bears the loved-one's name in the real world. Lovers squander their energies, their time, their lives on a factitious projection of their own personality; so many extraneous emotional associations are superimposed on the beloved ones that their identities are deformed out of all recognition. Love, Proust insists, wells up, satisfies itself, and then like all fantasy feelings, it evaporates. 'Happiness,' he concluded in *Temps retrouvé*, 'serves hardly any other purpose than to make unhappiness possible . . . Without happiness, if only the happiness of hope, there would be no cruelty and therefore no fruits of misfortune.'

À la recherche du temps perdu is a historian's novel. As well as unravelling the secret skeins of time, and tracing the personal stories and public trends of France under the Third Republic, Proust was ensuring that he became an historical personage in his own right. Artistic immortality was perhaps chief among Proust's motives in writing his novel: he wanted to be remembered long after his death for the words he had written. His ideas on art, memory and eternity were derived from John Ruskin, the English historian, critic and social reformer, of whom Proust made a personal cult. When Ruskin died in 1900, Proust cultivated a mood of 'healthy sadness', feeling confident (as he said) 'how little death matters when I see how powerfully this dead man lives on, how much I admire him, listen to him, try to understand him'. For Proust it was as inconceivable to repudiate a dead artist whom he admired as it would have been to denounce the memory of his mother. Memory honoured, preserved, even enhanced the reputations of the dead; above all, for Proust, the act of memory was a defining act of intelligence. 'You are one of those rare beings,' he wrote to Princesse de Caraman-Chimay after the suicide of her cousin, 'the only ones worthy of respect and commiseration, in whose hearts the dead live on.' At times he was hopeful: 'something may survive of a man after his death, if that man was an artist, and took pains with his work'; in other moods more doubtful: 'if art was indeed a prolongation of life, was it worth while to sacrifice anything to it, was it not as unreal as life itself?' As it proved, Proust succeeded in his strategy to preserve his sensibility and personal vision after his death, and thus avoid the oblivion of the world's forgetfulness.

'Proust,' a reader asserted after his death, 'was much more than a sentimental autobiographer of genius; he was a man trying to maintain his soul alive.' And a few years later, when Suzy Proust told Abbé Mugnier how much she still regretted her uncle's death, Mugnier replied: 'Marcel Proust, why no one is less dead than he is.' Mugnier said what Proust most wanted to be true.

Proust was a historian as well as someone who wanted to figure in history. He was steeped in tradition, fastidious in his historic sense, respectful of historic detail. He dissected and analysed the past as well as possessing a superlative gift for interpreting his own period. Despite being (with *Ulysses*) the most original novel of its epoch, *À la recherche du temps perdu* is, supremely, a historian's novel: 'The acuteness of his sense of time, with which his book is shot all through, out of which it arose, gives it a particular appeal for the historian,' according to the Oxford historian A. L. Rowse, for whom the sequence was 'the *Paradiso, Purgatorio*, and *Inferno* of the twentieth century'. Proust's Anglophone admirers, in particular, extolled him as a historian of the Belle Époque and of its grim, convulsive sequel, the European war. Edmund Wilson in the Great Depression year of 1931 pictured Proust as 'the last great historian of the loves, the society, the intelligence, the diplomacy, the literature and the art of the Heartbreak House of capitalist culture'. Similarly, the political theorist John Strachey praised *Temps perdu* in 1932 for 'reflect[ing] in a kind of agony the characteristics of the epoch' and for providing, besides much else, a history of the contemporary Death-Wish. 'Proust, in truth, sang a long agonised requiem mass over the highest expression of human life of which French bourgeois society under the Third Republic had been capable.'

Sex and drugs helped to shape his fictional sequence. 'No banishment,' Proust wrote in *La Prisonnière*, 'to the South Pole, or to the summit of Mont Blanc, can separate us so entirely from our fellow creatures as a prolonged residence in the seclusion of a secret vice, that is to say in a state of mind that is different from theirs.' Proust's sex life, for the most part, was dreamy and vicarious. It took place, largely, in an Ark of his own making: the crucial transactions were mostly interior fantasies with only the notional involvement of other people's bodies. 'The world of the possible is more extensive than the real world,' he told Violet Schiff. His imagination created a secluded private domain which was richer, because more privileged and illimitable, than reality. It could encompass anyone. He did not feel he needed to meet people to understand them: when a mutual friend offered to introduce him to the playwright Georges de Porto-Riche, he insisted it was unnecessary because, in his head, 'I'm already Porto-Riche [*Mais Porto-Riche, c'est moi*].'

Proust was an amateur toxicologist with a deplorable taste for experimenting on his own body. His lifelong companions, both consoling and destructive, were his anti-asthma cigarettes, his Legas fumigation powders, and his drugs. Amyl nitrate, valerian, opiates and barbiturates brought sleep's oblivion and afterwards a stupefied hangover from which pure adrenalin and caffeine revived him. He had the habitual drug user's cunning, and manipulated Louis Gautier-Vignal, who deplored his mentor's unhealthy diet and misuse of medicines, into obtaining a surreptitious supply of German and Swiss drugs despite these supplies having been severed by official war-time restrictions. Gautier-Vignal did Proust's bidding; but he did not want to. In *La Prisonnière* Proust depicted one of his noblest characters, Bergotte, a great novelist, in a version of his own habits. Stricken by pain and insomnia, Bergotte despairs of doctors and tries various narcotics – 'with success, but to excess'. Bergotte, like his creator, samples them all. One swallows a new drug, Proust reflected from direct experience, with delicious anticipation of the unknown. 'The heart pounds away like on one's first night with a new lover. Into what unknown sorts of dream will the newcomer lead us?' Proust personifies his drugs as a dominant male: 'He is inside us now, he has control of our thoughts.' Proust was submissive, eager and receptive: he wanted chemicals to penetrate, possess and overpower him. Drugs certainly mastered the moods and details of *Temps perdu*. The use of Veronal (a barbiturate sleeping-draught) and opiates does not prevent its narrator from recalling lines of poetry when awake in a hangover, after a night of narcotic sleep, but the drugs render him incapable of participating in everyday existence, sap his initiative and disrupt his memory. Proust's drug habits enhanced his powers as a novelist of dreams and trances and sustained his explorations in the exciting serendipitous jungles of the unconscious.

Proust said he was a novelist who had a 'unique need of precise information, who must have an exact knowledge of the things about which I'm talking'. His punctilious care for the minute accuracy of his book required enquiries to horticulturalists, dressmakers, astronomers, landowners, genealogists, pharmacists, soldiers, Society gossips, waiters, footmen, butchers and pimps. He once visited the Mexican-born literary intellectual Ramon Fernandez at midnight, in the middle of a Paris air-raid, to seek precise instruction on the pronunciation of *senza rigore*, a musical instruction that was to appear in *Jeunes filles en fleurs*.

This painstaking accumulation of details and allusions did

not turn Proust into a dry-as-dust pedant. Instead he remained a visionary who found rapturous transcendence in the most commonplace or chance events. He determined to unfold his views through a series of fortuitous events and trivial physical sensations that unexpectedly overwhelm the narrator with momentous enlargements of his understanding. These sudden intuitions of a moment are presented with pictorial vividness, and were intended to be as beautiful and suggestive as Old Master paintings. They were of utmost importance to Proust and his world, and were tantamount to a series of religious revelations: as Middleton Murry wrote in a tribute after Proust's death, 'this modern of the moderns, this *raffiné* of *raffinés*, had a mystical strain in his composition.'

These episodes of unheralded mystical insight mark the passage of time throughout successive volumes of *Temps perdu* but reach their apotheosis in a succession of minor incidents and colossal revelations in *Temps retrouvé* when the narrator attends a party given by Prince and Princesse de Guermantes in Paris. Entering the courtyard of their house, the narrator stumbles over some paving stones. Their unevenness provokes in him a dazzling, eruptive memory of some uneven stones at St Mark's in Venice. It is a transcendent moment for him: 'a deep azure intoxicated my eyes, a feeling of freshness, of dazzling light enveloped me'. His doubts about 'the reality of my literary gifts, and even regarding the reality of literature itself, were dispersed as if by magic.' He becomes confident that he can write his great novel: 'all my apprehensions, all my intellectual doubts were dissipated.' He associates this revelation with other timeless intimations that have occurred in his life. The savour of the madeleine steeped in an infusion of tea, described in *Swann*, is

the most famous of these epiphanies; but the narrator's feelings
on seeing the belfries of Martinville from Dr Percepied's trap
and the blissful transmuted consciousness conjured by three
trees glimpsed near Balbec from Madame de Villeparisis's carriage provide other moments of semi-magical intuition.

More than ever, at this final party *chez* Guermantes, the narrator is bombarded with revelations. As the narrator cannot be
announced to his host and hostess without interrupting some
concert-music, he is ushered by a footman into a small boudoir-
library to wait. There, in this library, the 'sudden chance' of the
footman accidentally grating a spoon against a plate summons
up, almost by enchantment, another imperious and intoxicat-
ing vision. 'The same sort of felicity which the uneven paving
stones had given me invaded my being; this time my sensation
was quite different, being that of a great heat accompanied by
the smell of smoke tempered by the fresh air of a surrounding
forest.' He has involuntary recall of a fleeting moment when
once he opened a beer bottle while a railwayman hammered at
the wheel of his railway carriage which was stationary near some
trees. Then, back in the library, a Guermantes servant brings
him a glass of orangeade, a plate of cakes and a starched napkin.
When he wipes his mouth with the napkin, its texture reminds
him of a towel with which he once dried himself while holidaying on the Normandy coast. 'Now, in that library of the Guermantes mansion, a green-blue ocean spread its plumage like the
tail of a peacock.' He rejoices in the colours, feels 'pure, disin-
carnated and freed from the imperfections of exterior perceptions'. He recognises this as 'an instant to which my whole life
had aspired'. Precious, sensual, subconscious memories of the
railway embankment and seashore have overwhelmed him in

the library of a princely Paris house. 'I felt that the happiness given me at these rare intervals in my life was the only fruitful and authentic one.'

Finally, from the shelves of the prince's library, he takes down, almost at random, a copy of *François le Champi*, a mediocre novel by George Sand. His mother had read it aloud to him during a night of childhood insomnia, and now it evokes memories that electrify him. 'A name read in a book of former days contains within its syllables the swift wind and the brilliant sun of the moment when we read it.' He rejects the 'vulgar temptation of an author to write intellectual works. A great indelicacy. A work in which there are theories is like an object upon which the price is marked.' Reality only counts when it is discovered at an intuitive depth where 'appearance matters little, as symbolised by the sound of the spoon upon the plate, the stiffness of the table-napkin, which were more precious for my spiritual renewal than many humanitarian, patriotic, international conversations.' These moments are the keys to *Temps perdu*.

Proust could not believe in an afterlife but was desperate to brave death and achieve immortality: he did this by writing a novel that reveals its meanings through futile characters and trivial details. In mundane moments and unexceptional incidents his narrator experiences moments of rapture or transcendent understanding, and finds reasons to rejoice. Despite all the selfishness, snobbery and vice that he encounters, despite his anguished jealousy, despite his culpability in wasting so much time, ultimately the narrator feels overpowering gratitude for the creative opportunity he has been given: to write a novel that will preserve his name and perpetuate his memory. Human beings misbehave, destroy good order, spoil their own happiness because of their spite or obsessions and collapse into helpless decrepitude: only art brings harmony; and art endures.

Proust believed that gratitude was a duty. One must be grateful for unhappiness and misfortune if they enhance one's perception and courage, grateful for the imaginative riches that one can develop, grateful for the difficulties in one's art – because in surmounting these hardships one makes a declaration of creative faith. *À la recherche du temps perdu* is a theological work for a secular world: it is a novel about the afterlife by someone who did not believe in Heaven or Hell. It is crucial to Proust's purposes that these final transcendent moments are provoked by the most mundane of incidents, although they occur at the most *mondaine* of parties given by the great Prince de Guermantes: a party, Auden once said, where all the guests are in Hell, though they don't yet realise it.

Thoughts of eternity preoccupied Proust as much as any seventeenth-century divine, and he transformed twentieth-century literary conceptions of Time and Memory, but some readers cannot stomach his approach. The fact that he located these moments of revelation in a princely mansion, and the profusion of duchesses, marchionesses and barons in his pages, induces them to indict him for snobbery. This is not a charge that it is easy either to rebut or to sustain because Proust's attitudes to the different social classes – so crucial to the structure and tone of his book – were sinuous and complex, like so much else that he thought. There is, though, a crucial question: is *À la recherche du temps perdu* a fantastic exercise of sustained name-dropping, or does his preoccupation with class distinctions and class loyalties – his analyses of the manners, vocabulary and habits of the different layers of French society – serve a deeper literary purpose?

CHAPTER 4

Footmen are Better Educated than Dukes

Proust was the first French writer since Molière to make a serious study of valets: he is also generally reckoned as an arch-snob. Gladys, Duchess of Marlborough, who knew him for years, said, 'His snobbishness was just snobbishness and there is little more to say about it.' In fact there is much to explain about both his personal class-consciousness and his keen scrutiny of the workings of a class-bound society. Proust's social climbing took him into the most cultivated circles of the most civilised nation on earth – the Comtesse de Noailles, whose hospitality and poetry he admired, once described their set of friends as useless but indispensable – yet he also idealised and sought intimacy with the servant class. Social distinctions provided the chords that vibrated through *Temps perdu* and were audible in all his meanings. The strongest notes were struck after the publication in 1921 of *Sodome et Gomorrhe I* with its detailed accounts of sexual contacts that transgressed the hierarchies of class, and defied orthodox notions of authority, deference, physical aloofness and social order. It is in such contacts, Proust suggests, that people begin to stop worrying about the opinions of their peers and perhaps free themselves for the possibility of change.

He studied the social classes like a naturalist and analysed their powers like a historian; but his purposes in writing an *Odyssey* of snobs were, like his veneration of commonplace details, reverential, even sacred. He wrote with rare subtlety about the specialised experiences of the nobility, with tender observation of the working classes and with respect for bourgeois energy. Whether depicting the French nobility as a 'historically-condemned luxury class' (to quote his German Marxist admirer Adorno), or demonstrating that snobbery was a basic duty for the early twentieth-century French bourgeoisie, Proust urged his belief that social loyalties generate human mediocrity, and that to allow one's friends and acquaintances to have priority in one's time and thoughts is to cramp and stultify one's potential. *Temps perdu* examines what happens when the impulse to social success is so exalted that it becomes the governing influence over humankind. During his lifetime religious faith and the desire to serve God had been relegated as forces controlling people's behaviour. After his first communion Proust never again attended mass, and failed to believe in a God or an afterlife; but he respected religious faith in others, honoured organised religion for its aesthetic and ethical influence, and was disgusted by the petty snubs that were directed at the priest of his father's native village as part of the triumph of the French government's anti-clericalism which prohibited members of religious orders from teaching in schools and achieved the separation of Church and State in 1905. *Temps perdu* is the work of an implacable and often anguished moralist who scorned the ways that people's conversation and behaviour were usually directed, regardless of their class, by neither the desire to be good nor to be truthful, but by the wish to affirm by their words the sort of people they wanted to be taken for. He presented social worlds where everything was for show, and described parties that were essentially theatrical, with the guests behaving like actors who talked solely for effect. In scenes of social comedy and of moral tragedy Proust explored the babbling, hypocritical, corrupt, decadent tendencies – the negative mass psychology – of his secularised age.

A few years after Proust's death, Wyndham Lewis published a fictionalised dialogue with the Schiffs in which he considered the deterioration in post-war life and fiction that had happened since incentives to social success, and the vanity of personal reputation, had superseded traditional religious morality. 'In place of Christendom – with all its faults and cruelties – is substituted the *salon*,' Lewis wrote. 'In this system,' he demanded, 'who become the *villains*, and who become the *heroes*?' It is a question that Proust posed, too. Petty cliques seem more destructive than the rigid national structures of class discrimination in his novel because they are entirely based on insular opinion and debilitating conformity. At least there are life-enhancing traces of human vitality and homogeneity in class tension. If people value the opinions of their peers more than the judgement of God, or subordinate their aesthetic sense and independent intellects to social pressures, it exterminates Love. This is the great lesson of Proust's most beastly clique, the Verdurin salon, whose members care so desperately about being accepted that they will subject themselves to cruel enormities. The Anglo-Irish novelist Elizabeth Bowen, who first read Proust in the 1920s, was transfixed by his understanding of how humanity is tormented by its narrow and exclusive social concerns. 'Cruelty infests, as might a malevolent fever a swamp or jungle, the universe of *À la recherche du temps perdu* – the marvel is that it does not poison it wholly.' One of Proust's themes, she divined, is heroic perseverance. His admiration for survivors, she thought, redeems his novel from its misanthropic vapours: 'the characters have an astonishing resilience, a fool-hardy, desperado quality which gives them panache: almost all of them are at bay.' Proust himself, as he fought to finish his huge book, showed astounding perseverance, had even the air of a desperado in his chaotic sick-room, but he also felt an intermittent animosity which shocked his friends. 'Often when I left Proust in the evening, I felt exhausted by the atmosphere that surrounded this extraordinary mind – an atmosphere redolent of . . . his "malice" and his "cruelty",' Prince Antoine Bibesco wrote.

It was crucial to Proust's creative powers, but also his most agreeable trait, that he ardently, sincerely found transcendent profundity in people and things that were generally dismissed as mundane. He had an omnivorous curiosity about every detail of people's lives. Sydney Schiff wrote admiringly that his friend 'spent a lifetime in the observation and accumulation of minute human refractions', but his insatiable inquisitiveness could be exasperating. It was critical to his profound humanity that he cared not only about people of exceptional creative talent, financial power and social splendour, but also cherished people whose lives were controlled by their limited social circumstances. He monitored, usually with disappointment, the classes whose money and privileges provided them with the greatest liberty of life choices, and studied with patient, tender respect those people who had no choice but to make their own living, and whose physical or mental energies were consumed in that task. The attraction for him of strong, competent waiters and chauffeurs, whom he convinced himself were more authentic in their experiences and more sincere in their behaviour – an attraction that he only seems to have acknowledged once his mother was dead – made him more inquisitive, questing and receptive: after 1905 his susceptibilities increasingly transcended social boundaries and conventional class assumptions so that he trusted or was drawn to socially inappropriate people. Possibly his mother's Jewish background, and his antagonism to the ruling authorities at the time of the Dreyfus case, contributed to his estrangement from conventional French class loyalties: certainly Proust, the reclusive valetudinarian who increasingly after 1905 lived vicariously and might be described as a recovering romantic, feasted on the lives of people with resilient nerves and robust bodies.

Romance, for Proust, was to be found in names, etymologies and pedigrees. Although he satirises a pedantic Sorbonne professor called Brichot who bores the Verdurin salon with interminable monologues about the etymology of obscure provincial towns and villages, his susceptibility to euphonious or evocative place-names, surnames and titles was irrepressible. He loved quizzing noblemen about their pedigrees and possessions. 'Marcel regarded with particular curiosity those whose names echoed the historic past', Comte Georges de Lauris thought; Society's 'alluring beauty', for Proust, lay in the sonority of titles. Gladys, Duchess of Marlborough recalled him 'succulently' murmuring resonant titles to himself. Once, when she told him that she thought the Duke of Northumberland's name sounded imposing, he grew excited: 'Hold on,' he exclaimed. 'I'm going to announce him.' He got up, flung open a door and yelled, 'Madame la Duchesse de Northumberland!', which provoked a fit of coughing. Proust spluttering over the titles of English duchesses recalls a memorable passage in *Temps retrouvé*. The narrator, returning to Paris after a long interval, encounters Baron de Charlus, who gives a litany of his kinsmen and

acquaintances who have recently died, and whom he has therefore outlived. Triumphantly, in tones seeming to resonate from
a sepulchre, he proclaims '"Hannibal de Bréauté, dead! Antoine
de Mouchy, dead! Charles Swann, dead! Adalbert de Mont-
morency, dead! Baron de Talleyrand, dead! Sosthène de
Doudeauville, dead!" And each time the word "dead" seemed to
fall upon the defunct like a shovelful of earth, the heavier for the
gravedigger wanting to press them ever deeper into the tomb.'

The names of the dead resonated for Proust; and the titles of
provincial nobility conjured for him all the elements of beauty:
the beauty of the French countryside, of old buildings, of heraldry, of historic traditions, of good manners and of cousinship.
In *Sodome et Gomorrhe* his narrator receives a black-bordered
notice formally announcing the death of a provincial noblewoman, Eléonore-Euphrasie-Humbertine de Cambremer,
Comtesse de Criquetot. It lists the names of the bereaved: the
Marquis et Marquise de Gonneville, the Vicomte et Vicomtesse
d'Amfreville, the Comte et Comtesse de Berneville, the Marquis et Marquise de Graincourt, the Comte d'Amenoncourt,
the Comtesse de Mainville, the Comte et Comtesse de Fran-
quetot, the Comtesse de Chavernay. This enumeration of Cambremer titles, this 'muster roll of the regional nobility', arouses
the narrator into thoughts that are sensual and reverential rather
than snobbish. Their names,

> those of all the countryside's interesting places, sang out
> their joyful endings in *ville*, or *court*, or sometimes in a
> more muffled *tot*. Clad in the roof-tiles of their château or
> the roughcast *crépi* of their church, their nodding heads
> barely protruding above the vault of the nave or of the main

building, and then only to be capped by the Norman lantern or the dovecot of their pepper-pot roof, they seemed to have sounded the rallying cry for all the pretty villages dispersed for fifty leagues roundabout and to have set them out in close formation, without one gap or one intruder, on the compact, rectangular chessboard of this aristocratic, black-edged letter.

Romantic Love yielded only imaginative triteness and personal disillusion, Proust thought; but romanticism about ideas or objects could be consolatory and imaginatively enriching because it entailed veneration of the past. People who fancied themselves romantically in love were deluded beings, in Proust's created world, and bound to end in disaffection. There is seldom anything tender, glamorous or impressive about the lovers in *Temps perdu*: they endure the grinding torture of jealousy, their sour mistrust cannot be eradicated, they are irreparably wounded by frustration and betrayal: in short they ruin themselves as human beings. Far better, Proust thought, to succumb to the Romantic associations and material solidity of medieval dates, historic names and venerable buildings than to cheat and debase oneself with those ephemeral, dishonest feelings that constitute conventional notions of romantic love. It was hateful to him when an ancient name or title was subsumed under a brazen new creation. Proust was indignant – even outraged – when his young friend Comte Pierre de Polignac, after marrying in 1920 Prince Louis of Monaco's recently legitimised daughter, who had been newly created Duchesse de Valentinois, abandoned his patronymic and title to become a bogus new Duc de Valentinois. 'A Polignac renouncing his own name to marry a washerwoman!' he exclaimed. 'Everyone knows the duchess's mother did Monaco's washing. I shan't see Comte Pierre any more.' He did not stop at ostracism; but inserted into *Guermantes* some disobliging, even scurrilous references to a Comte de Nassau and his relations by marriage – all of whom were evidently based on and intended to offend Polignac and the ruling family of Monaco.

Lucien Daudet presented his friend's approach to titled people as one of scientific curiosity. 'Fashionable society mattered to him, but in the manner that flowers matter to a botanist, not in the way that flowers matter to a man who buys a bouquet.' Once Proust had dedicated himself to writing *Temps perdu*, he wanted to observe, analyse and classify human types rather than to revel in frivolous elegance. 'It wasn't the fact of being invited that amused him,' Daudet explained, 'nor of going for lunch or dinner with people who were more or less well known, nor of going to great balls or obscure parties, as the careful verification by him of social mechanics – people adapting to their environment, or to neighbouring *milieux*, their alliances, their evolution.' Humans, like all other creatures, were best studied when adapting to their surroundings, Proust realised. There is a beautiful passage set at a gala evening at the Opéra in which the occupants of the theatre-boxes are depicted by marine metaphors as water goddesses or bearded tritons. It concludes with the Marquis de Palancy who seems as impervious and insentient as a fish:

> . . . his great round eye glued to the glass of his monocle,
> [Palancy] moved slowly around in the transparent gloom and
> appeared no more to see the public in the stalls than a fish

that drifts by, unaware of the crowd of curious visitors,
behind the water-tight windows of an aquarium. When
momentarily he paused, venerable, wheezy and moss-covered,
the members of the audience could not have told if he was
unwell, asleep, swimming, spawning, or simply taking breath.

At times Proust scarcely knew whether his methods were those
of an anthropologist or a biologist. Thus in *Temps retrouvé* he
described his character Robert de Saint-Loup's manner of
'throwing back his head so joyously and so proudly, under the
golden plumage of his slightly ruffled hair . . . that between the
curiosity and the half-social, half-zoological admiration he
inspired, one wondered whether one had found him in the
Faubourg Saint-Germain or in the Jardin des Plantes, and
whether one was looking at a *grand seigneur* crossing a drawing-
room or a marvellous bird walking about in its cage.'

Proust's remorseless curiosity about genealogical details
resembled a scientist's passion for classification and exactitude.
His insistence that in the social universe of the aristocracy there
was a huge distance between the orbits of provincial noblemen
like the Cambremers and the supreme tribe of the Guermantes
recalls a rosarian insisting on the difference between Gallica,
Damask, Noisette, Hybrid Tea and Floribunda roses. When
haughty Baron de Charlus (who deplores the fashion for naming
beautiful roses after such upstarts as Maréchal Niel and Baronne
Adolphe de Rothschild) explains to lower-middle-class Charlie
Morel, with whom he is ruinously in love, the hierarchies of
precedence among the French nobility he might be a fancier of
old roses explaining why one can plant Lady Waterlow or Lady
Hillingdon but not American Pillar, Benson & Hedges Special

or Many Happy Returns in one's grounds. 'There are a few prominent families, first and foremost the Guermantes, who claim fourteen alliances with the House of France,' declares the baron, whose brother is the Duc de Guermantes.

> Far beneath the Guermantes, however, one may mention
> the families of La Trémoïlle, descended from the Kings of
> Naples and the Counts of Poitiers; of d'Uzès, scarcely old as
> a family, but the premier peers; of Luynes, who are of recent
> origin, but have distinguished themselves by fine marriages;
> of Choiseul, Harcourt, La Rochefoucauld. Add to these the
> family of Noailles (notwithstanding the Comte de
> Toulouse), Montesquiou and Castellane, and, without for-
> getting any, that's all. As for all the little gentlemen who call
> themselves Marquis de Cambremerde [bow-legged shit] or
> de Vatefairefiche [Screwyou], there is no difference between
> them and the lowest private in your regiment. It's the same
> whether you piss at Comtesse Cacas or shit at Baronne
> Pipis: you will have compromised yourself and used a dirty
> rag instead of clean lavatory paper.

Ambivalence ruled Proust's attitude to Society according to Princesse Elizabeth Bibesco, who made an affectionate study of his closing years. 'His relations with the *monde* were a strange mixture of exaggerated taste and an exaggerated distaste. It provided him with delights and hates, each it seemed to me disproportionately great.' Undeniably he was a toady to princesses, a groveller to dukes and prone to laughable snobbery – as demonstrated by his pride in contracting a head-cold from the post-war British Ambassador in Paris, the Earl of Derby, a great territorial magnate whose title dated back to the War of the

Roses. Derby was a genial man whose gargantuan appetites were enough to kill a horse: at a time when he kept a stable of forty thoroughbreds and twenty grooms, he failed to save an expensive but ailing horse by putting it on what seemed to him a reasonable daily diet of three dozen eggs, a bottle of brandy and a bottle of port. He had a passion for hot baths, and during train journeys would take his ablutions in the station-master's office at wayside halts, using water piped from the engine of his private train into a portable bath: not a pleasing thought, for Derby's physique was likened by Lloyd George to that of a harpooned walrus. Proust delighted in the British Ambassador's company, and was gratified to be told that Derby found him the most intriguing man in Paris: less pleased, though, to discover the fascination for Derby was that Proust was the only man he knew who wore a fur coat during meals. When Proust caught a cold from the earl in 1919, he indulged in laughably prolonged sycophantic name-dropping: 'This English cold lasted all spring, which gave him a thousand opportunities to mention Lord Derby, which he liked to do often.' Proust's grateful doormat humility to Lord Derby's germs was the antithesis of his assertiveness about his literary status and creative powers. When, for example, the award to him of the Legion of Honour was gazetted in the *Journal des Débats* in 1920, he was distressed to find his name listed among (he considered) 'people of only slight literary merit' and asked an influential friend to arrange publication of 'another little paragraph placing me rather more among true writers like Madame de Noailles' who had received the same decoration. His request was accentuated by his steadfast determination to promote the greatness of his artistic achievement rather than personal pique.

It was not only Society that fed Proust's craving for personal details and compulsion to classify general types. He was intrigued by the duties and experiences of household servants. 'If there was a taste that Proust had almost to the level of perversion,' recalled his friend Marcel Plantevignes, 'it was what one might call *l'envers du décor*, to burrow into the underside of a household, and to penetrate into the most intimate, revealing secrets.' Proust cross-examined doormen, valets, footmen, hotel managers, waiters, cabmen and secretaries about their working lives and the confidential discoveries that they sometimes made. His enquiries covered every sort of background and taste. He was as eager to discover, said Plantevignes, 'the traditions upheld in long-established families as the rules for comfortable living recently adopted or copied by the newly rich.' Proust's enthusiasm for George Eliot's novels partly rested on her attention to mundane routines, which she made significant or illuminating. 'What strikes me in *Adam Bede*,' he noted, 'is the attentive, detailed, respectful, poetic and sympathetic portrayal of the humblest, most hard-working life. Keeping one's kitchen clean is a paramount duty, almost a religious duty, and a pleasurable duty too.' Insignificant routines hold immense inherent importance in Proust's universe: they provide the context that makes sense of mortality, memory and time.

Domestic service with Proust might seem monotonous and mundane, but the potential for profound discovery was inherent in it. 'I followed the daily routine, and I was happy to be in his household,' recalled Céleste Albaret, who was first employed by Proust as a courier, delivering complementary copies of *Swann* to his friends in 1913, and started working in what she called 'that great, strange, silent apartment' at 102 Boulevard Haussmann after Proust's valet was called up for military service following the outbreak of war. She did everything. 'I made the coffee, did the cleaning, went out to telephone or to buy something, delivered a letter, warmed up the linen, prepared or changed the hot-water bottles, tidied up the newspapers and manuscripts M. Proust left in heaps on his bed . . . lit the log fire in his room, heated the water for his footbath. I did all this as if I were singing, in a sort of joy, like a bird flitting from branch to branch.' Proust convinced her – for he was always manipulative – that fulfilling her domestic duties was nobler than going to Mass. 'Those ten years I spent working for M. Proust,' she said, 'I thank heaven for them – I couldn't have dreamed of a more beautiful life, though I didn't realise this at the time.' This is not sugary nonsense: this is what it could be like to work for Marcel Proust.

His respect for the hardiness of people who laboured at monotonous tasks was inseparable from his erotic susceptibility to working-class men. The English novelist Jocelyn Brooke, whose sensibility was transformed as a young man in the 1920s by reading Proust, recognised that his literary hero 'conformed to a familiar enough type: the "queer" who is socially a snob, but sexually an inverted one, with a taste, as often as not, for guardsmen and "rough stuff".' When Diaghilev's friend Misia Sert once asked Proust outright, 'Are you a snob?' his reply was sincere but ludicrous. 'If, among the few friends who have not dropped the habit of coming to enquire after me, an occasional duke or prince comes and goes, they are counterbalanced by other friends, of whom one is a footman and the other a chauffeur, and with whom I take more trouble. Besides, there is not much to choose between them. The footmen are better educated than the dukes, and speak prettier French; but they are more punctilious about etiquette, less simple, more touchy.' In his novel, too, Proust represented the idlers of the Jockey Club as less literate than electricians. 'I never discriminated,' declares his fictional impersonator, 'between *les ouvriers*, *les bourgeois* and *les grand seigneurs*, and I would have accepted any of them as friends, with a certain preference for the working men, and after them for the noblemen, not because I liked them better, but because I knew that one could expect greater courtesy from them towards the working men than one finds among the *bourgeoisie*, either because great noblemen do not despise workmen as the *bourgeoisie* do or else because they are inherently courteous to everyone.'

The room in Proust's apartment that served as his bedroom, workroom and sick-room contained all the accessories of his working life: 'a table strewn with phials,' Jean Cocteau recalled, 'a pile of exercise books, thick with dust like the other pieces of furniture,' and equally important an 'ebony table in the shadows covered with an accumulation of photographs of tarts, of duchesses, of dukes and footmen employed in great houses'. This welter of photographs had been amassed to provide models for the hugely diverse range of protagonists in *Temps perdu*: great noblemen, smart hostesses, dowdy provincial landowners, Sir Rufus Israels the powerful financier, Elstir the renowned painter, Bergotte the superb novelist, La Berma the acclaimed actress, lesser (sometimes contemptible) figures from the arts, literature and the stage, rich and cultivated Jews, professional soldiers, men-about-town, chatterboxes, controversialists, professors, physicians, diplomats, lawyers, Academicians, courtesans – to say nothing of the hotel employees, pages, footmen, chauffeurs, milkman, jeweller's assistant and military conscripts who serve the clients in the male brothel managed by Jupien, a waistcoat-maker turned pimp. The amplitude of Proust's characterisation is life-enhancing – although not for every reader. 'I had a shot at some Proust, but was bored to tears,' the academic lawyer Harold Laski confessed in 1926. 'I do not believe that the analysis, however consummate in power of handling detail, of people who have no real human value or significance can possibly be as important as is made out.' Proust in *Temps perdu* satirised this view as shallow and functional. 'I avow,' declares his character Bloch, pontificating with his usual clumsy, conceited bombast, 'that portraits of futile people are indifferent to me': Bloch wants novels 'to picture great working-class movements, or if not the crowd, at all events . . . noble intellectuals.' Yet it is central to the greatness of *Temps perdu*, essential to its claims to celebrate the entirety of creation, that futile people, with no great accomplishments, are the animating figures in Proust's invented world.

For Laski to have denounced Proust as a 'third-rate snob of no importance except as showing that third-rate snobs would in self-protection hail him as first rate' requires a hasty reading of *Temps perdu* and a distortion of the novelist's personal outlook. Proust's snobbery was rampant and undiscriminating in the 1890s, much more selective in the period after 1900 when he attached himself to Bibesco, Albufera, Guiche and Fénelon, and increasingly sardonic after he started writing *Temps perdu* in 1908. Though he continued to respect individual members of High Society, such as Guiche, and never lost his pleasure in sonorous and historic properties, his remorse at the amount of time he had wasted trying to impress people for whom he no longer cared (including, ultimately, Albufera) was expressed in his unforgiving satire of the Guermantes and other social sets. 'Despite my great desire to be fair and impersonal in *Temps perdu,*' he insisted in 1920, 'the most slandered class, the one that is always wrong, and only utters stupidities, the vulgar and hateful class, is the nobility and fashionable Society.' Proust tried to distance himself in his descriptions of them. He believed, as he told Lucien Daudet in 1916, that for the 'aesthetic discovery of realities, we must place ourselves outside them'. Accordingly, when writing the social scenes of his novel, he took 'care, when speaking of the Guermantes, not to present them from the standpoint of a man of the world . . . but to present them from the viewpoint of whatever *poetry there may be in snobbery.* I have not spoken of them in the casual tone of a man of the world, but with the wonderment of someone remote from it all.'

The romantic elation that titled people aroused in Proust is personified by his splendid character, the Queen of Naples. She was his representation of Maria Sophia Amelia, last Queen of the Two Sicilies, who died in the Munich palace of Duchess Charles Theodore of Bavaria in 1925. In real life the ex-queen, like Proust's version of her and several of his Guermantes characters, was a member of the Bavarian royal family: from her father Duke Maximilian von Wittelsbach she inherited her great beauty and indomitable spirit. She had been married by proxy at the age of seventeen in 1859 to the Duke of Calabria, who a few months later succeeded his father as Francesco II, King of the Two Sicilies. The young monarch was slow-witted, ungainly and inept: he did not understand his wife, whom he found so frightening that he hid behind palace doors when he realised she was approaching. The young queen wanted to slake her vitality by riding, swimming and long walks but found herself at the head of a bigoted society that condemned the impropriety of a lady leaving her own house except in a carriage. Art, music and literature, the solace of her winters in Munich, were banned as beneath her notice, but she was glorious in her candour and exuberant gaiety, and vainly tried to induce her husband to institute reforms in his kingdom. After Garibaldi launched an insurrection in May 1860, the King and Queen were driven from their capital of Naples, and retreated to the fortress town of Gaëta where, together with their courtiers and loyal soldiers, they were besieged by the Piedmontese for over three months from November 1860 to February 1861. Regardless of shot and shell, the young queen made a daily round of the batteries and fortifications to encourage their troops. She never flinched from nursing the sick and wounded: 'Men spattered with blood and mud gazed at her with almost religious adoration and kissed the hem of her skirt with almost feverish lips. The sight of her graceful figure stepping lightly through the stench of airless wards thrilled the poor wretches lying on straw pallets with an ecstasy of joy.' The siege at Gaëta, when Maria Sophia was not yet twenty, was the culminating phase of her life, although she lived another sixty-four years in exile, first in Rome, then in the Tyrol and Proust's suburban birthplace of Neuilly.

For Proust the queen evoked personal and literary associations. Like his mother she had endured months of privation in a siege – the bombardment, famine and epidemics at Gaëta were ten years before those in Paris – and the queen was almost killed by a shell just as Dr Proust was nearly killed by a stray bullet. Proust, the eager collector of celebrity snapshots, surely knew that the young queen had been the darling of portrait photographers, for whom she was avid to sit. Pictures of her in crown and robes, in a ball dress with a diamond tiara on her wonderful hair, on horseback and on foot were widely published in Europe of the 1860s, and continued to circulate when she was living in Paris during the 1870s. At that time she was ranked among the leading 'heroines of history', and was immortalised (somewhat romantically) as Queen Frédérique of Illyria in Alphonse Daudet's best-selling novel *Les Rois en Exil*. '*She* is the king, the true king,' Daudet's fictional royal chaplain declares. 'If only you had seen her on horseback riding night and day among the outposts! At Fort St Angelo, when the shells were raining down, she twice toured the ramparts to encourage the soldiers – upright and proud, with her riding habit and her crop, as cool as if she was strolling in her private park.' This description of the Illyrian queen is echoed in Proust's novel when he described his 'soldier-queen' of Naples: an impoverished yet still formidable exile, who had fired muskets from besieged ramparts, 'in whose veins flowed some of the noblest blood in history, the richest in experience, scepticism and pride'. Proust admires her fortitude and self-belief: she is 'a woman of great goodness' to whom he attributes 'an unshakeable attachment to . . . her immediate relations, to all the Princes of her family . . . and, after them, to all the middle class or humbler people who showed respect and proper deference to those whom she loved'. This intense family loyalty brought embittering anguish: the Queen of the Two Sicilies had to muster that astonishing resilience and desperado panache with which Proust liked to endow his characters. Her only child died in infancy; one of her brothers-in-law, like her cousin King Ludwig of Bavaria, drowned himself in a lake; her nephew Crown Prince Rudolf died mysteriously with his mistress at

Mayerling; her youngest sister the Duchesse d'Alençon was killed in a catastrophic fire that swept through a Paris charity bazaar in 1897; and a few months later another sister, Empress Elisabeth of Austria, was stabbed to death on the shores of Lake Geneva. Proust's fictional queen has a conception of good nature that, he concedes, might seem 'narrow, somewhat reactionary and increasingly obsolete', but she towers above the rest of fashionable Society because of the quality of her self-confidence: 'One of the mistakes of Society people is that they do not realise that if they want us to believe in them, they must first believe in themselves,' he contends. It is because the Queen of Naples has a regal indifference to opinion and reputation that she is singular among Proust's characters in defeating the vicious machinations of Madame Verdurin, whose middle-class *salon* is the nastiest group in the book.

Sidonie Verdurin, who has inherited 35 million francs, is a spiteful neurasthenic who controls her salon like a dominatrix in a sado-masochists' dungeon. Her chief consolation is the destruction of other people's happiness. The professional men, and their wives, who congregate in her salon and form her 'little clan' are browbeaten and bullied – in one case to the point of collapse. They, in turn, are collectively unprepossessing: conceited, ponderously facetious, pompous, pedantic, pusillanimous, cringing and snobbish. Their submission to humiliating abuse can only be explained by the intensity of their need to be included among the Verdurins' clansmen. Friendship among the middle classes is based on mutual respect for professional achievements and status: accordingly, Proust believed, there is no true friendship at the Verdurins because the host and hostess respect no one. All Madame Verdurin's relationships are abusive: she creates a vicious, vindictive ambience that degrades her guests. Proust's description of her husband and abetter, Gustave Verdurin, encapsulates his view of the human experience. 'The most spiteful of men,' Proust says; 'tormenting to the point of the most savage persecution, and so jealous of his domination over the little clan as not to shrink from the worst of lies or from fomenting the most unjustified hatreds.' Although relentless in enforcing his control, and primitive in his emotional barbarism, Verdurin is not a figure of absolute iniquity. 'He was,' Proust says, 'a man capable of disinterestedness, of unostentatious generosity, but that does not mean that he was a sensitive or pleasant man, nor scrupulous, nor truthful, nor even always good.' Verdurin personifies the ambivalence of Proust's universe and the self-contradictory moods of his protagonists as well as the genuine humility of Proust's moral judgements: 'We should never bear ill-will towards other people, should never judge them by the memory of some act of malice, for we do not know all the good that, at other moments, their hearts may have sincerely desired and realised.' Though evil is recurrent, 'the heart is far richer than that'.

Proust shows how inexorably the Guermantes were challenged, then sidelined and finally usurped by robust, egocentric bourgeoisie like the Verdurins. Sidonie Verdurin at first scorns the Faubourg Saint-Germain, then recruits Charlus to help introduce her into ducal drawing-rooms, and after repudiating Charlus, continues to push her way forwards until she can marry the impoverished old Duc de Duras, and assume the titles and privileges of a noblewoman. And, then, Proust who planned every detail of his novel meticulously, ambushes his readers. In *Temps retrouvé*, at the final, macabre masked ball given by the Princesse de Guermantes, the hostess seems very different from the princess of earlier volumes; for (as Proust suddenly reveals) the widowed Duchesse de Duras, the former Madame Verdurin, *née* des Baux, has lately married the Prince de Guermantes after his first wife's death. She has pierced the aristocratic carapace that had once (in every sense) repelled her.

Prince Antoine Bibesco depicted Proust as a heartless, inconstant friend who nevertheless showed compassion for collective human pain: 'I have seen him shed tears at the mere thought of the Armenian massacres.' Lucien Daudet gave a similar emphasis to his ex-lover's imaginative sympathy. 'If Marcel heard of anyone's misfortune, whether someone scarcely known to him or from his entourage, he wanted immediately to contribute to their assistance; he possessed that painful imagination which in an instant could conjure up every form of misery, and which drove him to give as much as possible, in order to blur the images which were torturing him.' The Verdurins, though, personify a detestable indifference to human anguish. They are so egotistical that they are oblivious to other people's feelings and pass through life without learning anything from suffering. They would not weep, as their creator did, over Armenians. In one passage Proust recounts how wartime restrictions prevent Madame Verdurin from obtaining croissants to dip in her coffee at breakfast. She gets a society physician to certify that she is suffering headaches for lack of these croissants: then an order is procured that bakers must supply her on medical grounds. The supply of croissants resumes on the morning that the Paris newspapers announce the torpedoing by a German submarine of the Cunard liner *Lusitania* with the loss of over a thousand lives. Carefully, Madame Verdurin arranges her newspaper to stay open without interfering with her consumption of the croissants, which she is dipping in her coffee. All the way through breakfast, as she utters conventional exclamations of horror, her face shines with placid satisfaction.

From boyhood Proust's relations with servants were odd and exaggerated. After falling in love with Lucien Daudet in 1895, he began to show eccentric solicitude for the Daudet family's servants. He invited their elderly maid to join him at the theatre one evening, gravely and without anticipating a refusal, and courted their Italian valet, shaking hands each time they met, discussing Dante, trying to relieve the old man of a heavy parcel of books. When Daudet betrayed embarrassment at these over-attentive courtesies, Proust retorted that he was 'violent, heartless'. Proust's solicitude for the disadvantaged was constant and unfeigned – during the war he sent tobacco, cakes and chocolates every week to soldiers at the front – and bewildered many of his contemporaries. His 'mania for huge tips' seemed deplorable to the Duchesse de Clermont-Tonnerre and her set. 'After dinner he wanted to give 300 francs to the head-waiter, and everyone would hurl themselves forward to prevent him from setting such a bad example.'

Proust admired, even adored his servants. His praise of them may seem excessive, but one cannot be sure that he was wrong for he possessed an intuitive genius for recognising exceptional properties in ordinary incidents and people. After the accidental death in 1914 of Alfred Agostinelli, he extolled his chauffeur-secretary as an 'extraordinary being who possessed perhaps the greatest intellectual gifts that I have ever known'. Proust also opened his heart to Gide about Agostinelli: 'Despite being of humble condition, without any culture, I had letters from him that were those of a great writer. He was a boy of delightful intelligence; although it was not for that reason that I loved him. It took me a long time to perceive this intelligence, though not as long as it took him. I discovered merits in him so marvellously incompatible with his situation in life, I discovered them with stupefaction, but without increasing the affection I already felt for him. After my discovery, I took a little extra joy in revealing it to him. But he has died before he could fully understand what he was.' It was like a sacred duty to Proust to find stupefying possibilities in prosaic circumstances. The trust, candour and unspoken mutual sympathy that existed between Proust and his housekeeper Céleste Albaret – first celebrated by Sydney Schiff in his story 'Céleste' and best commemorated in her vividly authentic memoirs *Monsieur Proust* – show his humanity at its most remarkable. For him, simplicity was a subtle and profound way of life: pretentiousness he equated with stupidity.

The meticulous observations and ultimate veneration of the old family servant in *Temps perdu*, Françoise, are indispensable to the novel's meanings. She first appears tending the narrator's invalid aunt Léonie, who is sequestered in a dim provincial bedroom: on the old woman's death she passes into service in the household of the narrator's parents. Françoise's smallest routines and opinions are gilded with significance by Proust. Her cooking:

> . . . like quatrefoils that were carved in the thirteenth century on cathedral porches, reflected the rhythm of the seasons and the incidents of daily life: a brill, because the fish-woman had guaranteed its freshness; a turkey, because she had seen a beauty in the market at Roussainville-le-Pin; cardoons with

marrow, because she had never done them that way for us before; a roast leg of mutton, because fresh air makes one hungry and there would be ample time to prepare it in the seven hours before dinner; spinach for a change; apricots, because they were still hard to find; gooseberries, because in another fortnight there would be none left.

Over the different volumes of his great sequence Proust depicts the hard work, strong emotions and stubborn prejudices of Françoise: he creates a portrait of highly individual immediacy, tender yet unsentimental, which is also a composite picture of all the faults and virtues of the old-fashioned French maidservant. Ostensibly she serves the narrator's family: actually, at times, she seems to dominate their lives. 'We were the ones who, with our virtues, our wealth, our style of living, our status, had to take it upon ourselves to devise little ways of appeasing her pride.' Françoise in all her simplicity has fulfilled the duty that Proust prized most in a creative artist, a workman or anyone else: she has recognised and accepted her vocation. 'Throughout her service with me and my parents, fear, prudence, alertness and cunning had instilled in her that instinctive and almost divinatory knowledge of us that the sailor has of the sea, the quarry of the hunter, and often the patient, if not the doctor, of the disease.' Françoise's vocabulary and diction – perpetuating provincial traditions, parochial loyalties and the rules of a semi-feudal existence – come to pervade the large Paris apartment in which she goes to work. To the ends, she preserves memories from her childhood that are distinct, accurate, evocative and uncompromised. She is an eternal figure – as idealised and yet authentic as the Queen of Naples.

Proust obtained his mastery of human characterisation, and collected his gallery of human types, at the same time that he was behaving like an obtuse, needy wretch, or ungrateful misanthrope, to his acquaintances. He knew, of course, his deficiencies. 'Don't scold me and don't tell me that I'm touchy,' he wrote in youth, 'not because it's false – for it's true – but because I know it already. I'm only like that though with people I love. You'll say that's a pretty way of treating them and that I'd be better off behaving that way with people I dislike. But what gave you the idea that one loves people to give them pleasure? One loves people because one can't do otherwise.' He was entrenched already in world-weary pessimism: 'I'm still too young to know what's going to be the happiness of my life. But already I know too well that's it not going to be love or friendship.' He tested his friends, weighed their fidelity against one another, taxed their loyalty with excessive demands for attention, until finally everything good between them was spoiled. He constantly declared his inconstancy. His exasperating behaviour to Prince Antoine Bibesco eventually drove this most Parisian of Romanians to writing a damning memoir entitled 'The Heartlessness of Marcel Proust'. From the outset Proust rejected as well as courted Bibesco. 'Friendship,' he warned the prince in 1901, 'is a thing without reality.' He professed to be 'weary of insincerity and, which is almost to say the same thing, of friendship'. During his breakdown of nerves and health in 1902, Proust inflicted on Bibesco preposterous letters, swerving between the aggressive and the obsequious, full of reproaches and self-pity, and often sly. His behaviour seems equally unappealing. He wept after a dinner party held by his mother for his friends in 1903, 'less because of the unpleasantness caused by Bibesco's ridiculous sally – and Papa's unjust repartee –

than at seeing that no-one can be trusted and that those who seem to be one's best friends have such incredible flaws that all in all they may be worse than other people.'

It was other people's emotional limits that hurt Proust: he wanted his best friends to cherish him infinitely. He was also so entrenched as a moralist – so much like a modern Jewish prophet – that he wanted to alter the direction of people's lives. 'I have been endowed,' he told Gide in 1914, when he was trying to impress him and thus promote *Temps perdu*, 'with the power of procuring happiness for others and quite often saving them pain. I have reconciled not only adversaries but lovers, I have cured the sick, though I can only aggravate my own ill-health, I have made lazy people work.' Georges de Lauris recalled the intensity of his attentiveness: 'No one else was ready to give as much thought and attention to his friends. Not to speak to him, not to ask him a favour, in short to evince some discretion, *that* offended him; I don't say that he was always sincere in his praises but there existed for him sacred ground where absolute candour was obligatory, a truthfulness which other people could seldom attain.'

Proust presented an irresolvable paradox: he was a sinuous and subtle social creature, with importunate human curiosity, who nevertheless insisted that chatter is spiritually depleting, and that the social impulse achieves only mediocrity. '*Savoir vivre*' he regarded as 'a bondage of the mind. He who cannot reject it remains a mere man of society. Yet elegant mediocrity is charming.' Artists, he instructed, are

> . . . under an obligation to live for themselves. And friendship is a dispensation from this duty, an abdication of self.

Even conversation, which is the mode of expression of
friendship, is a superficial digression, which gives us nothing
new. We may talk for a lifetime without doing more than
infinitely repeat the vacuity of a minute, whereas the march
of thought in the solitary travail of artistic creation proceeds
downwards, into the depths, in the only direction that is
not closed to us, along which we are free to advance –
though with more effort, it is true, towards a goal of truth.
And friendship is not merely devoid of virtue, like conversation, it is fatal to us as well.

The disappointing meeting at the Majestic between Joyce and
Proust – 'it didn't leave any impression on him, and he didn't
even mention the name,' Céleste Albaret recalled – vindicated
this viewpoint. Their conversation was vacuous because everything important in which they could engage was already in their
books.

It was a lifelong certitude for Proust that one must have
something more exciting than friends or else one is nothing. His
early essay on Ruskin depicted friendship as trivial, ugly and
dependent on those polite lies that are socially indispensable yet
spiritually catastrophic; and he harked on this point to the end.
'My duty to my work was more important than being polite,'
his creator resolves when finally he recognises that he must
repudiate 'the sterile pleasure of social contact, which excludes
all penetrating thought'. Proust's insistence that even a great
friendship is a paltry thing pierced young writers like Samuel
Beckett when they read *Temps perdu* in the 1920s. 'Friendship,
according to Proust,' Beckett explained in his perceptive Proust
monograph of 1931,

is the negation of that irremediable solitude to which every human being is condemned. Friendship implies an almost piteous acceptance of face values. Friendship is a social expedient, like upholstery or the distribution of garbage buckets. It has no spiritual significance. For the artist, who does not deal in surfaces, the rejection of friendship is not only reasonable, but a necessity. Because the only possible spiritual development is in the sense of depth. The artistic tendency is not expansive, but a contraction. And art is the apotheosis of solitude.

Most human emotions are derivative, not original, in Proust's understanding; people emulate other people's feelings or plagiarise their own. 'Falsehood is essential to humanity,' he believed; deception was as important to humankind as the quest for pleasure: 'We lie all our life long, especially indeed, perhaps only, to those people who love us.' One sentence in Proust reverberated for Beckett: 'Man is the creature that cannot come forth from himself, who knows only others in himself, and who, if he asserts the contrary, lies.'

Proust, who despaired of social communication and equated friendship with cowardice and self-negation, nevertheless gave his life to the human understanding that is transmitted by great art. From the outset he wanted *Temps perdu* 'to reach a wider audience, the sort of people who buy a badly printed book before getting into a train'. He did not get his mass sales all at once. When the first volume of his masterpiece, *Du côté de chez Swann*, was published in November 1913, its publisher Bernard Grasset was civil and diligent, but found the book unreadable, and never expected any profit (it was printed and marketed at

Proust's expense). The book's reception was a mixture of enthusiasm and bewilderment. 'Proust's book is not a masterpiece if
by masterpiece one means *perfection*, with an *irreproachable
design*,' Hahn wrote a few days after its appearance. 'But it is
without doubt . . . *the finest book* to appear since *L'Éducation
sentimentale*.' It was difficult, as Hahn conceded, to believe that
someone in Society was a genius, but 'from *the first line* a *great
genius* is revealed, and as this opinion must one day be universal, we had better accept it immediately.' Edith Wharton, who
had settled in France, was influential in achieving the unexpected success of *Swann*, according to Armand de Guiche, who on
several occasions during 1913 heard her insistent praise of the
book to Paris friends. Guiche believed that Wharton was the
standard-bearer around whom several of Proust's sturdiest sup-
porters mustered: her enthusiasm was such that she afterwards
consulted Gide about the possibility of Proust translating her
novel *The Custom of the Country* into French.

The fashionable denizens of Faubourg Saint-Germain were
slower than Hahn to appreciate the book, as Proust must have
expected: 'Society people,' he wrote, 'are so imbued with their
own stupidity that they can never credit that one of their own
set is talented. They only appreciate writers who are not in
smart society.' (When Anna de Noailles was very young, and
someone publicly extolled her poetry, Proust heard her mother
exclaim in alarm, 'Don't mention Anna's verses! You're going to
prevent me from marrying her off!' Even his hero, Lord Derby,
who had given him such a splendid English cold, was ruffled by
talk of his ancestors' Shakespearean connections).

Certainly, the Duchesse de Clermont-Tonnerre stalled over
the first volume, as she confessed. 'Sincerity obliges me to say

that this novel of 500 pages, with almost no blanks, alarmed me like a musical score covered in triple and quadruple crochets which one has to interpret. It was the first time that so dense a novel had reached me. Traditionally such a heavy appearance was reserved for works of philosophy and history, which one didn't read. It didn't seem that a novel merited such density. Moreover, the familiar, superficial tone of novels enabled one to run through them in an hour. At the end of an hour, one hadn't read more than 25 pages of Proust.' The English novelist Arnold Bennett, who had met Proust at Misia Sert's Réveillon party of 1910, read *Swann* shortly after its French publication too. 'The *longueurs* of it seemed to me insupportable, the clumsy centipedalian crawling of the interminable sentences inexcusable; the lack of form or construction may disclose artlessness, but it signifies effrontery too.' Yet when he re-read the book, a few weeks before Proust's death, he was 'absolutely enchanted' by some details. Delightfully for Proust, the book brought him new friends among the coming generation; and henceforth he always valued the company of younger readers who had cherished the book before they met its author. The rich young aesthete Comte Louis Gautier-Vignal, who was given the book by the Daudet family and read it in 1914 while recuperating from illness at the Hotel Majestic in Paris, had a similar experience to Bennett: *Du côté de chez Swann* required two readings to enjoy. 'Most of the early readers of *Swann* were disconcerted by a book destitute of action, in which the author unhurriedly noted with unusual meticulousness his slightest impressions and innermost feelings, using a style which, with its long sentences, slashed through by parentheses, made reading difficult.' Gautier-Vignal at first was deterred but soon became a fervent admirer of

Proust. His admiration was increased by a rendezvous with Proust at the Boulevard Haussmann apartment which ripened into a friendship that flourished until Gautier-Vignal went to live on the Riviera.

Publication of the sequence was suspended after the German invasion of France and Belgium in 1914, and during the war years Proust prodigiously expanded the scope and text of *Temps perdu*. The second volume of the sequence, *À l'ombre des jeunes filles en fleur* ('In the shadow of young girls in flower'), was ultimately published, after a delay of almost six years, by a more appropriate publisher, Gaston Gallimard, in June 1919. How ever, the Treaty of Versailles, which seemed at the time to have settled the world war, was signed in the same week as the book was issued, and commandeered journalists' attention: the reviews accordingly were respectful rather than rapturous. Proust overcame his disappointment by proposing himself, in September 1919, for the literary prize awarded annually by the Goncourt Academy. Léon Daudet was an influential Goncourt academician, and as a result of his strenuous advocacy, Proust was announced as the Goncourt prize-winner for 1919 on 10 December. *À l'ombre des jeunes filles en fleurs* sold out next day; after three days he had received 886 letters of congratulation. Proust revelled in his fame and sales. 'I don't know a single banker who hasn't found it on his cashier's desk, and all my travelling friends have seen it lying in their friends' houses whether in the Pyrenees, in the North, in Normandy or in Auvergne.' Yet even at this moment of triumph Proust was apprehensive about his future critical reception: he alone knew that some of his most dangerous themes and dominant characters were not yet fully revealed. *À l'ombre des jeunes filles en fleurs* was published between *Du côté de chez Swann* and *Le côté de Guermantes*; and from the outset of his novel's composition in 1908, Proust had intended that the Guermantes family would have hereditary tastes and specialised vices that some readers would find repulsive – indeed that might provoke some of his friends to repudiate him. A lifetime of reading, voyeurism, reflection, austere self-scrutiny and guilt had been used in his design of the Guermantes vices, which in 1919 were all still unsuspected by his readers: for them his hero was Charles Swann.

CHAPTER 5

Hide the Corpse in my Bedroom

When the Jewish playboy and patron of the arts Sydney Schiff began reading *Du côté de chez Swann* in 1916, he was especially attracted by its protagonist Charles Swann, a Jewish man-about-town and connoisseur. 'Swann is one of those personalities not easily understood,' Sydney Schiff felt. 'Though he is essentially Proust, he is not all Proust. And if to know M. Proust we must know Swann, it does not follow that because we know Swann we shall know M. Proust.' The character of Swann – inspired by Proust's glimpses, in his youth, of a Jewish collector and clubman named Charles Haas – was resilient, laconic and disciplined. Welcomed in the most exclusive ducal houses, Swann bears pain, indeed faces death, with the courage of a Spartan. Schiff, by contrast, moved among purely moneyed people, talked too much, was self-indulgent about his nerves and prone to whine. Katherine Mansfield nevertheless saw a resemblance between Swann's *mésalliance* with the courtesan Odette de Crécy and Schiff's elopement and marriage in 1889 with a Kentucky dentist's daughter. The story of the twenty-year-long misery of this first marriage is recounted in the two autobiographical novels that Schiff published under the pseudonym of Stephen Hudson, *Richard Kurt* (1919), which was dedicated to Proust, and *Elinor Colhouse* (1921). Proust, though, tried to discourage Schiff's emotional investment in Swann, who was 'not the principal character' in *Temps perdu*, despite its opening volume being named after him, as he warned Violet Schiff in 1919. Rather, his leading protagonist had been introduced, enigmatically, in *À l'ombre des jeunes filles en fleurs* of 1918: as became clear in the volumes published from 1921, Palamède, Baron de Charlus, a creation of supreme and grotesque originality, was the dominant figure around whom the sequence revolved. 'Baron de Charlus,' declared Céleste Albaret, who saw Proust working every day, 'was certainly the character to whom he was most attached, who interested and amused him the most, and whom he spent the most time analysing and refining.'

In *À l'ombre des jeunes filles en fleurs* the narrator is staying at the seaside with his grandmother and a fashionable young man called the Marquis de Saint-Loup. One day Saint-Loup begins to reminisce about his uncle Palamède. (He tells a story that Proust based on a scandal of 1824 involving the Marquis de Custine.) This uncle, when young, shared with two handsome friends a bachelor establishment to which they used to take women. One day a man-about-town, 'who was going through a regrettable phase during which he showed peculiar tendencies', arranged to visit Charlus at this place. There he began to make overtures to his host rather than to the women kept there. Charlus thereupon summoned his two friends: 'after they arrived, the trio seized the culprit, stripped him, thrashed him till he was bloody, and kicked him out into weather that was ten degrees below zero, where he was found half-dead.' The morning after the narrator has heard this tale, he feels that he is being watched as he goes for a walk. 'I turned round and saw a man aged about forty, very tall and rather stout, with a very black moustache, who, nervously flicking his trouser legs with his cane, scrutinised me with a fixed stare.' The stranger's gaze is so intense and unwavering that the narrator thinks he is a lunatic or a spy. After a final scrutiny, at once 'bold, prudent, swift and searching', the stranger swivels away, adopts a haughty air and makes an ostentatious pretence of studying a playbill on the wall. 'I thought,' the narrator concludes, 'he was a hotel confidence trickster who had been watching my grandmother and myself for days in preparation for some swindle.'

This conman proves to be Baron de Charlus. The first evidence about him seems mixed: he is experienced with women; he detests and violently punishes homosexuality; and his imposing yet louche manners suggest pent-up nerves, vigilant responsiveness, indeed some specialised and extreme eccentricity. It is only in later volumes of *Temps perdu* that Proust's purpose for Charlus becomes evident. The baron is to personify the 'strange, secret, refined and monstrous personal experiences' that constitute homosexuality. Like Charlus's, Proust's own sexual attitudes were volatile and contradictory: both the character and its creator, in successive moods, vehemently disavow homosexuality, betray a persistent fascination by it, act as its advocates, and sympathise with its practitioners. The number of Charlusiens became overblown during Proust's constant reflections on the subject – 'I am all too aware,' he announced to a friend, 'of the enormous, unsuspected number of men like Charlus in the world' – but the baron was indispensable to his conception of his novel, and an innovation of which he was especially proud. The magnificence of Charlus as a character, and the central role of Charlusiens in Proust's created world, only became evident with the publication of *Sodome et Gomorrhe I* in May 1921, just a year before the Schiffs' party at the Majestic. The last eighteen months of Proust's life proved to be dominated by two stressful, protracted processes: the public revelation, between hard covers, of his highly individual view of human desires; and afterwards his fight to complete his novel before his health fatally collapsed.

As early as 1912 Proust was explaining that he had devised a 'pretty original' character who might deter some potential publishers or readers: a 'virile homosexual [*pédéraste*], in love with virility, detesting effeminate young men, in truth detesting all young men, just as men whom women have made to suffer become misogynists. This character is sufficiently dispersed through different parts of the book so it is nothing like a specialist monograph such as Binet-Valmer's *Lucien*.' This last allusion was to a recent novel of 1910 about a young man's identity crisis. Its artistic, effeminate protagonist avows his homosexuality to his psychiatrist father and thereby arouses a family conflict. His misery, coupled with the risks that he runs in trying to satisfy his desires, make him propose marriage to a young girl and attempt suicide, although his final departure for Naples with his English lover carries a suggestion that he is on the brink of fulfilment. Proust's reference to *Lucien* is a reminder of how conscientiously he had considered the available literature on homosexuality, including, it seems, such minor English novels as Howard Overing Sturgis's *Tim: a story of Eton* (1891) and *Belchamber* (1904). He had determined to write more expansively than any of his literary forerunners and to create an array of characters that he was sure had no precedents.

Proust's project enabled him to explore his own impulses and analyse his experiences while retaining the liberty to abjure the

contents of his novel as abstract speculation or literary inven-
tion if confronted by uncomfortable or threatening personal
questions (for regardless of the French criminal code, a reputation for sexual deviance could lead to ostracism). Unlike Binet-
Valmer, he was not concerned with demonstrating the impact
on an individual of the dominant public morality. Instead, he
created a private imaginary domain in which many of his protagonists demonstrated the ambisexuality – the attraction to
both sexes, the curiosity about both genders – that characterised
his own wavering, evolving preferences and fantasies. He told
the literary critic and political agitator Charles Maurras that he
envied the nonchalance with which, in *Le chemin de Paradis*,
Maurras alluded to the Athenian sculptor Phidias, who loved
both a young man named Pantarces and a young woman Poly-
damia. Phidias represented Proust's emotional ideal. 'Such
tastes, nowadays so often attributed to mere fashion, were
accepted as natural in those days,' he explained approvingly to
Maurras in 1922. In the fictional world that Proust invented, he
expanded the significance of the inhabitants of Sodom and
Gomorrah until they metaphorically represented the whole
human condition. *Sodome et Gomorrhe* is a title derived from a
line in Alfred de Vigny's poem 'La colère de Samson' – 'the
women shall have Gomorrah and the men shall have Sodom' –
but its biblical origin is overpowering, and for Proust 'those valleys of sulphur and brimstone ringing with curses' were a hereti-
cal representation of the fall from grace that every human
suffers in Christian beliefs. With terrifying boldness Proust
makes inversion a substitute for religion. After reading *Sodome
et Gomorrhe I* the novelist Jules Romains sent Proust a message
of perceptive admiration. 'The richness of your gifts never ceas-

es to dazzle me,' he wrote, 'but you are, in my eyes, a magnificent heretic. I don't need to tell you why. You are not one of those who "falls" into heresy. You go forth to meet it; you espouse it.' The language, conduct and desires of Sodom and Gomorrah not only provided the heart of Proust's unique private universe: they offer, he suggests, the key to everyone else's. Even after losing his faith, Proust believed that we are all sinners (or transgressors in secular language), and constructed a parable from the disorders and misconduct of his Sodomites that was indispensable to understanding human loves and desires.

Male homosexuality was traditionally regarded as either an unmentionable abomination or as a marginal idiosyncrasy that gave lurid colour to the borders of fiction, and female homosexuality had been the source of either voyeuristic pleasure for men or the pretext for savage violence, such as befell the Princesse de Lamballe, who was murdered and hideously mutilated by French revolutionaries in 1792. *Temps perdu* however placed homosexuality more centrally in human experience than any previous novel or treatise, and used it to demonstrate the degenerative squalor of human emotions. Emmanuel Berl, who attested that during long philosophical discussions in Rue Hamelin Proust's 'coherence stunned me; he talked like he wrote', was shaken by Proust's preferred strategy to describe the human predicament and explain human experience: 'he was convinced that only homosexuality [*l'homosexualité*] caught in its toughness, its purity, the painful essence of truth.' It was partly from mischief, but also to bring sexual inversion in from the cultural margins to the centre of his created world, that Proust so often quoted or invoked Racine as a preliminary to sodomitical encounters. A young waiter who fascinates the old

Jewish financier Nissim Bernard is, for example, likened to a young Israelite in Racine's great biblical tragedies *Esther* and *Athalie*: his seduction by Bernard is described with comic incongruity through extracts from Racine's choruses.

In his fiction Proust usually refers to homosexuality as 'inversion', a word which betrays the context in which he formulated his ideas, for it was current in French medical parlance of his father's generation. The pioneering case-study by the leading French neurologists Jean-Martin Charcot and Valentin Magnan of a university professor of erect military bearing, utterly uneffeminate, with a life-long passion for looking at other men's penises, published in *Archives de Neurologie* of 1882, had the definitive title 'Inversion du sens génital'. Charcot and Magnan were not the only medical authorities who influenced Proust's novel. His conception of Charlus owed much to the German jurist Karl Heinrich Ulrichs, who in 1868 had published an influential treatise defining the male invert as someone with a woman's soul enclosed in a man's body, and reversing this formula to characterise women inverts. Following Ulrichs, and anticipating Proust, Valentin Magnan regarded homosexuality as a gender-confusion caused by heredity rather than environment: 'the beginning originates in the brain; it is in some way the brain of a woman with the body of a man and the brain of a man in the body of a woman.' This idea is evident throughout *Temps perdu*. 'I tried to depict a homosexual [*homosexuel*] besotted by virility because [Charlus], without knowing it, is a Woman,' Proust told Gide in 1914. Several of his other characters have women's souls in male bodies or female souls in men's bodies: Charlie Morel, for example, has a 'girlish air amidst his masculine beauty' while Mademoiselle Vinteuil is portrayed as a dual character: the 'shy suppliant maiden' co-existing with 'a rough conquering old soldier.' Even that champion of virility Charlus deteriorates into a grotesque old doll chattering about her appearance: 'It's horrible,' he exclaims, 'one looks so perfectly hideous, I know I'm not twenty-five any more and they won't choose me as Queen of the May, but one does still want to look one's best.'

'Like all homosexuals [*homosexuels*],' Proust maintained, Charlus 'is different from other men, in some ways worse, in others infinitely better.' His conception of Charlus as a character estranged from every milieu reflected his own situation as someone who always seemed a man apart. Georges de Lauris remembered first encountering Little Marcel when the latter was in his early thirties: from under his heavy eyelids Proust subjected the dinner guests of a rich banker's wife to his piercing scrutiny. 'How conspicuously different he was from the others! He was never confused with the others with whom he was being entertained. A sort of "aura" separated him from them. . . . Marcel was, in every respect, a human being who was the great exception.' At times Proust recoiled from any suggested correlation between specialised sexual tastes and artistic sensibility, but in his novel he affirmed that the 'special taste' of the inhabitants of Sodom, 'inherited by them like an aptitude for drawing, for music, a weakness of vision, is perhaps the only living and despotic originality.' Proust conceived Charlus as a paradigm of the sensibility and perception that can be found in some men who are attracted by other men. He was 'convinced,' he told Gide, 'that it is to his homosexuality [*homosexualité*] that M. de Charlus owes his understanding of so many things which are closed to his brother, the Duc de Guermantes, that make him so much shrewder, more discriminating and sensitive.' The same might be said of Marcel Proust and his brother Robert:

although the former's complicated sexual outlook was only one of several traits that set him apart and brought him such distinction, it was at the core of his sensibility.

The adolescent Proust did not hide his sexual interests from the more intelligent boys among his fellow pupils at Lycée Condorcet. He was not abashed when his school-friend Jacques Bizet rebuffed his suggestion, in 1888, that they explore each other sexually. 'I admire your wisdom while simultaneously regretting it,' Proust told Bizet in a message written surreptitiously during a history lesson. 'I am not fatuous enough to believe that my body is so precious a treasure that it required great strength of character to renounce it.' Seventeen-year-old Proust rationalised that sexual behaviour was permissible between adolescents of the same sexes although similar acts in adulthood were reprehensible. 'I always find it sad,' he told Bizet, 'not to pluck the delicious flower that soon we shall be unable to pluck. For then it will already be fruit – and forbidden.' Proust continued to idealise and extol inversion to his more trusted school-friends. When his fellow Condorcet pupil Daniel Halévy reproached him for being 'jaded and effete', Proust protested that he did not deserve Halévy's 'contempt, which would have been better directed at a lecher surfeited with women and seeking a new type of orgasm in pederasty'. He was candid about Halévy's attractions: 'You have bright, pretty eyes which reflect the grace and refinement of your mind with such purity that I cannot love your mind without kissing your eyes; your body and mind, like your thoughts, are so slender and supple that I feel that I could mingle more intimately with your thoughts sitting on your lap.' But he defended himself by invoking Platonic ideals of young masculine affinities. 'I pride myself on having some highly intelligent friends, with great moral delicacy, who once amused themselves with a friend: it was when they were young men. Later on they reverted to women.'

During the early 1890s Proust had intense loving friendships with several gifted youths: Edgar Aubert, who succumbed to appendicitis in 1892, Comte Robert de Flers (a gifted drama critic, theatre director and playwright who survived as a lifelong friend), and Willie Heath, who died of typhoid in 1893. In 1894 he met Reynaldo Hahn, who was three years his junior. Hahn had been born in Venezuela, was admitted as a child prodigy to the Paris Conservatory at the age of eleven, and composed some of his most memorable songs as a teenager. He afterwards had a distinguished career as composer, conductor and sometime Diaghilevien collaborator. Proust and Hahn ultimately enjoyed a deep, loving and mutually sympathetic friendship, which long outlived its early fleshly excitements: 'A year or a year and a half', Proust later explained, was for him 'the term beyond which such affection, or should I say infection, recedes and dies.' But there were fraught phases in the 1890s because Hahn, who wanted to concentrate his powers on his music rather than to submit to other men's emotional demands, found Proust's needs too intense. 'To have you tell me everything,' Proust nagged, 'has been my hope, my consolation, my support, my life.' Unless confident that he knew every detail and individual in Hahn's existence, he was devoured by jealousy. With Hahn as with other men, Proust proved too possessive, volatile and exacting for anyone with a life or interests of their own.

Proust flirted with men, doubtless had arousing conversations or exciting tussles with some of them, but throughout his early manhood he also cherished sentimental admiration for several women: charming girls of his own age such as Marie de Benardaky and Jeanne Pouquet as well as beautiful older women such as Geneviève Straus and Comtesse Elisabeth Greffulhe. In his late thirties he still gazed, admired and rhapsodised like a moonstruck youth. In 1908, for example, he lingered absurdly at a ball trying unsuccessfully to wrangle an introduction to 'the prettiest girl I've ever seen', Oriane de Goyon. He despaired afterwards that he would never be invited to another ball, never see her again: 'How marvellous she looks, how intelligent she seems.' His wistful, idealised heterosexual crushes can seem as clumsy as his narrator's early infatuation with the Duchesse de Guermantes, who is stalked with nervous doggedness on her daily walks in Paris. Gilberte Swann proves that Proust could create a girl character of authentic charm and vitality; but he betrays himself on at least one occasion when depicting her adolescent flirtation with the narrator. The incident in which Gilberte wrestles with the narrator in the Champs-Élysées until their *frottage* climaxes with his orgasm is improbable in a girl of her class and generation, although plausible if one imagines that the narrator's wrestling partner is another boy. Gilberte in the Champs-Élysées is perhaps what Proust wanted the girls in his private universe to be like: androgynous fighters, wrestlers who are not that tough.

Often in *Temps perdu* Proust is feeble, even ludicrous, when trying to describe heterosexual action. His fictional impersonator's trysts with Albertine are seldom convincing.

> I half-opened her night-dress. Her two little upstanding breasts were so round that they seemed not so much integral parts of her body as to have ripened there like two fruits;

and her belly (concealing the place where a man is made as
ugly as the metal pin left sticking out of a statue that has
been taken down from its fixture) was closed, at the junc-
tion of her thighs, by two valves of a curve as sleepy, repose-
ful and retiring as the horizon after the sun has set.

Proust's ripe fruit is more convincing when men are somewhere
in the background: as when, during summer holidays, the narrator and Albertine go spooning in the countryside.

> I recall the hot weather that we had then: from the brow of
> the farm-boys labouring in the sun there would fall, vertically,
> regularly, intermittently, drops of sweat like the drips from a
> cistern, and alternating with the fall of the ripe fruit from
> the trees in the adjoining orchards; they have remained for
> me, to this day, together with a woman's mystery, the most
> substantial part in any love that is offered to me.

If Proust's narrator's fantasies about women conjured up other
men's sweat, it is equally true that the sight of sweating men re-
awoke the narrator's memories of his desire for Albertine. This
is an imaginary world in which sexual distinctions are only
important for the tricks they play on human sensibility.

Hahn introduced Proust to Alphonse Daudet's family, who
found him intriguing. Daudet himself, with his novelist's pene-
tration of other people's secrets, said with a smile, 'Marcel
Proust, he's the devil.' By 1896 Proust's devotion had transferred
from Hahn to Daudet's eighteen-year-old son Lucien. As with
Hahn, the emotional intimacy between the two young men
proved more important and enduring than their ephemeral
erotic charge, but their early involvement provoked one inci-

dent of outward drama. As their mutual desire was petering out in 1897, a *fin-de-siècle* journalist and novelist called Jean Lorrain made snide newspaper insinuations about Proust's affection for Lucien Daudet. In Paris, after Oscar Wilde's downfall in 1895, there was 'only one invert of mark', Elisabeth de Clermont-Tonnerre recalled, and that was this same Jean Lorrain. He 'wore scarab rings on each finger, bouffant ties, and hennaed his hair; he chattered in terms both crude and poetic of the secret charms of the bargemen of Billancourt'. This amusing and able man had a pitiful weakness for denouncing homosexuality in his articles despite his own taste for rough trade: this self-repudiation was paralleled in *Temps perdu* by Charlus and Saint-Loup who both, on different occasions, assault men who have propositioned them. Proust challenged Lorrain to a duel, and showed calm resolve in the days before it was fought. He chose as his seconds neither a soldier nor a noblemen, but the painter Jean Béraud and (although the duellists agreed to fight with pistols) a semi-professional swordsman called Gustave de Borda. Proust and Lorrain met at a quiet and secluded location, near l'Ermitage de Villebon, in the Bois de Meudon, picturesque and extensive woodlands east of the Palace of Versailles, and just across the Seine from Billancourt, where Lorrain had so often sought out his obliging bargemen. At twenty-five paces, one after the other, they both fired two shots without wounding their adversary. Robert de Flers and Hahn, who accompanied their friend to Villebon, thought Proust showed admirable sang-froid and determination: many other friends rejoiced at his safe passage through this ordeal, and denounced Lorrain as a cowardly wretch. The affair imbued Proust with lifelong pride at this evidence of his masculine courage, and during recurrent paroxysms of nervous irritability during the next quarter-century he challenged several other men to duels which mercifully were not fought: the insolent young Henry, Vicomte de Vogüé, who provoked him at a party in 1903; Camille Plantevignes in 1908; and Jacques Delgado in 1922. He also liked to make muffled threats of duels to such men as Jean de Pierrefeu, who gave him an unflattering review in 1919.

All these youthful friends – Aubert, Flers, Heath, Hahn and Daudet – were creative, artistic, brimming with aesthetic ideals and ambitions rather like Proust himself. The sexual feelings were reciprocated or at least acknowledged. But after 1900 he moved towards intense, slightly hysterical but more sublimated friendships with young noblemen like Antoine de Bibesco, Louis d'Albufera and Armand de Guiche, who were 'unassailable' in their 'fundamental purity', as he wrote. Proust also befriended Bertrand, Vicomte de Fénelon with whom, in 1902, he visited the Netherlands on what proved to be his last foreign excursion. Their journey, which ostensibly was to study paintings and architecture, was both fervent and frustrating, for Proust had no intuition that Fénelon was secretly an invert. He never lost his susceptibility to intelligence and charm in young men: at the end of his life he still derived warm pleasure from the spirited energy and bright minds of Paul Brach and Jacques Benoist-Méchin, two men in their twenties whom he encountered during 1922. Brach and Benoist-Méchin were, in some senses, replacements for Louis Gautier-Vignal: Proust's attachments and dependence seldom lasted, and of Gautier-Vignal he had seen enough. In his novel, he generalised the tendencies that he observed in himself towards young men to cover all love affairs: 'the woman to whom one devotes everything is so rapidly replaced by another, and one astonishes oneself by a constant, hopeless fervour that is renewed all over again.'

With these new friends Proust was sometimes candid about his interest in inversion but sometimes touchy. His ambivalent responses are evident from two contradictory letters sent to Bibesco in 1901. In the first he called himself an 'old coquette of intellectual friendship (a Salaist)' – his private word for an invert, which punned on *salacité* while making an in-joke about the flamboyant behaviour of Comte Antoine Sala. But only three days later he was protesting semi-scientific neutrality to Bibesco. 'Salaism,' he insisted, 'interests me in the same way as gothic architecture, though much less': his personal life and friendships were free of it. He was equally upset when Bibesco publicly referred to Fénelon using the compromising nickname 'His Blue Eyes'. 'If you're going to start dropping innuendos to Lauris or to others! Think a second of the impression that it would make, of what people would think of me . . . it's not only on my account, I owe it to my family not to let myself be taken for a Salaist gratuitously, since I'm not one.' He was, indeed, so scared, that he ended by enjoining Bibesco, 'Keep this letter carefully hidden and return it to me when you next see me.' These feints and denials were requisite acts of self-protection, but the reason for Proust's constant, ardent interest in Sodom and Gomorrah was blatant. According to Bibesco, 'Marcel kept a register of all the famous and infamous sodomites not only of Paris but also from abroad' and felt that a man's attitude to inversion was as important as his partisanship in the great controversy of the epoch. 'Dreyfusard, anti-Dreyfusard, Salaist, anti-Salaist, are just about the only interesting things worth knowing about an imbecile,' he told Bibesco.

There is a passage in *Sodome et Gomorrhe* that describes the emotional isolation of inverts in terms which recall Proust's predicament with Bibesco. They are, says Proust, 'friends without friendships, despite all those which their charm, frequently recognised, inspires and their hearts, often generous, would gladly feel; but can we describe as friendship those relations which flourish only by virtue of a lie and from which the first outburst of confidence and sincerity in which they might be tempted to indulge would make them be expelled with disgust.' Given Proust's belief in the impossibility for him of an enduring, honest friendship, it is not surprising that his novel and correspondence include so many denunciations of friendship as a false, degrading experience. Bibesco, too, came to feel equivocal about Proust's alternating avowals of affection and misanthropy. Ultimately, in old age, the prince felt reluctant to discuss Proust's 'emotional abnormality' but mocked his visit with Fénelon to a brothel where he professed to be disappointed by the women's attractions presumably so as to avoid performing. Proust complained that the brothel was freezing cold, and threw the establishment into disarray as he ordered hot-water bottles and blankets – presumably the only client that evening who needed to be thus equipped and armoured.

Proust's touchiness about his sexuality, his fear of being shamed or shunned, and his desire to protect his family, confirm Violet Schiff's view that he could not begin to write his great novel during his mother's lifetime. As Proust recuperated during 1906 from his mother's death, he began to make up for lost time in the matter of sexual curiosity. Instead of loving upper middle-class aesthetes or admiring unobtainable young noblemen, he betrayed for the first time an interest in working-class youths. In July he asked

Lucien Daudet for the name and address of a valet working at the Swedish legation. In August he started fussing over a young corporal who was his cook's nephew, and in September he asked a railway company chairman, Henri de Blarenberghe, to trace a youth who worked at Gare Saint-Lazare. Even Albufera, ultimately, was asked the identity of that 'young telegraph operator who was related to one of your servants' (whom Proust professed to need for purposes of literary research). Further opportunities to satisfy his curiosity about young working-class men came in the summer of 1907 when Proust felt strong enough for a summer holiday. After cancelling a visit to the Cévennes, he went to the Grand Hôtel at Cabourg where he watched, gossiped with and overtipped the lift-boys, pages and waiters. There was a trace of Proust in his character Nissim Bernard, who falls for a young waiter at the Grand Hôtel in Balbec. 'With Oriental atavism he adored a seraglio,' Proust wrote of the elderly Jewish financier. 'He loved the labyrinth of corridors, secret storage rooms, salons, cloakrooms, larders and galleries that comprised the hotel at Balbec.'

These were tastes that could jeopardise a man's existence: Proust felt the vulnerability of his position long before he became a financial underwriter and client of a male brothel which was often raided by the Paris police. Indeed, the police surprised him there, during a raid on the night of 11–12 January, drinking champagne with two soldiers, and recorded him in their police report as 'Proust, Marcel, rentier, 102 boulevard Haussmann.' The authorities' rooted objection to young men from the lower classes consorting with moneyed men, as happened in male brothels, had already proved fatal to Oscar Wilde. While it was permissible for the rich to seduce servant girls, or to keep mistresses from the poorer classes, because the women remained subordinates, affection or sexual contacts between men of widely different classes defied notions of hierarchy and masculine authority, and so were intensely threatening to social order – especially if the men from the governing classes subordinated themselves or encouraged poor, uneducated men to be insubordinate. When Wilde was on trial, Sir Edward Carson, the prosecuting counsel, attacked his association with Alphonse Conway, an eighteen-year-old working-class 'loafer' whom he met on the beach at Worthing and took for a night to a smart hotel in Brighton. Carson denounced Wilde's 'disgraceful audacity' in giving Conway a blue suit and straw boater with a band of red and blue ribbon so he would not be ashamed of his appearance at the hotel. 'Mr Wilde procured a suit of clothes to dress him up like a gentleman's son, put some public school colours upon his hat,' Carson fulminated. It was an act of class imposture which could only subvert social order. 'If Mr Wilde were really anxious to assist Conway, the very worst thing he could have done was take the lad out of his proper sphere, by giving him champagne luncheons.'

Proust felt vulnerable to rumours, aspersions and social shame during 1908 at precisely the moment when he began to write the volumes that became *À la recherche du temps perdu* with their developing theme of sex between men of widely different classes. At times he felt such openness might be the ruin of him. His anxiety that he might be harried or ostracised for what he was proposing to do in his novel – or might be thought to have done in the flesh – was worked to a higher pitch in 1908 because all newspaper-reading Europeans were being startled by the revelations of a male sex scandal. Proust was fascinated by the social fall of the German courtier Prince Philipp von Eulenberg-Hertefeld, and felt apprehensive about his own social survival. The Eulenberg case was a press stunt engineered by Isidor Wittkowski, a renegade Polish Jew who transformed himself into Maximilian Harden, a reactionary journalist, anti-Semite, patriot, chauvinist and Christian reformer. Harden had vowed to avenge the fall from power of his patron, Bismarck, and sought to ruin Eulenburg and his close friend Count Kuno von Moltke, the military commander of Berlin, both members of the Court camarilla surrounding Kaiser Wilhelm II, with accusations of political misjudgement and moral degeneracy. In 1907 he embroiled them in criminal trials during which Eulenberg – a devoted husband and a delightful, over-indulgent father – swore that he had never committed 'filthy' practices. This led to the prince's arrest on a charge of perjury in May 1908. The most incriminating evidence against him (dredged up from twenty years earlier) came from Jakob Ernst, a fisherman whom Eulenberg had recruited as his manservant, and from Georg Riedl, a former fisherman, ex-convict and milkman. It was the class anarchy as much as the physical facts that seemed so criminal: to Harden, discussing a cuirassier supposedly debauched by Eulenberg, it did not seem 'strange that a commoner, who was on terms of champagne and bottoms [*popo*] and Du and Du among counts, should become a delinquent. Who degraded him?' These protracted legal proceedings broke the prince's health and seemed to vindicate Harden; although the criminal trial was abandoned because of Eulenberg's illness, he and his friends were irretrievably disgraced.

Eulenberg's trials of 1907–9 provoked much discussion of sexual inversion in France: indeed they gave wider currency in Europe to the German neologism *Homosexualität*, as mentioned by Charlus. Amongst the press outpourings, Rémy de Gourmont in *Mercure de France* tried to infer some of the governing principles of human conduct from his analysis of Eulenberg's trials. 'Nothing shows more clearly the incoherence of Nature, the absence in the world or above the world of any governing intelligence. Nothing shows more clearly the incompatibility of abstract morality with the blind monster of real life. Human efforts to impose a little order on the chaos of forces, desires, passions, baseness, frenzies are beautiful but also laughable.' Proust, who was a voracious reader of newspapers, agreed with Gourmont that Sodom could reveal some of the governing forces of humanity rather than merely provide marginal salacious excitement.

During the spring and summer of 1908, when the Eulenberg case was being publicised, just after Proust had resolved to explore these toxic subjects in his projected novel, he felt justifiably frightened about exposing his reputation to Hardenesque calumny and was hypersensitive to any suggestion that he was an invert. 'It's so boring to have to explain what one is,' he protested to Albufera early in June, apparently answering reproaches about sexual attitudinising. 'As to what you say about my friends, if you're thinking of Reynaldo, you're right to believe that he's the dearest friend to me, the best, a brother. If he murdered someone I'd hide the corpse in my bedroom so that people thought that I had done the deed.' Suspicions might be prevalent about several of Proust's creative friends, but he assured Albufera that 'it isn't only in the theatre world or literature that malevolent rumours fester.' High Society was implicated too. 'I don't want to accuse anyone, especially as I know there are some young men with vices who are very nice, but in your generation only a few are . . . beyond the reach of calumny.' Proust's accusations and suspicions about other men were swiftly followed by confusing denials about himself. A few days later in June, at a ball given by Princesse Edmond de Polignac, Proust remarked to Princesse Alexandre de Caraman-Chimay on the svelte good looks of François, Vicomte de Paris. The viscount, who felt uncomfortable at being complimented by a man in this way and mocked Proust's remark, received next day a seven-page tirade of protests and recriminations. Repeatedly invoking the memory of 'poor Mama', 'whom I loved more than anyone else in the world', Proust ended: 'You are not worth the effort that so exhausted me in writing all this . . . Goodbye strange being who inspires affection without knowing how to be a friend.'

The crescendo of Proust's paranoia was reached later in the summer of 1908. While holidaying at Cabourg, he befriended Marcel Plantevignes, an intelligent and cultured nineteen-year-old. In the evenings Plantevignes used to visit Proust's hotel bedroom where he was favoured with long conversations and readings from the draft novel. Then one day Plantevignes received a letter that was, to him, alarming, inexplicable and preposterous. 'Monsieur', it began coldly, 'Since you used to lavish on me with a tenacity and persistence that were sometimes worrying – because I wondered whether one day these virtues might turn to perfidy – signs of the most sincere devotion, I scarcely imagined that you were preparing yourself for the dastardly act of stabbing me in the back.' After this confused, excitable opening Proust almost spat his 'disdain and refusal ever to see you again' at the dumbfounded teenager: 'you have clumsily ruined a friendship that might have been very beautiful.' When Camille Plantevignes, a manufacturer of ties, who was the boy's father, visited Proust to express his family's bewilderment, he was challenged to a duel. Vicomte d'Alton and the Marquis de Pontcharra, who were selected by Proust as his seconds, regarded his behaviour as foolish histrionics, especially as he refused to explain what insult had provoked his outburst. After days of pompous muddle, it emerged that Proust was enraged because the young man had curtly dismissed, rather than formally contradicted, a tedious woman who had accosted him on the Cabourg promenade with warnings of Proust's dangerous sexual reputation. When, at a reconciliatory meeting, the boy remarked that the woman's accusation was a common rumour in Balbec, Proust paled and fell silent before rallying himself with sorrowful, sardonic banter.

Proust's fear of being labelled as an invert during 1908, his pain at becoming the object of sexual innuendo, are crucial to appreciating his courage in publishing *Sodome et Gomorrhe* in 1921, and to assessing the temper of the final eighteen months of his life. The decision to write about Sodom caused him years of uneasiness, but also imbued him with artistic confidence: he knew his book served a public need by filling a literary vacancy. He wrote in *La Prisonnière* of 'the invert [*inverti*] who has been unable to feed his passion except on literature written for men who love women, who think of men when reading Musset's *Nuits*' (romantic poems of the 1830s about emotional identity). He resolved to give his readers a literature that did not ignore, misinterpret or discard the significance of inversion. 'For the last nineteen hundred years', he again wrote in *La Prisonnière*, 'all conventional homosexuality [*homosexualité*] – that of Plato's young friends as well as that of Virgil's shepherds – has disappeared, what survives and increases is the involuntary, highly-strung kind, which we hide from other people and disguise from ourselves.' He was determined to acknowledge, if not celebrate, 'the homosexuality [*homosexualité*] that survives in spite of obstacles, shameful and besmirched, that is the only true form, the only form that can be found in a person of refined moral qualities.'

When Freudianism was still a respectable analytical tool in literary criticism, Proust used to be complimented for being a Freudian *avant la lettre* whose theories of the unconscious anticipated those of the Vienna School. It is more pertinent to notice, and applaud, how unFreudian was Proust's treatment of sexuality. He never attributed inversion to cankered parental love: he never insisted that over-possessive mothers or ineffectual fathers have poisoned their children's sexuality by bad parenting. Instead he presented homosexuality as a familial trait or a quality transmitted by heredity. In the crucial opening section of *Sodome et Gomorrhe* describing Charlus picking up Jupien, Proust explains that their convergence has been ordained by their ancestry as much as their temperament. The sexual tastes of Charlus's nephew Robert de Saint-Loup are presented as the 'hereditary malady' of the Guermantes. 'One can easily imagine a *grand seigneur* from this ancient family, blond, golden, intelligent, dowered with every prestige, harbouring in his depths a secret taste, unknown to anyone, for black men.' Hereditary determinism, it seems, makes both Charlus and then Saint-Loup fall in love with Charlie Morel, while their cousin Prince de Guermantes, 'a jolly king of the fairies', also lusts after the young violinist.

Unlike Freudians, Proust does not say that inverts are emotionally stunted people whose sexual behaviour is a sign of arrested development and disordered emotions: instead he stresses the sophisticated diversity of inverts' development. 'His nature was like a piece of paper folded so many times, and in so many directions, that it would be impossible ever to straighten it out,' he writes of Morel. Proust's inverts are not – like Freud's – narcissists who seek reflected images of themselves in their sexual partners. Much more excitingly, and inclusively, they seek difference – even opposites. 'Morel, being exceedingly dark, was necessary to Saint-Loup, as shadow is to sunlight.' The estimable Jupien is attracted by older men; Charlus desires young toughs rather than young gentlemen; one should not be disappointed (Proust instructs his readers) when a man whose 'delicacy, gracefulness and affability touch all hearts chases after boxers'.

Sex, for Proust, was a matter of translation. From adolescence onwards he had a taste for merged, confused, perhaps even dissembled genders. At the age of twenty, answering a personality test, he replied to a question about the quality he most sought in a man, 'Feminine charms'. The traits he preferred in women, he next answered, were 'manly virtues and sincere camaraderie'. Proust's pleasure in translated genders remained fixed. One can surmise that when he lay with Louisa de Mornand in 1904, he was thinking of Albufera and Fénelon as much as of her; certainly he was frank with her about the importance of translation in his sexual imagination. He was 'always curious about what transposes a friend's face from the masculine sex into the feminine, and vice versa,' he told her; adding that he yearned to see photographs of her dead brother, and the dead brother of Marie de Bénardaky, 'the great love of my youth and for whom I wanted to kill myself'.

Sydney Schiff once pictured the room in Rue Hamelin where Proust worked, nursed himself and slept: 'the bed was surrounded by books of every size as by a rampart which only left just enough space to approach'. Proust referred to his sources – found ideas or inspiration in other people's books – at every stage of his work. The volume that he published in 1921 revealed gender transposition as a central technique of *Temps perdu*, and ambisexuality as a central theme; but although his treatment was more emphatic and extensive than any previous writer, he was following an established tradition of gender translation among French novelists. Chevalier d'Albert, the protagonist of Théophile Gautier's *Mademoiselle de Maupin, double amour* (1835), is a twisted aesthete who finds beauty in 'an excitable little Italian beggar, the colour of a lemon, with enormous flashing dark eyes, who looks almost like an unframed canvas by Murillo'. Although d'Albert is still young, he already professes to have 'become so jaded that I can now only relish what is queer or extreme'. He has a mistress, but plays such mischievous identity games, causing such disarrayed preferences and erotic combinations, that there is no doubt where his curiosity is tending: he craves to become a woman so that he can discover 'new kinds of carnal bliss'. *Mademoiselle de Maupin* develops into a witty masquerade of gender confusion and role reversal in which the sexual transpositions become giddying.

Maxime Saccard in Zola's early novel *La Curée* (1871) (*The Quarry*) is another fictional invert who plays a game of gender exchange with his woman lover. As a schoolboy of thirteen, Maxime, who is a rich Paris property speculator's son, already 'had vices before he knew the meaning of desire'. As a young man Maxime looks and behaves like a kept woman. 'His long, limp-wristed hands betrayed his vices. His hairless body had the languor of a satiated woman . . . his spineless, flacid being . . . submitted passively.' Succumbing to his 'hereditary corruption',

Maxime is seduced by his stepmother whom he meets at night in the stifling heat of the conservatory to copulate on a black bearskin rug. 'Renée enjoyed her domination, and . . . played the part of a man,' Zola wrote. 'Maxime submitted; this epicene being became a great girl in Renée's arms. He seemed born and bred for perversion.' Nearly thirty years later, among the characters of one of his final novels, *Paris* (1898), Zola included an 'androgynous abortion' called Baron Hyacinthe Duvillard. 'He diverted himself with poetry and music, he lived in an extraordinary set of artists, whores, madmen and bandits, boastful of all his crimes and vices, affecting horror of women, professing the worst philosophical and social ideas, always going to extremes, by turns collectivist, individualist, anarchist, pessimist, symbolist, even sodomite.' Hyacinthe has, in certain essentials, a female identity: women physically revolt him and he cannot reciprocate when a *déclassé* princess, Rosamonde, becomes infatuated with him. They develop, though, a conspiratorial friendship, and tour the low dives of Paris in search of shocking novelties. Ultimately Hyacinthe induces Rosamonde to become the lover of his father's courtesan Silviane.

The amusing gender exchanges in Huysman's novel *À rebours* (1884) have particular significance as Proustian antecedents because the novel's protagonist was partly modelled on Comte Robert de Montesquiou, who was Proust's prototype for Charlus. An effete nobleman, Des Esseintes, becomes excited as he watches the performance of a circus acrobat called Miss Urania (whose name plays on a contemporary medical term for male inverts, 'uranists'). He fantasises about her transmogrifying from a woman into an androgynous creature before ultimately becoming an utter man, while he simultaneously turns female:

'this exchange of sex between Miss Urania and himself aroused him tremendously.' Later Des Esseintes finds a ventriloquist girl 'with greasy hair parted on one side near the temple like a boy's'. His difficulties in copulating with her are solved when, from their bed, she projects an angry man's voice, which seems to be yelling from outside the bedroom door. 'Open up, damn you!' shouts the ventriloquist. 'I know you've got a john in there with you! Wait a minute, you slut, and you'll get what's coming to you!' Immediately, says Huysman, Des Esseintes, 'like those lechers on the river bank, in the Tuileries gardens, in a public lavatory or on a park bench, would recover his powers, and hurl himself on the ventriloquist, whose voice went blustering on outside the room.' These threats of violence coupled with gender transposition excite Des Esseintes so much that finally he can perform sexually with the ventriloquist girl – and perform, moreover, playing 'the man's part'. (When *À rebours* was first translated into English in 1922, these passages were omitted.)

Proust, then, though he drew certain ideas about Sodom from French psychiatrists' characterisation of women's brains trapped in men's bodies, and his depiction of Gomorrah from the reverse formula, could find literary precedents in Gautier, Zola and Huysman for men whose women lovers play the part of men, or whose gender identity becomes a game of exchange. Morel is the flying trickster of this sexually equivocal world. There comes a moment when Charlus intercepts a licentious letter sent to Morel by Léa, a lesbian actress. Léa's teasing way of writing to Morel, applying feminine phrases and grammar to him throughout, such as 'Dirty slapper!' or 'Pretty love, you *are* one and no mistake!', indicates to the narrator that Morel has a similar taste for women as the women of Gomorrah. Another revelation confirms that there are no more boundaries to Morel's sexual adaptability than to original sin itself. After Albertine's death in a riding accident, the narrator hopes to recover the sensations of his lost love for her by having sexual relations with Andrée who has also been Albertine's lover. When he has enticed Andrée into fulfilling this fantasy for him, and as they lie caressing one another, she produces a tormenting tale about Morel's involvement with Albertine. It has that polymorphous sexual temper that gave Proust such pleasure – especially when pursued with ruthless, unapologetic perversity. Andrée describes to the narrator how, during Albertine's summer holidays in Normandy, Morel used to seduce young laundry-maids and fisherwomen who would have rejected a woman's advances. Once the girls were under his sexual influence, he would take them to a secluded rendezvous for sport with Albertine. 'Fearing that they might lose Morel, who of course joined in the act, the girls always did what they were told,' Andrée reports.

There were scientific as well as literary precedents on which Proust drew as he expanded his treatment of Sodom and Gomorrah. He had lived in a medical household for over thirty years until his father's death in 1903: his approach to many subjects was informed by the conversation and opinions that he heard, he was a pretend-scientist as well as an aesthete and he fancied himself a more perceptive diagnostician than many physicians. This background fostered his tendency to treat sexuality as a branch of pathology. 'After so many centuries of disapproval,' he explained to Charles Maurras in 1922, such propensities are only 'left to survive among the sick who are powerless to cure themselves. That is why, in my books, as I plod joylessly through the valleys reeking of pitch and sulphur,

I appear to blame something that personally I do not blame.' Holding these views, Proust familiarised himself with the views of his father's contemporaries who claimed inversion as an area of expertise, and consulted expert opinion on sexuality as he did other types of specialist knowledge when researching and writing his novel. Proust, in the volumes of his novel published from 1921, followed the medical orthodoxy of the preceding generation when developing his characters and plot. One can recognise, for example, the conventional medical wisdom on inversion reproduced by the French psychiatrist Charles Féré in *L'Instinct sexuel* (1899) as permeating Proust's treatment of the subject. 'Love between inverts has a characteristic one seldom finds in true friendship, jealousy,' Féré declared. Jealousy, of course, is a dominant power in Proust's created world: when, to cite one instance, the Prince de Guermantes makes a sexual assignation with Morel, the flat surface of Charlus's mental landscape is (we are told) transformed into a 'mountain chain', but mountains that have been carved by a sculptor to represent vast, writhing depictions of 'Fury, Jealousy, Curiosity, Envy, Hatred, Suffering, Pride, Horror and Love'.

Féré noted, too, that inverts' 'passion often makes all social distinctions disappear for them'. Proust's novel described kings and lackeys, dukes and cabmen, artists and footmen, diplomats and lift-boys, young girls, married women, actresses, bus conductors, a fireman and a policeman on points duty, who all reveal an unsuspected side to Paris street life. When Baron de Charlus is relaxing after his first sexual encounter with Jupien, he asks the tailor about the sexual availability of the cyclist who delivers parcels for a local pharmacist and of a chestnut vendor ('not the one on the left, he's a horror, but the other way, a great dark strapping lad'). In Proust's depiction, this expansive and thriving underworld existed not only throughout cities but in the countryside and hence throughout the world. Class barriers and geographic frontiers are weakened by inversion, as Proust shows in the furtive gossip at a reception between two dukes, a general, an eminent physician, a leading advocate and an author about Prince de Guermantes's fair-haired footman, dressed in fetching knee-breeches, whose gender they encipher by transposing him into a woman.

> 'I believe she's altogether against it, certainly she plays hard to get, you like to get to essentials quickly so she would disgust you. Anyway, I know there's nothing doing, a friend of mine tried.' 'That's a waste, I thought the profile very fine, and the hair superb.' 'Really, as good as that? I think, if you had seen a little more of her, you would have been disillusioned. But two months ago, you would have seen a real marvel serving at the buffet, a great hunk of six foot six, with gorgeous skin and really up for it. But he's left for Poland now.'

'Sodomites,' Proust wrote, 'form in every land an Oriental colony, cultured, musical, scandal-mongering, which has charming qualities and insufferable defects.' Here, again, he was following the conventional medical wisdom of his father's generation: inverts, so Féré noted, 'often manifest a taste for the arts and in particular for music. Male inverts are often effeminate; the women, to the contrary, have a virile character . . . Often inverts like cooking, knitting, embroidery; they love jewellery, clothes that are striking in colour or design, and follow fashions slavishly. They often display an affected politeness, with a great tendency to lying, vanity, gossip and indiscretion.' Charlus conforms to these stereotypes. He paints beautiful pictures on fans. In his youth he took musical lessons from Stamati who forbade him from going to hear Chopin play at his aunt Chimay's. He can still play Fauré's sonata for piano and violin in the purest style. Though Morel is musically well-endowed, it is Charlus who enlarges the young virtuoso's knowledge and purifies his technique.

'Uranists,' declared Féré (using the term adapted by Huysman for his circus acrobat), 'are often attracted by normal men, and feel a true sexual repugnance, as intense as for women, for their fellow inverts.' From the outset, as we have seen, Proust conceived Charlus as emphatic about his own virility and idealising manliness precisely because his own temperament was so feminine. The finickiness of Charlusiens during their indefatigable search for partners is risible in Proust's portrayal. On one occasion, for example, the Baron picks up a bus conductor, whom he asks if he likes concerts. When the young man replies that he sometimes visits a concert-hall where the singer Félix Mayol performs, Charlus snaps back that he detests Mayol's effeminacy and hates his camp humour. Any hint of passivity provokes Charlus into furious repudiations, and for him the bus conductor's attractions pall.

Féré identified 'a need to submit, a searching for ill-treatment, or the pursuit of masochistic brutalities' as a common trait among uranists. This exaggerated a tendency in some submissive men, including Proust, a spiritual masochist who affirmed that the 'whole art of living is to regard people who cause us suffering as enabling us to accept its divine form and thus to populate its daily life with divinities.' The short but controversial scene in which the narrator glimpses Charlus, chained to a bed in Jupien's brothel, being flogged with a whip studded with nails, was Proust's bold acknowledgement of some inverts' tendency to masochistic passivity. Féré attributed sadism to lesbians as the counterpart to male inverts' masochism. In *Swann* there occurs the first instance of the narrator's fortuitous voyeurism in which he watches Mademoiselle Vinteuil's lovemaking with her girlfriend and profanation of her father's photograph. The narrator intuits, though, that this is posturing without any profound commitment to cruelty. 'Sadists of Mlle Vinteuil's sort are beings so purely sentimental, so naturally virtuous, that even sensual pleasures seem to them something bad, the privilege of the wicked.' They are indulging with their partners in a plagiarism of other people's wickedness 'so as to have the illusion, for a moment, of escaping from their scrupulous, tender soul into the inhuman world of pleasure'.

Féré is only one example of contemporary medical opinion. The Paris physician Émile Laurent, for example, also investigated those who had 'sinned against Sodom' in his researches for *Les bisexués* (1894), and found, among other phenomena, Paris rent-boys who lived in long-term relationships with older men. They were, Laurent reported, 'a band of a dozen young men, from fourteen to twenty years, all of them living by pederasty, under the protection of some sinister toughs who were for the most part double their age, forming in this way couples in which the man was the husband and the adolescent was the wife; the former fructifies the latter, whom he treats as an object.' Laurent's choice of the verb 'fructify' to describe what these men do to their youths recalls Proust's use, in his momentous description of Charlus's first encounter with Jupien, of a sustained metaphor involving an insect's fertilisation of a flower.

Proust, who had once daydreamed of a sort of companionate marriage with his employee Alfred Agostinelli, gives a touching glimpse of other possibilities which Morel briefly seemed to offer Charlus and which were very different from the male husbands and male wives described by Laurent. After the Baron conceives an exclusive devotion to Morel, he is charmed when a distinguished Academician (perhaps inspired by Fauré), who is only attracted to women, understands the relationship between the young violinist and his older patron, but is discreet, affable and professionally helpful. On first meeting the couple at a Verdurin dinner, the Academician asks another guest, casually as if he was talking of any man and his mistress, 'Have they been together long?' This morally disinterested dignitary is an honourable figure in the Proustian universe.

The creation of *Sodome et Gomorrhe* required Proust to consult literary precedents and medical texts; but also to use the traits of some of his contemporaries when devising his composite characters. Various Parisians contributed to the creation of Charlus, including Comte Robert de Montesquiou, Comte Aimery de la Rochefoucauld and Baron Jacques Doasan. Although one must accept the primacy of Montesquiou in the formulation of Charlus's character – 'the kernel of the whole business,' Proust said – one must also acknowledge Serge Diaghilev's component influence on Charlus. Proust and the impresario had met long before the Schiffs brought them together at the Majestic, and corresponded intermittently, although their letters have not survived. Moreover, Hahn worked with Diaghilev, and doubtless gossiped about him to Proust. Certainly the violent intensity of Diaghilev's affair with Nijinsky has parallels with Charlus's infatuation and desertion by Morel. Undeniably Diaghilev – so gifted, admirable and grotesque – reminded some of his collaborators of Charlus. Stravinsky, recalling imperial St Petersburg, pictured Diaghilev 'entering the Leiner restaurant on the Nevsky Prospect, where Tchaikovsky had caught cholera, and bowing to people right and left like Baron de Charlus'. Charlus's possessive pride over his protégés was Diaghilevien: 'the mere fact that I take an interest in him and extend my protection over him, gives him a preeminence and wipes out the past, 'the Baron declares of Morel. In other ways Charlus behaved like the Russian Ballet's autocrat: he instigates 'violent scenes, in which he was overwhelmingly eloquent, and crafty intrigues', and advises Madame Verdurin on the arrangements of her musical evening 'in a peremptory tone which blended the rancorous pride of a crotchety nobleman with the dogmatism of the expert artist'.

Although Montesquiou and Diaghilev were men of extraordinary gifts and flaws, their parts are only dust in the balance of *Temps perdu* compared with Proust's own experiences, observations, mishaps, eccentricities and adventures. The real-life models for Charlus, for his nemesis Morel, his carer Jupien and the others are nugatory compared with Proust himself. Proust read widely, watched all the antics of the Guermantes world, but he could have made no sense of it until he had put all his data and impressions under the clarifying lens of his contacts with men from the servant class. This is what made Proust feel so vulnerable when he wrote of *Sodom et Gomorrhe*. He had to step out of his class, acknowledge his dependence on men who ought to have been his subordinates, and behave with social indecency.

At Cabourg in the summer of 1907 Proust met a nineteen-year-old chauffeur-mechanic Alfred Agostinelli, the son of a

Monaco hotelier. Agostinelli took him motoring in the country (including a memorable visit to the Clermont-Tonnerres, where Agostinelli shone his headlights so that his client could admire the roses at night-time). Proust was so delighted that he contributed a rather overwrought article on country motoring to *Le Figaro* in November 1907. When Agostinelli sent a complimentary letter about the article, Proust was beguiled by its vocabulary and intelligence. The two met occasionally during 1908; but Agostinelli's influence on Proust was dormant until January 1913 when he reappeared in Proust's life, seeking a job as a chauffeur, and was hired as a secretary and typist to decipher the confused, untidy drafts of *Temps perdu*. Agostinelli moved into Proust's apartment in Boulevard Haussmann with his ugly, harsh common-law wife whom Odilon Albaret, another taxi-driver, nicknamed the 'flying louse'. The ensuing months brought Proust some rapturous moments interspersed in longer periods of jealous anguish: he lavished money on Agostinelli, and adored his physical proximity. The extent of their contact is unknown, although one of Proust's biographers, Ronald Hayman, fancies that Proust found a 'satisfyingly sacrilegious' replacement for the ritualised goodnight kiss that he had received as a boy from his mother: 'before the two men separated at night, Agostinelli's tongue would slide into his mouth like a slice of bread.' Agostinelli, one suspects, was flattered by Proust's attentions, liked the money and was genuinely kind. Proust, as usual, fretted about what people might say. 'Avoid mentioning my secretary (the former mechanic),' he instructed one confidant. 'People are so stupid that they could discern in this relationship . . . something homosexual [*pédérastique*]. It wouldn't make any difference to me. But it would be heartbreaking to wrong this boy.' And then, further to cover himself, he described a ravishing blonde woman whom he had admired in a restaurant.

There is a poignant passage in *Sodome et Gomorrhe* which conveys the awkwardness of Proust's feelings for Agostinelli. A certain type of male invert is described: 'lovers to whom there is little possibility of love, the hope of which gives them the strength to endure so many risks and so much loneliness, because they fall for a type of man who has nothing feminine about him, with a man who is not an invert and cannot, in consequence, reciprocate'. Inevitably Agostinelli's relationship with his employer became troubled: Proust could so easily become pettish and manipulative. *Swann* was published on 14 November 1913, and a fortnight later the Agostinellis left Proust's apartment and fled to Monte Carlo. Proust wanted to recruit private detectives to shadow Agostinelli and sent hysterically extravagant telegrams to the intermediary whom he enlisted to inveigle the fugitive back to Boulevard Haussmann. During this period Proust re-learnt the limits of his control and was overwhelmed by unhappiness. After contacts were resumed, Agostinelli coaxed a reluctant Proust into paying for aviation lessons, and in the spring of 1914 enrolled in a flying school at Antibes under the name of Marcel Swann. Proust was prevaricating over the purchase of an aircraft for Agostinelli, which the younger man offered to name *Swann*, when on 30 May the trainee pilot crashed into the Mediterranean on his second solo flight. The accident happened only a few hundred yards from land at Antibes, but Agostinelli could not swim: clinging to the wreckage he made pitiful gestures for help, but drowned before rescuers could reach him. Supposedly his pockets were crammed with bank-notes that Proust had sent him.

Proust blamed himself for Agostinelli's death: 'If he had never met me and had not earned so much money from me, he never could have afforded to learn aviation.' To Gide he lamented: 'He died before fully knowing who he was, and before fulfilling what he might have been. The whole affair is shot through with such frightful circumstances that, crushed as I already am, my grief is unbearable.' Like most great creative spirits, however, Proust used his love objects for the purposes of his work, and his grief was soon being constructively exploited and thus assuaged. His experiences with Agostinelli intensified his design and characterisation of his narrator's affair with Albertine Simonet, which many readers find interminable or obsessive, although a minority feel that *La Prisonnière* and *Albertine disparue* enhance the emotional universality of *Temps perdu*. It is facile, though, to pretend that Albertine is simply Agostinelli with his gender transposed: the chauffeur, after all, is vivid, comprehensible and brimming with vitality in Proust's letters about him, whereas Albertine is often an anaemic, encrypted character. She is not a real individual so much as a symbol of desire and deceit presented in semi-human form. 'She represents Love itself, and each reader can impose on her the image of whoever means most to him,' wrote Maurice Sachs, who began reading Proust in 1925.

At the time of Agostinelli's death it was intended that Grasset would publish the second volume of *Temps perdu*, which was still projected as a trilogy, later in 1914. Proofs of the book, which was to be entitled *Le côté de Guermantes*, were sent to Proust, but publication was postponed after the outbreak of war in August. 'I shan't go out again,' he announced to his housekeeper Céleste Albaret in September. 'The soldiers do their duty, and since I can't fight as they do, my duty is to write my book . . . I haven't time for anything else.' His declaration was too absolute and austere to be persisted in: actually, during the war years, he often left his apartment to seek new opportunities to enrich his novel. The deferral of its publication enabled him to expand its features. Chief among Proust's wartime accretions was the massively enhanced prominence given to Albertine, which necessitated the insertion of a new volume, *À l'ombre des jeunes filles en fleurs*, between *Swann* and *Guermantes*. He also made important new additions to *Guermantes*: he installed the illness and death of the narrator's grandmother at the heart of the volume; and he put passages about Charlus at either end of the book, developing the character revealed in *À l'ombre* and foreshadowing the Baron's dominant position in the next volume, which he decided to add to the sequence, *Sodome et Gomorrhe*. After 1914, then, Proust seized his chance to double the length of his manuscript. If *À l'ombre* was the result of Proust's reflections on the meaning of his year with Agostinelli, *Sodome et Gomorrhe* was fashioned out of war conditions and Proust's adventures in wartime Paris.

Elisabeth de Clermont-Tonnerre recalled French military mobilisation in the summer of 1914. 'The men went off with a light-hearted pride. The war was for them an affirmation of virility. They vanished in an instant, brothers, husbands, and servants with only a casual wave of the hand in the English manner, equal for all; no tears, no kisses.' She recalled one woman sobbing in her house: 'There's not a single man left, you hear, not one. Even the gardener has gone.' The individual deaths in action of men like Fénelon, and the mass slaughter, made Proust grieve: Louis Gautier-Vignal, who saw him intermittently during the war years, thought he was anguished by the worldwide suffering and lonely because many of his acquaintances were dispersed in different theatres of war. Whenever Gautier-Vignal visited Proust's sickroom, he found the bed littered with newspaper maps of the different strategic Fronts. Nevertheless, the war did not greatly disturb Proust's interior life, and certainly conditions in wartime Paris provided him with rich creative opportunities, notably in observing the insistent, even frantic affirmations of virility by men living in or passing through the capital. He had always felt that one does not need to journey to look at new landscapes so much as to look with new eyes, and the war provided him with new vision without him having to leave his district. Edmond Jaloux had described an unforgettable conversation with Proust – the first of many – as they stood at midnight in the hall of the Ritz, which had been plunged into total darkness by an air-raid alert. They would have felt that they were in utter black solitude if it had not been for the red glow from the points of cigarettes which some Americans were silently smoking in the shadows. The eeriness of the situation must have impressed Proust, as it did Jaloux, even as he closely interrogated the younger man about himself and his acquaintances. Proust, as a nocturnal creature, thrived in the wartime black-out. Paris was darker than villages at night-time: 'When people went calling on each other, it felt like visiting neighbours in the country.' Proust included in the final volume of *Temps perdu* lyrical descriptions of moonbeams glittering on the heavy snow lying on the Boulevard Haussmann because the labourers who might have shovelled it away had all been conscripted, and of searchlights scouring the night skies during German air-raids. He inserted moments of social comedy, too, such as the Ritz guests who have been evacuated from their bedrooms during a night-time bombing raid, and who congregate downstairs: 'American Jewesses in their night-gowns, clutching to their withered bosoms the pearl necklaces that would enable them to marry a decrepit duke.'

The war, as Proust also recognised, was a time of erotic adventures and tantalising sexual chances. Saint-Loup's pre-war 'martial ardours' had been '*démodé* and absurd, like the caperings of a heraldic lion', E. M. Forster wrote in 1929, 'and when the Great War does come it is a monster, indecent and imbecile, shaggy with dispatches, in whose foetid darkness M. de Charlus waddles about seeking pleasure.' Charlus is delighted when Paris fills with foreign soldiers in brilliant uniforms, making the streets seem as colourfully contrived as theatrical scenery, and becomes as exciting as an international port. For Proust, too, war conditions were pictorially exciting. He likened the streets of Paris to the Baghdad of the *Arabian Nights*, and saw Parisians sheltering in underground railway stations from the aerial bombardment as heirs to the inhabitants of Pompeii upon whom volcanic fire rained. In *Temps retrouvé* he wrote lusciously of the sexual opportunities in the Métro during air-raids. In the murky gloom there, he said, 'whether the object of desire be a woman or a man,' the Pompeian refugees could dispense with all sentimentality or tedious preliminaries. 'In the darkness, the whole of this old-fashioned routine is jettisoned, and hands, hips and bodies can start their game at once . . . a body that does not withdraw, which presses closer, thrills us with the idea that the woman (or man) whom we are silently confronting is debauched and without inhibitions.'

It is doubtful that Proust ever descended into the Métro, but he had an infallible wartime informant called Albert Le Cuziat, whose conversation incited him into such daring writing. They had first met in 1911 when Proust was a guest at Count Orloff's, where Le Cuziat was employed as a footman. Born in 1881, Le Cuziat had left Brittany at the age of sixteen for Paris: his looks attracted Prince Constantin Radziwill, who recruited him as one of his dozen footmen, each of whom was presented with a pearl necklace. Radziwill was an energetic (married) debauchee, who confided to Montesquiou that male blackmailers cost him 70,000 francs a year. Proust had been gleeful – both at the sexual comedy and at the confirmation of his ambisexual view of human desire – when in 1911 Radziwill 'was surprised while busily engaged in being sucked off by Lady Pirbright'. Proust was convinced that Radziwill's footmen, in their blue velvet livery, adored 'their Master' and were usually willing to comply with his tastes. When one footman, who was untrained in the necessary responses of menservants in the Radziwill household, resisted a princely overture, and seemed on the point of hurling the prince from a window, Princesse Radziwill intervened. 'My good man,' said the princess to the recalcitrant footman, 'if you don't want to do it you only have to refuse. But one can't go about killing people just for that.'

In appreciation of Le Cuziat's wry stories, genealogical expertise and punctilious etiquette, Proust resolved in 1917 to amuse himself by investing in a male brothel to be operated by the footman, who was then employed by the Duc de Rohan. Le Cuziat's pit of Sodom was first opened in Rue Godot-de-Mauroy in the Madeleine district: Proust helped furnish the premises with some old belongings of his parents. Afterwards the brothel moved to the Hôtel Marigny at 11 Rue de l'Arcade. A fascinating memoir of Le Cuziat's establishment was subsequently written by Maurice Sachs, who translated into French

Schiff's Proustian memoir *Céleste*. Born in 1907 (and destined to die in a Nazi camp), Sachs was a former seminary student who discovered Le Cuziat's amenities in 1928. 'Someone showed me an establishment on rue [de l'Arcade], which, under cover of a bath-house, harboured male prostitutes, boys too weak and lazy to seek regular work, who earned money which they took home to their women by sleeping with men.' The premises were reached through 'a paved courtyard, decorated with bay-trees and privets in pots like a vicarage, with a little flight of four steps under a narrow glass porch and the word BATHS on the glass-paned door,' Sachs recalled. Le Cuziat when young had been 'handsome, tall, thin and without doubt of a submissive and affectionate character', but by the time Sachs befriended him he was a bald middle-aged man, with 'very thin lips, very blue eyes, a very sharp profile'. Le Cuziat, Sachs realised, 'liked to serve as others like to command. It didn't seem to him much like punishment to serve in more than one way.' He had been 'dazzled' by working for Radziwill, Prince d'Esseling and Count Orloff, and had developed a passion for the nobility. 'He knew the heraldry, the illnesses, the adulteries of three generations, and had discovered that in the provision of vice he could secure the only sure intimacy between a great nobleman and a little peasant. He first became a catamite and procurer out of snobbery, but then he got a taste for it.'

Chez Le Cuziat, and elsewhere, Proust enjoyed – and learnt from – vicarious sex. He liked to listen as well as to watch. In 1919, when he was obliged to leave his apartment in Boulevard Haussmann, he temporarily occupied the spacious fourth floor of a building near the Bois de Boulogne owned by the great actress Réjane. There he was distracted, and surely excited, by the sound of an actor called Le Bargy pleasuring his wife. 'The neighbours on the other side of my partition make love every day with a frenzy which makes me jealous. When I think that for me this sensation is weaker than that of drinking a glass of cold beer, I envy people who can scream such that the first time I thought someone was being murdered, but very soon the woman's cry, repeated an octave deeper by the man, reassured me as to what was happening.' The Le Bargys raised a 'din which can be heard from as far a distance as amorous hump-backed whales', but it was their post-coital routine that offended him most. 'The last gasp has been scarcely emitted before they rush off to take a hip-bath and their murmurs recede in the noise of water. The absolute absence of any transition exhausts me on their behalf, for if there is anything that I really detest *after*, at least *immediately after*, it is having to move.' He did not like a warm mouth to be swiftly moved away after it had received. He re-invented the coupling of the Le Bargys for the opening of *Sodome et Gomorrhe* in which the narrator hears, through a partition, Charlus in a sexual encounter with Jupien, and the two men washing afterwards: an episode that jolted many readers in the 1920s by its unprecedented explicitness.

Amongst the transactions watched by Proust in Le Cuziat's establishment was the flogging of an industrialist, which inspired the brief scene in which Charlus is flagellated by a nice young jeweller's assistant, who looks like Morel and is posing as a murderer in order to feed the baron's fantasy. In the 1920s this episode disgusted, among others, Edmund Wilson, although Jaloux in 1927 reckoned 'this frightful scene is of the very greatest art', indeed akin to 'Shakespearean tragedy'. Masochism is as idealistic – 'a dream just as poetic' – as the desire to visit Venice, Proust suggests. When Céleste Albaret asked Proust how he could watch such things, he replied, 'precisely because it could not be made up'. She detested the Breton pimp – 'you only had to look at Le Cuziat to see he never did anything for nothing . . . he still had the soul of a servant' – and denounced him to her employer. 'Incredible as it is in a monster, as you call him,' Proust explained, 'he loved his mother dearly and did all he could to make her happy.' When Proust sent a note of condolence on her death, he received a touching reply, he said, 'one of the best letters I have ever read about the death of a mother. So it proves he has a heart somewhere . . . you can't help feeling sorry for him.'

The Proustian primacy that Schiff tried to foist on Swann belongs to Charlus, but behind the Baron there lurks a figure without whom the Charlusiens are incomplete. Charlus remains unfulfilled, with his life trajectory still obscure, until he loves Morel. Though his love for Morel ruins him, it confirms his destiny. The foreground of Charlus lacks all perspective and sense without Morel in the background. And if there is one Proustian character whose subtleties and meanings were refined at the Hôtel Marigny, it is surely Charlie Morel. Morel brings Charlus to his apotheosis, Morel transforms Saint-Loup and Morel solves the riddle of *Temps perdu*. Instinctive vice and deliberate wickedness provided, Proust thought, a way to fathom human nature and to understand the motives that govern human conduct. Instinctive vice and deliberate wickedness – together with real artistic gifts, spasmodic bursts of conscience, a mercenary soul, driving ambition and sensitivity to other people's opinions of him – are the major ingredients of Charlie Morel. When the narrator watches him first being approached by Charlus on a railway platform, Morel seems 'frank, imperative and resolute', but deeper acquaintance shows him also to be morose and mistrustful: algebra provides his only effective respite during attacks of neurasthenia (which excite in him nervous aggression). 'He resembled,' Proust says, 'an old book of the Middle Ages, full of errors, of absurd traditions, of obscenities; he was extraordinarily composite.' So composite, indeed, that he is loved by Charlus, kept by Saint-Loup, flees from the Prince de Guermantes, joins Albertine in her romps with the Normandy laundrymaids, becomes engaged to marry Jupien's niece, writes newspaper denunciations of homosexuality and is teased like a sister by Léa. Charlus is Proust's character-in-chief; but it is Morel, so despised and repudiated by many readers in the 1920s, who is the representative figure of human sexuality in *Temps perdu*. Morel incarnates original sin.

CHAPTER 6

The Permanent Possibility of Danger

Among his compatriots Proust became renowned, almost overnight, when he was awarded the Goncourt Prize in December 1919; and throughout 1920 he was the most prominent of the writers in the foreground of French literature, as confirmed by the government in the autumn when he was gazetted as a Chevalier de la Légion d'honneur. London, for once, was not lagging behind Paris: by 1919 the English cognoscenti had already claimed him for themselves. In the early decades of Modernism, educated Londoners looked to Paris rather than New York for avant-garde leadership and creative brilliance, and even during the patriotic fervour of the war were neither complacent nor insular. It should be a cause of pride that Proust so quickly came to matter to certain Londoners. 'Long ago,' wrote an English reviewer in June 1921, '"everybody who is anybody" was reading M. Proust – or at least was valiantly pretending to read him, since among other exacting social duties the absorption of thousands of pages of complicated psychology expressed in very elaborate prose was to be avoided if possible.'

A memoir by the novelist Violet Hunt helps to date this process. She recalled waiting one dark Kensington afternoon, during the winter of 1918–19, in the warm boudoir of 'a foolish Society woman' who had invited her for tea but was late. 'On a table near

me, by the powder-puff and the cigarettes, I found an author who
had not yet swept the board as he has done since' (she was writing
in 1923). A copy of *Du côté de chez Swann* was lying there, borrowed from the London Library, 'that accredited emporium
founded for the reading of the Intelligentsia', as Violet Hunt says.
The Library's first copy of *Swann*, bought as recently as November 1914, had been handled by so many of the Library's readers
that its original yellow backing had already had to be replaced:
certainly, even if Proust was not yet ubiquitous, he had captivated the discriminating, elegant-minded subscribers to the London
Library. The book, in its shabby, black rebinding, looked 'dull
and forbidding among the brocade and tinsel of the bibelots' in
the Society woman's boudoir, but Hunt opened it idly.

> At once I became involved in an *enchevêtrement* [tangled
> mass], a leash of moods, a congeries of complexes, of cranki-
> ness, all that goes to make up a man – Swann. There was no
> breathlessness, no sense of hurry, yet it was 'good going'.
> There were hairbreadth but quite actual escapes from
> bathos, ugly grazings averted, artistic difficulties compound-
> ed: this author backed his sentences in and out of garages
> like a first-class motorist.

Within minutes she felt initiated into the cult: 'Proust is a fashion – a disease,' she wrote afterwards, 'a Proustian, so-called, is
an Opium-Eater.'

It is suggestive that Violet Hunt found the book in the
boudoir of a foolish Kensington socialite in the winter of
1918–19. The fashion for *Temps perdu* flourished, it seemed to
Wyndham Lewis, who lived in a dismal Kensington mews and
became increasingly antagonistic to Proust in the 1920s, because

the novel resembled a 'high-brow *private news-sheet*, the big "Gossip" book – the expansion of a Society newspaper-paragraph – of the Reigning Order.' Some, at least, of Proust's early readers in England, as much as in France, liked to feel they were eavesdropping on Society figures rather as his narrator eavesdropped on Charlus and Jupien. The Countess of Granard, for example, read all the volumes in turn, but without any intelligence or grasp of their purpose, according to Harold Nicolson. Yet there are easier ways to be snobbish than to skim *Le côté de Guermantes*, and it is impressive how many English people read, or tried to read, Proust in French: for the first English translation of *Swann* was not published until September 1922 just two months before Proust's death. As the Duc de Guiche reported after visiting England in June 1921, 'London "intellectual" women have only two topics of conversation: the scientific ones talk about Einstein, the literary ones about "Prrrr . . . oust" – that's the way they pronounce your name.'

Proust thought he was risking it all – his success in France, the plaudits from London – by the course that he had fixed for *À la recherche du temps perdu*. 'When M. de Charlus appears,' he wailed, 'people everywhere will turn their backs on me, especially the English.' The publication in October 1920 of the first part of *Le côté de Guermantes* was a major literary event in Paris, but for Proust it was ominously overshadowed: he was already apprehensive about the coming out of *Sodome et Gomorrhe*. Part I of this section of *Temps perdu* was eventually published together with part II of *Le côté de Guermantes* on 30 April 1921 and appeared in Paris bookshops on 2 May. Its publication, and that of Part II in May 1922, marked the outward climaxes of the closing years of Proust's life. (The typescript that Proust spent the last months of his life revising was provisionally entitled *Sodome et Gomorrhe III* although it was renamed by him and ultimately published posthumously as *Le Prisonnière* in November 1923.) The worry aggravated his ill-health: in the early months of 1921 he had bronchitis, rheumatic fever and other ailments for which his physician prescribed 'morphine, aspirin, euvalpine, spartéine: in a word all the medicines that you can – or I hope cannot – imagine,' as he wrote in April. He grasped at encouraging news – such as the inauguration of Proust admiration societies, or Swann clubs, in Britain and the Netherlands – to assuage his anxiety. The book's publication revived his confidence. On 9 May he went to the Ritz: 'the first time I've got myself out in 35 days' – although he was soon again lamenting his 'hellish existence', and told Gide on 14 May that his life was 'nothing but a slow agony.'

There were sound reasons to worry about press reactions. Binet-Valmer's *Lucien* (with which Proust compared his novel) had been widely denounced on its publication before the war. 'Was it really necessary,' demanded *Le Temps*, 'to show us this unhappy boy falling step by step into the lowest regions of Sodom and Gomorrah? These are things that should be left to treatises on pathology or to handbooks destined for the guidance of confessors in their exploration of the impurities of human nature.' Proust knew, too, that he would displease some inverts. 'If, without mentioning homosexuality at all, I depicted healthy adolescents, if I portrayed tender, fervent friendships, without implying there was anything further, then I should have all the homosexuals on my side, because I would be giving them just what they like,' he had predicted in 1913. But instead of cautious hints and softly-hued sentimentality about youths,

Proust portrayed adult desires and fleshly impulses, and investigated compulsive behaviour and clandestine acts, with an explicitness that seemed startling. Proust had felt daunted by the risks to his reputation of seeming to proselytise on behalf of the inverts, and had chosen homosexuality as a secularised representation of humankind's fall from grace. Accordingly he had decided to depict inversion as a 'sickness' and to present the sodomites' 'dream of masculine beauty' as a 'neurotic disorder'. He based his plot on a proposition – the 'best proof' that inversion is a neurosis being that 'a homosexual man adores men but detests other homosexuals' – that was untrue of himself, since he was far from detesting Reynaldo Hahn, Lucien Daudet or Diaghilev, and untrue of many other men.

Proust's tetchy trepidation before the unveiling of *Sodome et Gomorrhe* was evident for months. He was swift to remonstrate when, in November 1920, Paul Souday alluded to him as a 'highly-strung aesthete, a little morbid, almost feminine', while reviewing part I of *Guermantes* in *Le Temps*. 'At the moment when I am about to publish *Sodome et Gomorrhe*, and when, because I discuss Sodom, no-one will have the courage to defend me, you are clearing the path (without malice, I am sure) for all the mischief-makers, by calling me "feminine". From feminine to effeminate is just one step. My seconds in duels can tell you if I behaved like an effeminate man.' When Souday tried to make amends by sending Proust a box of chocolates – perhaps a tactless gift to a man who has objected to being thought feminine – Proust cried, 'Put these on the fire, Céleste, the man who sent them is capable of anything.' It did not seem to him, in his hypersensitive state, a large step from distilling poisonous rumours to sending poisonous bonbons.

Equally Proust tried to minimise pre-publication gossip. 'I remind you that *Sodome et Gomorrhe I* must be shown to nobody (I mean nobody),' he adjured his publisher Gaston Gallimard in January when the book was in production. 'There have already been some indiscreet glimpses of it that have dismayed me.' Once the proofs were corrected and the publication date approached, his editors tried to bolster him with supportive remarks: 'at times Charlus speaks to Jupien in language that is almost transcendental,' wrote Jacques Rivière of the *Nouvelle Revue Française* in April.

Until the appearance of *Sodome et Gomorrhe I* in May 1921, the subject of inversion had been impalpable in *Temps perdu* except for the Vinteuil lesbian scenes and Charlus's thrashing of a man who had propositioned him. But in May 1921 the centrality of inversion was suddenly revealed to Proust's readers. The title of his new volume was explicit enough: 'scabrous', Elisabeth de Clermont-Tonnere called it, although she noted that the phrase 'Sodome et Gomorrhe' had been current during the Second Empire 'to condemn all lazy and extravagant behaviour', and in the 1920s was still used in that sense by 'several noble old wrecks of that epoch' whom Proust knew. (Binet-Valmer, a loyal admirer of the volume, disliked the provocative word 'Sodom' in its title.) Even more explicit than the title was the book's opening scene in which the narrator watches Charlus picking up Jupien, and eavesdrops on the violent moaning that accompanies their sexual activity. Prince Antoine Bibesco, for one, was a 'bit shocked at the acoustic effects of Charlus-Jupien', he confessed to Proust in an otherwise zestful letter. Proust, though, was amused by an Italian fan-letter which he received: 'I love all your books,' declared his admirer, 'but my wife has a marked preference for Charlus's first meeting with Jupien.'

Looking back from the perspective of 1925, Léon Pierre-Quint decried the reviews of *Sodome et Gomorrhe* and its successor volume *La Prisonnière* as 'a conspiracy of silence indicative of the most blatant literary incomprehension'. He himself had heard a Paris journalist, who had previously prided himself on being an early discoverer of Proust, exclaim in 1921: 'It's frightful! All of a book on this one subject!' Similarly, another reviewer, who also been a Proustian pioneer but shrank from Charlus as a 'loathsome monster', demanded of *La Prisonnière*: 'Why choose *that* subject? Why portray *that*, of all types? . . . Authors have no right to choose themes that are bound to disgust the majority of men.'

Many reviewers of the 1921 volume pursued a policy of sanitisation and suppression. Souday, who was doubtless chastened by Proust's reproaches about his use of the word 'feminine', scarcely mentioned Charlus or inversion in his review for *Le Temps* on 12 May. 'The writing of M. Marcel Proust is not always entangled, and the present volume is, in general, easier to read than its predecessors,' he declared as the preamble to a discussion of Proust's favourite theory of 'the contingency and the relativity of our states of consciousness . . . including the flight of time, the instability of things, the deformities of memory'. Souday flung laudatory epithets at Proust: 'a Bergson or an Einstein of the psychological novel'; 'pre-eminently the novelist of mobility, of perpetual change and of universal illusion'. He praised Proust's 'assimilation of the arts and sciences' and said Proust's 'heroes resemble him like a brother'. But as to inversion, he only mentioned that one chapter tended 'in a direction that is a little difficult to follow', and that its subject matter had been treated 'more summarily' in Saint-Simon's memoirs. Proust thanked Souday for the gracious compliments before reproaching him for having 'skirted round . . . my Baron de Charlus. But I know that you are speaking from on high in the pulpit to a large congregation and therefore have to speak with reserve.' While he acknowledged that Souday had shown 'rare courage' in public support of 'Wilde during his misfortune', he regretted that the review seemed to commend Saint-Simon's more cursory allusions to sodomy. Proust explained that he could no more treat Charlus summarily than he did any of the Guermantes. He had to be as exact, meticulous and detailed about the baron's sexual adventures as about the Duchesse de Guermantes' red shoes.

Souday's evasions were followed by many other critics. The fact that the 'new lump of Proust', as Ezra Pound called it in 1921, comprised 'the tail end' of *Guermantes* affixed to the beginning of *Sodome* meant that reviewers could focus on the social side and disregard the sexual – despite a title indicating the centrality of inversion. In two separate reviews Pound, who was then living in Paris, ignored the opening sections of *Sodome et Gomorrhe* containing revelations about Charlus and Jupien as well as Proust's long, powerfully written disquisition on homosexuality. 'The second chapter of *Sodome et Gomorrhe* devotes nearly two hundred pages of close type to a dinner, one only, at the Duchesse de Guermantes', is all that Pound would reveal. 'The pages of Proust's beautiful boredom roll on, readable, very readable, and for once at least the precise nuance of the idiocy of top-crusts is recorded.' Pound never mentions inversion, never names Charlus, never concedes the bold originality of Proust's sexual themes. In private, though, he was willing to assess Jupien and Charlus as well as the Faubourg Saint-Germain. 'The little lickspittle wasn't satirising, he really thought his pimps, buggers and opulent idiots were *important*, instead of the last mould on the dying cheese,' Pound mused to a friend.

Some reviewers' omissions were intended to protect Proust's reputation or to widen the appeal of his novel. The *Observer*, a staid English newspaper, praised the volumes that were published in Proust's lifetime for revealing 'adolescent boyhood with an imaginative insight never surpassed in modern fiction'. The novel's preoccupation with inversion was discounted by fastening on the fact that its narrator – Proust's fictional self – lacked any tendency to unnatural vice. Admittedly, the narrator is 'passionately aware of beauty in sight, sound and smell, but above all in books', which might have seemed suspicious to citizens who read the *Observer* on Sundays; but his susceptibility to beauty is never suspect. 'He is terribly sensitive and alarmingly acute; but he is not abnormal. He merely represents, in a high degree, the qualities that are latent or expressed in all children.'

There were exceptions to the prevailing evasions in public print: some admirers shared Proust's trepidation about the effect on his reputation of *Sodome et Gomorrhe*. 'It seems,' an English reviewer predicted in June 1921, 'to be inevitable that the glory showered upon M. Proust while he merely analysed manners will not be showered at all, and may even turn into a shower of mud, now that . . . he is about to expose the curious machinery of morals.' Most good Proustians judged they must keep quiet or talk in code. Some felt that it would be crass to insist on extensively discussing a subject that should not perturb intelligent adults: others were chary of publicly compromising the reputation of *Temps perdu* although their intimate, personal comments were more candid. A third group of readers regarded Proust's sexual outlook as vicious, perverted, a degrading infection or a moral tragedy, which corrupted his novelist's vision. Harvey Wickham, for example, who was an early American advocate of *Temps perdu*'s greatness, nevertheless condemned its author for his 'moral diseases'. Proust, to Wickham, seemed a 'less witty and more theoretical Oscar Wilde', a miscreant 'whose crimes were committed only on paper' and in solitude. 'His probable habits one does not like to think of. Yet auto-eroticism has this in common with homo-eroticism: it viciously avoids nature's saving differentiation.'

Proust himself indulged in denials during the summer of 1921: it was 'absurd' of people, he maintained, to say that he had portrayed Montesquiou in Charlus. 'Although I have known an enormous number of inverts in society whom nobody else suspected, in all the many years I have known Montesquiou, I have never ever seen him, either at home, in a crowd, anywhere at all, evince the faintest hint of it.' At other moments he was more relaxed about his subject-matter, and during the summer of 1921 started using the word 'charlusiennement' as a synonym for 'homosexually'. He continued, though, to insist on the masculine integrity of the new book: 'Nothing,' he told Binet-Valmer in November 1921, 'is less effeminate than *Sodome et Gomorrhe*.'

Proust's denials and evasions were forced upon him by his fear of whispered accusations and latent prejudices. Although *Temps perdu* was not a direct, faithful representation of Proust's life, denial is at the heart of his world of unanswerable suspicions and obsessive jealousy, and the novel is splattered with versions of its author's defensiveness. Fear of exposure, panic when confronted by opportunities to be honest with oneself, genuine personal confusion, changing tastes and adaptive habits create an atmosphere of contradiction and deceit in the novel. 'Andrée and I are both horrified by that sort of thing,' Albertine retorts to the narrator, when he has been nagging her with his 'sickly doubts' about her relations with a girlfriend. 'We haven't reached our age without seeing women with cropped hair and mannish ways who do the things you mean, and nothing revolts us more.' Saint-Loup (like his uncle before him) hits a man who has propositioned him, although he has previously been attract-ed by the Grand Hôtel de Balbec's lift-boy, with whom he immures himself in a dark room on the pretext of developing photographs. The lift-boy, by the time war is declared, will not for any amount of money accept overtures which now seem to him as offensive as the Germans, whereas by 1914 Saint-Loup's life has become dominated by his feelings for Morel. Morel, in turn, sneers with his friends when Charlus – his mentor if not his lover – joins them in a railway carriage, and does not protest when they make unpleasant, derisive noises intended to offend the old man. Proust gives collective examples of Sodomists' denials and self-repudiations as well. Whenever, he declares, a Sodomite candidate for election to a club is blackballed, most of the vetoes are issued by other Sodomites, who punish sodomy for a variety of motives: anxiety for their reputations, projected self-hatred, cowardice, vindictiveness, hypocrisy, conformity.

Despite his evasions, Proust resolved to give a clear pointer that the publication of *Sodome et Gomorrhe I* should carry vital signif-icance for attentive readers. In the months before its appearance, he prepared his essay 'À propos de Baudelaire' for publication in the *Nouvelle Revue Française* of June 1921. This piece contains some intensely personal passages, providing a clandestine *credo* for his sympathisers, but less meaningful to those who lack affinity with him. Proust gave repeated signals of the personal and artistic importance to Baudelaire of Sodom, although he refrained from claiming publicly that (as he insisted to Gide in May) Baudelaire had been an invert too. Proust opens the essay with a gratuitous allusion to Balzac's character Lucien de Rubempré (who is destroyed by another man's love for him) and recalls how Alfred de Vigny was enflamed with jealousy by Marie Dorval's friendships with other women. He cites Baudelaire's line, 'Hypocrite lecteur, mon semblable, mon frère' ('Hypocritical reader, my kind, my brother'), which might aptly be applied to so many cautious early readers of *Sodome et Gomorrhe*. In *Les fleurs du mal*, writes Proust, Baudelaire created a domain where virtue and vice seem reversed. Piety is inverted in this 'sublime but painful book, where the compassion is sniggering, where the debauchee makes the sign of the cross, where the task of instructing in the most profound theology is confided to Satan'. Proust recalls that his generation originally knew *Les fleurs du mal* only in expurgated editions. Many readers treated Baudelaire's 'Femmes Damnées' as if it was a semi-pornographic 'secret little publication', and were 'stunned' when they first obtained an uncensored edition to find that it included 'the rawest, most licentious pieces about love between women' which Proust ranked 'among the greatest poems of the book'. Indeed, as he stresses, Baudelaire, 'the great Poet, with the innocence of genius', assigned such pre-eminence to these poems that he 'wanted to call the whole volume not *Les fleurs du mal* but *Les Lesbiennes*.' Proust is telling his more sympathetic readers that his account of Sodom and Gomorrah has just such primacy for him.

'Beneath any carnal pleasure of any profundity, there is the

permanent possibility of danger,' Proust wrote. He felt intimi-
dated in his life by the hostility that he also felt threatened his
novel. What was this constant, muted menace?

In the 1890s Elisabeth de Clermont-Tonnerre was beseeched by
a dismissed concièrge to help him get his job back. When she
raised the man's case, her father the Duc de Gramont replied,
'Don't get mixed up in this', and muttered to her stepmother, 'It's
a business of the Oscar Wilde type.' At the time the young woman
was mystified by what could possibly connect a foreign dramatist
with a Paris janitor, although later she came to understand that the
Wilde case proved the dangers of sexual or emotional intimacies
between men of different classes. The physical facts of male homosexuality made people squeamish, but it was the destruction of
class barriers among some inverts, the negation of the physical
aloofness upon which masculine dignity and authority depended,
and hence the subversion of all established hierarchies, that
seemed so threatening and was fought with such aggression. In the
early 1890s Proust had met Wilde, whose catastrophe remained for
him a terrifying, inhibiting memory. In *Sodome et Gomorrhe* he
invoked Wilde to show how inverts faced the constant risk of
imprisonment or dishonour. 'Their honour precarious, their liberty provisional, lasting only until the discovery of their crime; their
position unstable, like that of the poet who was lionised in every
drawing-room, applauded in all the theatres of London, and next
day was hunted from every lodging, unable to find a pillow on
which to rest his head, turning the mill like Samson.'

Proust's trepidation was peculiarly acute during 1921, as it had
been in 1908 when the Eulenberg case, coinciding with the
months during which he began to write *À la recherche du temps
perdu*, had so upset him by showing the dangers of such topics.

But throughout his adulthood he suffered recurrent spasms of fear that – even if he was in no danger of the treadmill – his honour was precarious and his position unstable. As early as 1897 he had fought a duel with a flamboyant invert called Jean Lorrain, who had made public insinuations about his relationship with Lucien Daudet. (It was one of time's cruelties that by 1921 Gide thought Proust had grown to resemble Lorrain, 'fattish, or rather bloated'.) His nervousness about his reputation never diminished. Thus, in 1913, after consulting Vicomte Charles d'Alton about his 'delicate situation' with Agostinelli, he beseeched d'Alton, in order 'to avoid any dangerous gaffes', to refrain from mentioning that he employed Agostinelli: 'In a word . . . don't speak of him to anyone.' In his novel Proust depicted the self-loathing of many inverts of his epoch, and in his life he reflected the anxious self-doubt of those same inverts. He considered his own position to be delicate if not dangerous, and stressed the perils for his protagonists. Charlus, it must be remembered, is destroyed by homophobia as much as by his own increasing excesses. In a brilliant chapter of *La Prisonnière* Charlus organises a performance by Morel of the Vinteuil septet at Madame Verdurin's. This vindictive, unscrupulous woman retaliates for the careless slights of Charlus and his haughty friends by destroying the baron's relationship with Morel and then attacking his reputation. In a melodramatic frenzy of deceit she warns Morel that he is destroying his position by his 'disgraceful promiscuity with a tainted person'. Morel weeps as she tells him, 'another month of this life and your artistic future is shattered.' After Morel has repudiated his mentor publicly, she starts a whispering campaign full of fantastic lies, sly half-truths, clichés and fake moral indignation. Before the war Morel writes monstrous libels against Charlus, including a pamphlet that Madame Verdurin circulates among her friends entitled *The Misadventures of a Dowager whose Name Ends in –us, or the Old Age of the Baroness*. During the war she repeatedly denounces Charlus and his cousin the Queen of Naples as German spies. 'If we had a more energetic government, these kinds of people would be in a concentration camp,' she shrieks.

As Madame Verdurin's tirade signals, the fact that sexual contacts between men often transcended nationalities was more threatening in wartime than their class subversion. The cosmopolitanism of homosexuality was a distinct refrain in late-nineteenth and early-twentieth-century confessional memoirs. 'In Paris, Italy, Vienna, and everywhere I found poor creatures like myself!' recalled a German of Proust's generation. 'On the Righi [above Genoa], in Palermo, in the Louvre, in the Highlands of Scotland, in St Petersburg and in the docks at Barcelona I found people I had never seen before but who became attached to me in an instant, and I to them.' Distinctions of classes or nationality were erased by Sodom if perhaps not so much by Gomorrah. 'The congenital bent of my temperament,' wrote the Victorian poet John Addington Symonds, drew 'all kinds of young men – peasants on the Riviera, Corsican drivers, Florentine lads upon Lungarno in the evenings, *facchini* at Venice, and especially a handsome Bernese guide who attended to the strong black horse I rode'. Twenty years later the young economist John Maynard Keynes drew up a list of his Edwardian sexual partners:

Stable Boy of Park Lane
Auburn haired of Marble Arch
Lift boy of Vauxhall
Jew boy

The Swede of the National Gallery
The Baron of Mentone
The Young American of Victoria Station
The Blackmailer of Bordeaux
The Grand Duke Cyril of the Paris Baths
The French Youth of the Baths
The chemist's boy of Paris
David Erskine MP

Proust's crusade for accuracy in his novel required him to depict the cosmopolitanism of Sodom.

Supremely, though, the Charlusiens are champion transgressors of class boundaries. Their defiance of social distinctions is keenly reprobated, as Proust shows. On one occasion Charlus takes an immaculately dressed young footman to dine with him in a private room at the Grand Hôtel in Balbec. The other hotel guests mistake the footman for a smartly attired foreigner, for his clothes are not quite right, but the hotel staff recognise him as a servant immediately, just as animals scent one another from a great distance. The servants resent Charlus's disregard of traditional class demarcations: old Françoise is appalled to see him arm-in-arm with the footman; the wine waiter makes a coarse remark, which everybody hears. Although the footman knows how to behave, he is the object of opprobrium which would not be meted out to a poor woman who has come under the protection of a rich man. The Balbec lift-boy's sister is just such a mistress – ostensibly 'a fine lady', the lift-boy boasts, because she can play the piano and employs a maid – but actually a foolish delinquent who enjoys urinating or defecating in hotel wardrobes so as to humiliate the chambermaids who have to clean the mess. Above all, though, Sodom's threat to class demarcations is encapsulated by the altered destinies of the young seamstress who is Jupien's favourite niece. She is a charming woman who becomes engaged to marry Morel: after he breaks with her, Charlus (out of gratitude to his pimp and former lover Jupien) adopts her, bestows upon her the Guermantes name of Mademoiselle d'Oléron, and under that style of shamnobility, she marries Léonor, Marquis de Cambremer. The infiltration of the Cambremers, whose lineage has never included a single commoner, by a seamstress whose uncle runs a male brothel is just the sort of social topsy-turvydom that sexual subversion was predicted to cause.

Proust's voyeuristic visits to Le Cuziat's brothel enriched his sexual imagination so that *Sodome et Gomorrhe* became the first novel to present human sexuality as a continuum including bisexuality and the homosexual behaviour of married men. Until then homosexuality had been treated in fiction and by public moralists either as a rare phenomenon or as the effete taste of people surfeited by expensive comforts. 'Generally,' declared the French polemicist Jacques Georges-Anquetil in the 1920s, 'this is a vice of luxury, and not practised by humble people. The pure air of the countryside protects our peasants from these miasmas just as the wholesome tiredness of working men protects them from such temptations.' Yet homosexuality was a country pleasure too: Addington Symonds, for one, had been intimate with peasants, postillions, carters, porters in country hotels, Alpine herdsmen, masons, hunters, woodmen, carpenters and stable-boys. To reflect this reality, Proust included a beautiful passage, much admired by Colette and others, about two country neighbours who have regular sexual encounters together at a remote cross-roads. The passage is so striking that it later inspired W. H. Auden's poem 'Who's Who'.

It was exciting for Proust to present the inverts as a vast secret society that no frontiers of class or nationality could contain. Back in the 1760s the military commander and womaniser the Prince de Ligne, who became a freemason because Masonic lodges were open to nobles and commoners, Christians and deists and therefore dissolved the social barriers erected by Church and state – the same Ligne who observed that 'one is not a bugger just because one fucks one's manservant from time to time' – had compared the secret signs and gestures of sodomites and masons. Proust made a similar comparison in a spirit of triumphant celebration: the inverts, he asserted, formed a 'freemasonry far more extensive, more effective and less suspected than that of the lodges, for it rests upon an identity of tastes, needs, habits, dangers, apprenticeship, knowledge, commerce, vocabulary.' Its members identify each other by signs that may be natural or imitative, involuntary or deliberate. By these gestures and nuances a 'beggar sees one of his own kind in the great nobleman whose carriage door he is shutting, the father in his daughter's suitor, the man who wants to be cured, absolved or defended in the physician, the priest or lawyer; all of them obliged to protect their own secret, yet sharing in other's secrets, which the rest of humankind never suspects.' This clandestine world, with its arcane signs and ciphered messages, is populated with venturesome men and women in revolt against authority. 'The ambassador is friends with the convict, the prince, endowed by his noble breeding with an independence that no timid petit bourgeois could show, confers with a thug [*apache*] after leaving a duchess.' It is, declares Proust, 'a reprobate part of humanity, but an important part, suspected in places where it does not exist, flaunted, insolent and unpunished in places where it is never detected; numbering its adherents everywhere, among the common people, in the army, in the Church, in prison, on the throne'. Reading this passage after Proust's death, the critic Harvey Wickham condemned its 'melodrama'. If this 'vast secret horde' was really so numerous and ingenious, Wickham demanded, how could they permit themselves to be subjugated and demeaned as 'outcasts in the eyes of the law' by the crude majority of 'embourgeoised conventionals, too dull to have invented secret grips and passwords with which to recognise one another?'

Proust applauded the way that inverts can be invisible, flourishing and unsuspected by most of society, yet instantaneously recognisable to one another by covert signs and allegiances. In one passage of *Sodome et Gomorrhe* he describes a type of young man who comes to Paris from the provinces full of hopes of distinguishing himself. Such men would be entirely derivative in their ideas, conversation, clothes, tastes and manners – emulating the leaders of the profession in which they hope to succeed – but for one redemptive divergence: 'their special inherited proclivity [*goût*]'. He pictures an otherwise conventional young lawyer or physician who on certain evenings congregates in a café with other ambitious young men, who all look so inscrutable that no one in the café can surmise their common interest. They might be members of

an angling club, sub-editors, or sons of the Indre, so correct is their attire, so cold and reserved their manner, so covert their glances at the fashionable young men a few feet away, the

young 'lions' who are clamouring about their mistresses, and
among whom those who admire without daring to look up
will learn only twenty years later, when some will be on the eve
of election to an Academy, and others ageing clubmen, that
the most seductive among them, now a stout and greying
Charlus, was in actual fact one of themselves, but elsewhere, in
another world, beneath other exterior symbols, with alien signs.

Effeminacy spoils the clandestine life that so fascinated Proust. In
Sodome et Gomorrhe he denounced extremists who allow a
bracelet to protrude from their cuff, or sometimes a necklace
from the opening of their collar, who, by their insistent stares,
their giggling, their laughter and their mutual caresses, force a
band of students to flee in haste, and who are served with a ser-
vility beneath which there seethes indignation, by a waiter who,
as on the evenings when he serves Dreyfusards, would delight in
summoning the police if he did not profit by pocketing their tips.

Despite the positive notes in Proust's presentation of the Charlusiens, and his avoidance of moral indignation, his treatment of
the subject surprised or disappointed several of its literary apolo-
gists. Binet-Valmer, who was a steadfast public supporter of the
book, for example, reckoned that its inverted men and women
were 'anti-social types, and in consequence noxious'. But when,
in December 1921, Proust acknowledged that he had 'annoyed
sodomites by the way I have withered them in *Sodome et Gomorrhe*', and claimed that his approach was necessary for the structure
of his book, with its rueful themes of loss and waste, he was thinking most of André Gide. Gide, who had written an apologia on
the love of adolescent boys entitled *Corydon* in 1911 but then
locked it in a drawer, was alternately impressed and aghast at the

success of *Sodome et Gomorrhe* ten years later. He pelted Proust with letters and visits, assured him that wherever he went in Paris he heard nothing but talk of Proust, approved of the novel's forthrightness, accepted the need for Charlus's character to be ignoble and tragic so as to appease public morality, and even sympathised with Proust's lack of personal candour; but his rivalry made him grudging and suspicious. If, on 3 May, he conceded to Proust that he had been 'right to introduce uranism first through the most revolting figure, in a way that excluded right away from the mind of the public any idea of leniency on your part', nevertheless privately, in his journals, he recorded different views. According to Gide, Proust reproached himself, during a long conversation in May 1921, for 'transposing . . . all his charming, tender and delightful homosexual recollections' into his volume about girls, *À l'ombre des jeunes filles*, 'so that he has nothing left for *Sodome* but the grotesque and the abject'. Six months later, when an extract from the forthcoming second volume of *Sodome et Gomorrhe* was published, Gide's reservations were stronger.

Knowing what he thinks, what he really is, it is hard for me to see anything but a dissimulation, a desire to protect himself, a skilful camouflage, because it can be to no one's advantage to denounce him. Moreover, this offence against truth is likely to please everyone: heterosexuals, whose prejudices it justifies and whose repugnance it flatters; and the others, who will exploit the alibi provided by their lack of resemblance to his characters. In short, given the general cowardice that will help it along, I know of no piece of writing which is more likely to implant false opinions than Proust's *Sodome*.

Staunch Catholics were especially offended by Proust's preoccupations as they became evident in 1921. Louis de Robert, from whom Proust had become estranged, complained to a friend on 10 June: '*Sodome et Gomorrhe* profoundly disgusts me. What is this aberration of the mind and of the temperament?' Paul Claudel insisted to his fellow Catholic poet Francis Jammes, 'It's the light of God that shows the best of human nature, and not, as in Proust, the phosphorescence of decomposition.' Jammes himself, Proust half-joked two months before his death, 'has started to offer Masses, imploring the Seraphim and all the heavenly powers, to make me quit the caverns where my sole companion is the Prince of Darkness.' Arguably the most sustained Catholic criticisms came from the novelist François Mauriac, whose feelings were divided about the new book. In a letter that he sent Proust on 15 May he reported that the opening section of *Sodome et Gomorrhe*, featuring the mutual sexual discovery of Charlus and Jupien followed by the narrator's powerful soliloquy on inversion, had excited in him 'contradictory sentiments: admiration, repulsion, terror, disgust'. Mauriac told Proust candidly that he preferred the repressed Charlus of *Jeunes filles en fleur* to the rampaging figure in *Sodome et Gomorrhe*, which he thought had a distorted emphasis. 'One feels that Sodom and Gomorrah are confused with the entire universe. A single *saintly* figure would be enough to re-establish the balance.' He conceded though that Proust's depiction of a 'blatant' sodomite in Charlus was 'vivid, terrible, eternal. I admire you more than any of my contemporaries, but have a reservation about the *choice* of subject in your work. But, then, do we choose our subjects?' It was the secular treatment of religious themes that distressed Mauriac. 'God is terribly absent from

Marcel Proust's work,' he lamented in a major assessment that he published a fortnight after Proust's death. 'We are not among those who rebuke him for having pierced into the flames and debris of *Sodome et Gomorrhe*; but we deplore that he ventured there without adamantine armour.' Mauriac attributed 'the sometimes hideous daring' of *Temps perdu* to the fact that Proust lacked 'Divine Grace.' A year later, when *La Prisonnière* was published in 1923, Mauriac gave high praise to much of the book, but denounced the coming out of Charlus: 'The secret Charlus of the earlier volumes, whose disease only betrays itself by an odd look, a liking for flowers and too flamboyant hand-kerchiefs, here erupts like the pus of a burst abscess.' In *La Prisonniére*, Mauriac protests, one is confronted by 'a horrifying Charlus: too appalling! who is not a sick man but a sickness'.

The resentment of Gide and the Catholics was tempered by more positive reactions from other readers. 'The publication of *Sodome et Gomorrhe* was like the staking out of new ground by an adventurous colonist,' wrote Joyce's friend Sisley Huddle-ston, the correspondent in Paris for both the *Observer* and *The Times*. 'Something had changed. In the social world there was a stirring of curiosity. The telephone, which is used for gossip, constantly rang. At luncheon parties passages were read amid laughter. Names were mentioned and anecdotes invented.' As Gide reported to Proust on 13 May, 'Princesse Murat is giving readings of certain gobbets of Charlus – by telephone.' Some of the praise for Proust in 1921 now seems absurd. 'You accelerate and slow the rotations of the Earth by your will-power; you are greater than God,' a Swedish admirer assured him in 1921. In another reader's assessment, 'Proust's influence was like the Earth on its habitat, atmospheric, geological, electric.'

Geneviève Straus reassured her lifelong friend on 21 May that she was 'not in the least scandalised by the subject', and in the same month Proust's calm and urbane admirer Walter Berry likened *Sodome et Gomorrhe* to Krafft-Ebing's treatises. Edith Wharton's assessment at this time to Bernard Berenson was more qualified. 'The last Proust is really amazing; but I think he has *fourvoyé* [gone astray] in a subject that can't lead anywhere in art, & belongs only to pathology. What a pity he didn't devote himself to the abnormalities of the normal, which offer a wide enough & untilled enough field, heaven knows.' Wharton praised Proust's creation of 'the great, the abject, the abominable and magnificent Monsieur de Charlus' and scorned an English critic who recommended to timid readers of *Temps perdu* the expedient of 'thinking away' M. de Charlus – as if, she said, one can think away Falstaff from *Henry IV*. She loathed, though, as she explained in 1925, the opening scene in *Sodome et Gomorrhe* in which Charlus and Jupien first have sex. 'There is one deplorable page where the hero-narrator, with whose hypersensitiveness a hundred copious and exquisite passages have acquainted us, describes with complacency how he has deliberately hidden himself to spy on an unedifying scene.' In this and several other episodes 'marked by the same abrupt loss of sensibility . . . Proust's characters invariably lose their *probableness* and begin to stumble through their parts like good actors vainly trying to galvanise a poor play.'

Not all women were as squeamish about the all-male action as Edith Wharton. 'The beginning of *Sodome* is stunning,' Colette wrote to Proust, whom she had not liked or admired when they first met in the 1890s. 'No one in the world has written pages like those about Inversion, no one! . . . I swear that no one, after you, or other than you, can add anything to what you have written. Who would dare to touch on, after you, the arousal, lepidopterist, botanical, ornithological, of a Jupien at the approach of a Charlus? Everything is magnificent – and the portrait of the Princesse de Parme! How I admire you.' This was sincere praise; but in *Le Pur et l'Impur* (1932) she gave her reservations: she thought, with justice, that lesbians are misrepresented in *Temps perdu* (though it is impressive that they were not ignored completely). Although 'overwhelmed by respect' for the way that Proust 'enlightened' his readers about Sodom, with its 'hounded beings, who had to be so careful to cover their tracks', she thought he betrayed himself as 'ignorant when he assembled a Gomorrah of unfathomable, vicious young women' behaving with the 'fury of fallen angels'. In Proust's created world, she wrote, 'Sodom, with its indispensable solidarity, irresolvable, enormous, eternal, looks down from a great height on its puny counterfeits.'

Sodome et Gomorrhe made subsequent allusions to homosexuality easier in France and elsewhere. Proust's path-breaking in 1921–2 showed the way for many other travellers, as was realised at the time, although the memory has receded now. François Porché had the idea to write his influential monograph *L'amour qui n'ose pas dire son nom* in 1923, shortly after Proust's death, although it was not published until 1927. A few years later, in her brilliant memoirs of Paris, Elisabeth de Clermont-Tonnerre felt no inhibitions about describing the rent-boys who served the needs of both the bourgeoisie and nobility. 'Connoisseurs of male lechery found an unequalled savour in the easy prostitution of youths who, to make some francs to spend on a girl, abandoned themselves without shame or remorse. Milkmen, telegram boys, lift attendants, young builders powdered like clowns, corrupt "innocents", easy to pick up, were more fascinating than the phoney sailors [*faux-marins*] of Paris.' The Catholic propagandist Anquetil complained about the greater visibility of these activities in the early 1920s: Proust's outspokenness was very much of its time. 'This vice, formerly contained in brothels, or in the shadows of public urinals, flaunts itself now in plain view, under the blazing lights of public rooms, before the eyes of a crowd seeking spicy thrills,' Anquetil remonstrated in his fulmination against the collapse of public morals in post-war Paris, *Satan conduit le bal* (1925). 'In the public promenades, in the arcades, in the cafés, music-halls, everywhere that female prostitution is tolerated, male prostitution displays itself today with a scandalous lack of shame and incredible audacity. Every day, on all the great boulevards, on the Champs-Elysées and in the Bois de Boulogne, and especially on Sunday, there's an incessant coming and going of these *petits messieurs* questing after a soul sister.'

In contrast to Parisian plain-speaking, the English were chary of these topics intruding into polite conversation. Arthur Walkley, the drama critic of *The Times* in London and pioneering Proustian, felt obliged in 1922 to issue a 'frank' warning to potential readers of *Temps perdu*. 'There is an ingredient in M. Proust's later volumes that one finds it very difficult to "stick". It came into the story with M. de Charlus, who is, surely, one of the most repulsive brutes ever conceived by a novelist.' Walkley could not brook the relentless analysis of the Baron's vices. 'My taste is not catholic enough to take in the peculiarities of that filthy brute and amazing cad, M. de Charlus. That the author finds so evident a pleasure in patiently analysing and faithfully reporting such a character leaves me stupefied. But there the thing is, "fox-ing", as it were, page after page – and I won't utter another word on the subject.' Arnold Bennett conceded in 1923 that Proust's 'psychological portrait of the type-pederast' [*sic*] was 'an unpromising subject according to British notions', but insisted that Proust handled it with 'beauty and heart-rending pathos. Nobody with any perception of tragedy can read these wonder-ful pages and afterwards regard the pervert as he had regarded the pervert before reading them. I reckon them as the high-water of Proust.' Still, Proust's treatment was so controversial in the 1920s that Clive Bell opined that the English translation of *Temps perdu* escaped prosecution for obscenity only because it was a translation: 'No Englishman, writing in English, would be allowed to publish in England so complete a picture of life.' Proust, said Bell, was an aristocrat of the intellect and senses who surpassed 'those intellectual lower-middle classes from which are drawn too many of our magistrates, judges and legislators'.

Despite Bell's confidence that an English translation of Proust would not be prosecuted, the publication of the first English translation of *Sodome et Gomorrhe* – euphemistically entitled *The Cities of the Plain* – was deferred in Britain until 1929, when it appeared – not under the imprint of Chatto and Windus, who had published the earlier British volumes of *Temps perdu* – but from the more daring American firm of Alfred Knopf. Even so, Knopf packaged the book as a limited edition of 2,200 copies – each numbered – to prevent any accu-sations that it was a mass-market book that would corrupt the wider reading public. (Chatto took courage and published their edition of *Cities* seven years after Knopf). The literary editors of some periodicals, such as the Tory *Spectator*, ignored *The Cities of the Plain* in 1929: other magazines, such as the progressive *New Statesman*, decried it as pornographic. 'Proust's method is long-windedness itself,' explained the reviewer E. E. Kellett, author of *A Short History of Religions* and of volumes of Victorian nostalgia. 'A worse fault is that of discharging at us, without warning, a "filthy parbreake" of indecency or vulgarity. No one of sense will object to plain speaking when it comes in the natural course of the story. But half Proust's indecencies are entirely gratuitous, and still further hamper his narrative. Lubricity is one thing; lubricity for the sake of tediousness is another.' Kellett's summary of Proust's plot has the harshness of a man who felt he had been sullied. 'A neurotic and asthmatic weakling, afflicted in addition with a snobbery almost sublime, has a succession of diseases which he imagines to be love-affairs.' Although protesting 'flabby and unstable devotion to a girl called Albertine . . . he has a penchant for the keyhole, a genius for spying; and these volumes, though eked out with descriptions of the salons of duchesses, are really engaged with his discoveries and suspicions of what is called "inversion".' Kellett (echoing Edith Wharton) urged that such topics should 'be reserved for the pathologist' and suggested that Proust chose his subject in order to earn money and notoriety: 'few, probably, would have read him had he adopted a pleasant theme.' Kellett conceded that there was 'something to admire in the psychological analysis of [Proust's] degenerates, and in the kind of poetry . . . into which he sublimates their malady', but this did not outweigh 'the repulsiveness of the theme'. Kellett likened Proust's sodomites to 'earth-worms', and concluded his review of *The Cities of the Plain*: 'one escapes with relief to the sturdy, virile world of Fielding, or even to the coarse naturalism of Zola. It is not necessary to be a Puritan in order to detest the atmosphere of a horrible book . . . like this.'

Other readers felt unconvinced by Proust's sexual experience rather than outraged by his frankness. Vladimir Nabokov, for one, objected that the narrator's jealousy of Albertine's excursions to Gomorrah was implausible. 'It makes sense if the reader *knows* that the narrator is a pansy, and that the good fat cheeks of Albertine are the good fat buttocks of Albert'; but otherwise, Nabokov argued, 'if the reader knows nothing about Proust's perversion, the detailed description of a heterosexual male jealously watchful of a homosexual female is preposterous because a normal man would only be amused, tickled pink in fact, by his girl's frolics with a female partner.' However, most early objections were moral rather than aesthetic or structural. Charles Briand, a French magistrate who believed himself to be an admirer of *Temps perdu*, wrote an unpleasant book, *Le secret du Marcel Proust*, which expressed all the indignant shock of French bourgeois values when confronted by Proust's outlook. Proust was a human failure – and a potential source of contamination – because he was unmanly, Briand maintained. 'His temperament predisposed him to impotence: his solitary life turned him into a masturbator; his masturbatory habits, his worldly illusions and deceits, his total incomprehension of female intelligence and sensibilities, his ignorance and disgust at femininity, all this made him an invert. But, invert and masturbator, he was above all, according to both his inherent nature and his nervous system, an impotent man.' Albertine, Proust's so-called 'great love', was no more than 'a guinea-pig who masturbated him', Briand added: 'all his behaviour towards her is superabundant proof of his physiological incapacity to do anything else with her.' Briand's views on Proust's virility could, he promised, 'be confidently confirmed by observation of many psychiatric cases in clinics'.

Harvey Wickham felt that Proust's failures as a novelist came 'by trying to make a lyric out of a lie, and an epic out of a lyric [and] by turning pseudo-scientist'. For him Proust did not make lust seem 'devilish' enough. He cited 'two gilded youths' from Chicago, Richard Loeb and Nathan Leopold, the lovers in search of thrills who kidnapped, murdered and disfigured a fourteen-year-old boy called Bobby Franks in 1924. 'Really, one should listen to some evidence in the criminal courts before writing too sweetly about the vagaries of lust.' Wickham's highly personalised attack on Proust's morality emphasised, like Briand's, its distaste for masturbation as much as for homosexuality. Proust was a 'half man, or half woman if you prefer', who lay in his 'cork-lined room' creating ever 'grosser fancies' taken from 'the region of forbidden things' and his own 'infernal knowledge of himself'. It was with similar associations of self-pollution that a character in Aldous Huxley's novel *Eyeless in Gaza* (1936) denigrated Proust: with

> richly comic eloquence he proceeded to evoke a vision of that asthmatic seeker of lost time squatting, horribly white and flabby, with breasts almost female but fledged with long black hairs, for ever squatting in the tepid bath of his remembered past. And all the stale soapsuds of countless previous washings floated around him, all the accumulated dirt of years lay crusty on the sides of the tub or hung in dark suspension in the water. And there he sat, a pale repellent invalid, taking up spongefuls of his own *thick* soup and

squeezing it over his face, scooping up cupfuls of it and appreciatively rolling the grey and gritty liquor round his mouth, gargling, rising his nostrils with it, like a pious Hindu in the Ganges.

The British need to confute Proust's morality persisted long after his death. To some his outlook resembled a toxic effluvium that made the Third Republic sick. 'Proust was enough in himself to cause the fall of France in 1940,' opined the poet Alfred Noyes (now only remembered for his efforts to suppress *Ulysses* and prosecute Joyce's distributors). In 1954, when the possibility of increasing criminal penalties against male homosexuality was being mooted in the British parliament, a distinguished social reformer called Lady Beveridge, 'finding the subject so much to the fore in the newspapers', decided to investigate the topic. 'I've been reading Proust – the book "Sodom",' she told the *amateur de Proust* A. L. Rowse, 'but I was so *outraged*, Leslie, so outraged.' In Britain during the 1950s male inverts were routinely denounced as 'predatory' or 'proselytising', so for the novelist Pamela Hansford Johnson writing in 1956 it was a virtue that Proust, 'unlike Gide', was not 'a propagandist for his own way of life. He is like a man living in Sodom, resigned to the coming of the fire from Heaven and depressed by the prospect, but feeling nevertheless, out of his innate objectivity, that Heaven has more than a little right on its side.' In the moral temper of the 1950s it extenuated the sodomites' crimes if they hated themselves for – or were ashamed of – what they did. It therefore seemed laudable to Hansford Johnson that – again unlike Gide – 'Proust detested his inversion and wished that with him it had been otherwise.'

Yet many British readers, from the 1920s onwards, found *Temps perdu* personally redemptive. 'How amazingly,' E. M. Forster exclaimed in 1925, 'does Proust describe not only French Society . . . but the personal equipment of the reader, so that one keeps stopping with a gasp to say "Oh! how did he find that out about me? I didn't even know it *myself* until he informed me, but it is so!"' Men of a younger generation than Forster had an even stronger reaction. 'For me Proust is the greatest of all novelists,' wrote Jocelyn Brooke. 'When I first read *Swann*, at the age of nineteen or twenty [in 1928], I experienced a sudden revelation – or what Joyce might have called an epiphany.' He devoured successive volumes until the sequence seemed to him 'not only the novel to end all novels, but, more especially, *my* novel; it might, I felt, have been written for myself alone . . . and there were times – so uncannily did Proust echo my own thoughts and feelings – when it seemed to me that I must, in fact, have written it.' Even so, when Brooke compared *Swann* and *Jeunes Filles*, 'in which the theme of homosexuality remains latent, with the shoddiness of the later volumes,' he wished that Proust's treatment of sex had been 'orthodox'. Despite such reservations, the politician Francis Birrell, both as the father of a gentle, contented homosexual son and as one of the earliest serious readers of the novel, was thankful to Proust, 'the first author to treat sexual inversion as a current and ordinary phe-nomenon, which he describes neither in the vein of tedious panegyric, adopted by certain decadent writers, nor yet with the air of a showman displaying to an agitated tourist abysses of unfathomable horror'.

Temps perdu became a companion for young men in the posi-tion of Birrell's son. When, in 1926, the incipient English novelist Christopher Isherwood wanted to dramatise his feelings, he ran away to a cottage in Wales where he spent his days gazing from the window across a rain-sodden landscape and trying to read *Swann's Way*. He also bought a revolver with which, perhaps, to kill himself; but he later put Proust to the better use by recommending that his young lover Wystan Auden should read *Sodome et Gomorrhe* while they were both exploring the underworld of Weimar Berlin. Auden modelled himself on Charlus, and together with Isherwood adopted 'crook', the word used in the first description of Charlus in the English translation, as their codeword for a male homosexual. In short, Proust wonderfully succeeded in one of his stated aims: to write a book that finally made sense for men who, in the past, when they read a novel by Walter Scott, desired Scott's sturdy outlaw hero Rob Roy rather than his vivacious, pretty heroine Diana Vernon. Proust, for all his nervousness about his reputation, would have been inexpressibly touched by how warmly, in the end, such readers took him for one of their own. So much so that a London *littérateur*, in 1957, regretted that a 'special cult has now been established in his name, that he has been made the high priest of unsavoury rites'.

The Parisian Maurice Sachs, related by marriage to the Bizet and Straus families, was among the earliest acolytes of these rites. 'Each generation has found, in one way or another, its own particular magic and its own unique imagery,' he recalled. 'Ours came partly from Cocteau: stars, sailors, serpents, madness, antiquity, the heart, choirs, incest, glass panes, snow and Greece; part from the Surrealists: sacrilege, dreams, the surreal, shit, revolution, roses, and guillotines.' Then, in 1925, Sachs read Proust, and was transformed by *Sodome et Gomorrhe* and the volumes that followed. 'This double revelation of a work of art and of easy pleasure pitched me into an atrocious promiscuity which ultimately became obsessive.' He became a client of the boys in Le Cuziat's brothel, where his sexual pleasure was enhanced by its aesthetic, or Proustian, associations. 'There I could re-encounter, on the other side of death, Marcel Proust whose name enchanted all our young set. My imagination created a carnal complicity between his adored work of art and this haunt of ruffians where the clanking of Baron de Charlus's chains still seemed to resound.' It was, for Sachs, thrilling to watch, like Proust, clients 'with wolfish steps and marauding airs leave the bedrooms after their pleasure like people sidling from a wood after a crime.' The names of Proust's protagonists 'took on a strange heightened significance when one heard them pronounced by Albert who had, more intimately than other people, collaborated in their creation, by reporting to his master the traits and language that were the secrets of his office.' The brothel became a sleazy detour for sensation-seekers who hoped to hear Le Cuziat retell his anecdotes of Proust, such as the novelist's visit to a butcher's shop where he demanded of a young butcher, 'Show me how you kill a calf.' Le Cuziat had other tales which seemed to reveal to Sachs 'an unknown man, this Marcel Proust, with great terrible depths . . . devoured by a masochism which made him pay with his life for the successful completion of his work, tormented by an anguish which was whipped into sadism as when he had someone stab a living rat with hat-pins in front of him.'

Céleste Albaret denied some of Le Cuziat's – or Sachs's – stories, and other admirers prefer to eschew their hero's night-time researches, which were so much more practical than those of Krafft-Ebing or Freud. 'Maurice Sachs's and Proust's characters are vermin,' Paul Claudel noted in 1948 after reading the former's memoirs of Le Cuziat. Jean Cocteau conceded the probable creative significance of Proust's visits to the brothel but preferred to suppress the details. 'Do not expect me to follow Proust on his nocturnal ramblings,' Cocteau told Proustians in the 1950s. 'Proust returned at dawn, folding his cape round him, pallid, his eyes ringed with dark lines, a bottle of Évian water protruding from his pocket, his black fringe over his forehead, one of his button boots undone, his bowler hat in his hand like the ghost of Sacher-Masoch.' In the 1970s Louis Gautier-Vignal, who had enjoyed a relationship of late-night wartime *tendresse* with Proust, devoted a section of his memoirs to denying, or at least dismissing, evidence of his mentor's proclivity for other men. Attitudes have relaxed since then; and in doing so, they have obscured a crucial fact: the heroism underlying Proust's feelings and experiences in 1921–2.

At the close of 1920 Proust commanded an unrivalled literary reputation in Paris, and was an enviable success in London; but he jeopardised all the acclaim that mattered so much to him with the volumes that he was determined to begin publishing in 1921. His misgivings, as it transpired, were over-stated, but not absurd; and ultimately his hardiness was vindicated. Proust's readers should honour, not forget, the reality of his life at this time. Mauriac in 1922 delighted him by likening his courage and grace to the great French champion boxer Georges Carpentier, and it was an apt comparison. This puny, reclusive neurasthenic showed, in 1921–2, magnificent audacity: he proved himself – more than in any duel he fought or threatened – what he always most desired to be, a brave and resolute man.

CHAPTER 7

My Awful Clairvoyance

The final eighteen months of Proust's life were a period of gathering pace and urgency, ultimately of desperate creative crisis and abject sickroom scenes. He felt that his life was slipping away – 'I have been dying for the last year,' he claimed in April 1922 seven months before his death – and was anguished by the brevity of that segment of eternity that belonged to him. The intensity of his vocation – his debilitating distress over wasted time and frittered chances to work as he fought to finish his novel – became even more ferocious in this closing phase of his life. Though he retreated behind an emotional as well as a medical *cordon sanitaire*, he did not sever all social contacts. Both by letter-writing and tightly controlled meetings with a select few, he maintained his intimacy with the best of the old world: Anna de Noailles, Princesse Soutzo, Armand de Guiche, the latter's sister Elisabeth de Clermont-Tonnerre and sundry Bibescos. With publishers, too, there was a steady exchange of business messages. This was a discomforting, unhappy period for many of his admirers and visitors. Princesse Elizabeth Bibesco recalled her final meeting with Proust at the Rue Hamelin apartment in 1921. 'First there was the hideous cold ante-room, where everything that could be plain was a pattern and everything that could be flat was an excrescence. In the middle stood a portrait

of his father on an easel. Hard, varnished and ugly, permitting –
like the rest of the room – no compromise with beauty. The
cold was so great that one felt like a fish being kept fresh.' Finally she was shown into the squalid icebox of a room where Proust
spent all his days and most of his nights: its displeasing décor
and arrangements seemed to assert that it was a room 'you leave
with your thoughts and return to with your pains'.

   Although, during these last months, Proust was more than
ever an ailing recluse, secreted away in his sickroom, nocturnal
and practically invisible, he remained the consummate historical chronicler, watching and recording the final aristocratic
splendours and the noisier mass movements to be seen in Paris
in the early 1920s. 'His senses were not like those of other people,' wrote Sydney Schiff. 'Lying in the shuttered and curtained
room, the walls of which were lined with cork to prevent noises
reaching him, he yet seemed to know everything that went on
outside.' His exceptional working methods were both expressive
of his temperament and intrinsic to the mesmerising prose of
his novel. 'The last word of its time,' that bewitching stylist
Joseph Conrad called *Temps perdu* a month after Proust's death.
Conrad was baffled by the inexplicable success of its language:
'In that prose so full of life there is no reverie, no emotion, no
marked irony, no warmth of conviction.' Proust's work, despite
the vital force of its characters, its swarm of exuberant imagery
and the opulence of its sensations, was composed of words that
seemed sanitised and drained. By a similar paradox he lay in his
sickroom, secluded from the living, yet he knew their lives. The
pell-mell impetus of Proust's creative existence in 1921–2, its
purposive intensity and febrile effort, paralleled the hectic surge
of Paris outside his apartment. Proust and the city in which he

lived provided interior and exterior forms of restless anxiety. In the final act there was a concentration as well as a culmination of the themes of Proust's life and work.

À la recherche du temps perdu was the last great nineteenth-century European novel – nineteenth-century because Proust had begun preparing in the 1890s for the life work that he only began in 1908 – as well as among the foremost works of the twentieth century. His bridging of the two centuries was hailed by his early readers: '*Temps perdu* is a reviving and even recreating of old matter and old method into new effects,' as one reviewer summarised in 1921, although Wyndham Lewis, with characteristic negativity, railed against 'the last pitiable success of the ancient régime dressed up to look like *new*'. After 1921 some of Proust's readers, like Lewis, implied that his interests were degenerate, by which they meant perverted. Certainly his interests focused on degenerative processes. His fiction is a prolonged study of class degeneration, of moral degeneration and of physical degeneration. In his novel, the influence of the Faubourg Saint-Germain declines, the confidence of the nobility recedes and the Guermantes so falter in self-respect that Prince de Guermantes marries that poisonous *bourgeoise*, Sidonie Verdurin. Charlus degenerates into a man of predatory, obsessive lusts; bodily or mental decay have overwhelmed the protagonists by the closing sections of *Temps retrouvé*. 'The old Duc de Guermantes,' reports the narrator, 'was now no more than a ruin, but a superb one, or perhaps not even a ruin so much as that most romantic of beautiful objects, a rock in a storm. Lashed on all sides by waves of suffering, of anger at his suffering and by the rising tide of death by which he was surrounded, his face, crumbling like a block of stone, still kept the style and confidence that I had always admired.' The duke, it must be said, is of one of the most dignified of the ruins in Proust's world. It is only at this final stage, when he realises what old age signifies, that the narrator can finally understand 'the meaning of death, love, the pleasures of the intellect, the uses of suffering, vocation'.

Proust was born in the right epoch to be a Modernist, but at the wrong end of it. Of the Schiffs' leading guests at the Majestic, Proust was born in 1871, Diaghilev in 1872, Picasso in 1881, Stravinsky and Joyce in 1882. Although much of *À la recherche du temps perdu* is set in the 1890s or in the aftermath of the Dreyfus case, it reaches a revelatory climax in the Paris of the wartime black-out, and closes with scenes that seem to be set around 1932. The apotheosis of Proust's world was in Paris immediately after the Great War. In 1919 Renoir died, Rutherford split the atom, Alcock and Brown flew the Atlantic, Walter Gropius founded the Bauhaus and the Weimar Republic was constituted as the successor to the Hohenzollern Empire in Germany. Five years later, in 1924, a *bloc des gauches* replaced the *bloc national* as the rulers of France, the first Labour Government took power in Britain and André Breton issued his Surrealist *Manifeste*. In between there had been the death in 1920 of Eugénie, the last Empress of France, and the deaths in 1922 (the publication year of *The Waste Land* and *Ulysses*) of Karl, last Emperor of Austro-Hungary, and Benedict XV, known as the great Pope of the world tragedy. The first years of peace were a period of keen contrasts and contentions, backward-looking, progressive, idealistic, sullen, with ominous tendencies and auspicious trends. Throughout this provisional, historically unsettled period the dukes and duchesses, princes and countesses still seemed to shine with untarnished glamour in a Paris where the streets were being taken over by chauffeurs, motor-cars and the sort of petty crooks who as youngsters might have worked *chez* Le Cuziat. It was the Paris of Picasso and Pirandello, of Diaghilev and the Dolly sisters (Hungarian-born dancers from Brooklyn), of Stravinsky and Gertrude Stein, of James Joyce and Josephine Baker, of the Ballets Russes and the shimmy, the one-step, the mambo and the Charleston. Money and frivolity seemed to dominate the Parisian ambience of the 1920s: the most prominent of the post-war self-made multi-millionaires was a perfume manufacturer named Coty. As always the Arts were dancing round Money and the rich were encircling the artists. Paris was never more artistically vital, dazzling and dominant: its galleries and dealers displayed every week paintings and sculpture that had no equals in the world.

Proust's different worlds – social, creative, intellectual, historical – were co-existent and co-inherent in the Paris of the early 1920s. Everything that was intrinsic and essential to his novel became intrinsic and essential to the capital: not least the collapse of some class boundaries and the cheapening or confusion of others. 'Paris is capricious in accepting some social-climbers and not others,' explained one hostess, who had overheard a baffled, real-life counterpart of Madame Verdurin complaining, 'We are not getting on: Mrs KGC has always the best people, and she has not half my money.' A veneering of literary taste helped to secure the position in Paris of precarious social-climbers. In 1922 the nefarious international armaments dealer Basil Zaharoff, a major investor in the casino at Monte Carlo, who lived in a magnificent house on Avenue Hoche and had previously under-written Ballets Russes productions, endowed a new literary prize worth 20,000 francs called the Prix Balzac, which Proust lobbied should be awarded to Jacques Rivière, who needed the money.

Paris was a city of words: lawyers' conversations in antechambers of the courts, confidential interludes between politicians and journalists, chatter in restaurants and cafés, the perpetual buzz of opinions and rumours that daily appeared in the newspapers. For Parisians conversation was the cheapest and best entertainment, and amongst the educated, conversation was an art. The French ability to spin words, to reverse, invert, pervert and confound ideas, and to divine character, thrilled visitors to Paris. Talk – brilliant, prosaic, self-serving, spiteful or indiscreet depending on the speaker and the mood – provided the essence of Paris salons and the oil that ran its political machinery. Without inside information, there would have been nothing for its politicians, its army of small investors, its racing men, its theatre-goers avid for backstage gossip and for all the idlers whose lives were devoted to the pleasures of conversation. There was 'published every day in Paris', Proust wrote in *La Prisonnière*, 'a sort of spoken newspaper, more terrible than its printed rivals', one which took a cruel, capricious pleasure in creating crass new celebrities or destroying established reputations. 'This verbal press reduced to nothing the power of a Charlus who had fallen from fashion, and promoting above him a Morel who was not worth a millionth of his former protector.'

When Proust could not venture out to hear the verbal press, he kept *au courant* with Paris life through the newspapers and magazines that were brought to him daily by Céleste Albaret and lay heaped on his sick-bed. His weakness for newspaper opinions, and his respect for the power of journalists to make reputations, showed in his ruthless use of contacts and shameless persistence in trying to ensure good publicity for his novel. He had, for example, been an occasional contributor to *Le Figaro* under the editorship of Gaston Calmette, and dedicated *Swann* to Calmette as an adroit means of ensuring that *Le Figaro* was a steadfast publicist of his work. Proust remained an inveterate consumer of journalism throughout his years of invalid seclusion, and an avid monitor of all the artistic novelties and intellectual spasms that Paris offered in the early 1920s – as well as of the daily fluctuations in the share price of Royal Dutch and other market leaders on the Bourse. It was as typical of his alertness to contemporary culture as of his personal generosity that during the summer of 1922, when he was in rapidly failing health, he took the trouble to send a delicately phrased, encouraging letter to Julien Benda about the latter's recent novel, *Les Amorandes*, which he thought had been unjustly handled by reviewers and perhaps the Paris verbal press. Around the same time he sent an admiring, astute letter to Jules Romains about his new novel *Lucienne*, which he had read and the reputation of which he had monitored, for he tried to be responsive to every new success in the arts or in life. In his own novel he celebrated the heartless sensuality of sipping *café au lait* while reading newspapers, and transforming world cataclysms, wars, murders, suicides, divorces, fires and all the other possible human dramas into objects of amused curiosity.

Proust's involvement with the press was noted, exaggerated and used against him by Wyndham Lewis. 'Fiction,' Lewis complained, had become 'the private publicity-machine of the Ruling Society' since the Great War. *Temps perdu* was, he alleged, the literary climax of this corrupt tendency. 'Was not Proust for years the Gossip-column writer upon the staff of *Le Figaro*? Is it not as a Gossip-columnist that he got his information?' Actually

Proust was never a gossip columnist, although in 1903 he had contributed to *Le Figaro* several society sketches, with such titles as 'Un salon historique' (describing the salon of Princesse Mathilde Bonaparte, the wise old daughter of Jérôme-Napoleon, ex-King of Westphalia) or 'Le salon de la Princesse Edmond Polignac: musique d'aujourdhui, échoes d'autrefois' ('music of today, echoes of other times'). Partly to spite the Schiffs, against whom he turned, Lewis insisted that there could be no objective truth in Proust's work because it reproduced too obediently 'the hot and immediate interests of "real" everyday social life' in modern Paris, 'the life of the Gossip-column, the fashionable studio, the freak-party'.

Paris in the early 1920s, with its freak parties and its publicity, was in the hangover of *la belle époque*. Its confidence and vitality had suffered in the war, during which even Proust's sanctuary, the Ritz Hotel, had endured bombardment. War nerves, and post-war nerves, had also made the city more frenetic. Peaceful horse-drawn cabs, known as 'fiacres', were being superseded by irate taxi-drivers: in 1922 the Paris authorities decided not to renew licences for horse-cabs as their slowness was obstructing the city's motor traffic. The cars and vans were faster, louder and seemed more urgent in Paris than in London. One-way streets, and designated traffic routes, were proliferating in the narrower quarters of central Paris. As Sisley Huddleston reported in April 1922, 'Paris is a hubbub of ceaseless sounds; the air vibrates deafeningly, and the buildings shake. To live in the busy centres in Paris is to be driven mad.' The despised, perpetually-broken French speed limit of 30 kilometres an hour was temporarily abolished in 1922. When people talked of the Salon, Huddleston noted, they now meant the annual motor-show in the Grand Palais rather than the older-established art exhibition. The avenue des Champs-Élysées had evolved from a street of superb private houses to a street of expensive hotels, and in 1922 was being colonised by huge new banks and emporia in which expensive motor-cars shone behind plate-glass windows. Paris pavements had deteriorated as much as the roadways. Handbag-snatchers patrolled the *trottoirs* that previously had been the preserve of boulevardiers. Those idle, malicious, nonchalant men-about-town, brandishing canes, who had once sauntered in the boulevards and loitered in the cafés, were now submerged by productive citizens hurrying along on business clutching attaché cases. Parisians bustled, throbbed, and cheated; they sought out films and novels that extolled speed or glamorised crime.

A young English visitor who went native in Paris in 1919–23, Lord Derwent, noted the 'quiet wrath' of the typical respectable French bourgeois 'at the Sodom and Gomorrah his beloved capital was being turned into. It was no longer the old, almost elementary appeal to the man from Manchester or Amsterdam of the nudities of the Folies Bergère, the Rue Chabaneix, or the more secret but still banal "houses" of the Montmartre Heights themselves.' Instead Paris, like Berlin, submitted to

the contortions and darting of all that had crept out of the rubbish-heap of Europe at the impulsion of that great kick, the War. It was not only bad champagne and gilt-framed mirrors and worn plush and crudely-painted, mechanical houris; it was cocaine –

Ashes to ashes, dust to dust,

If the cocktail don't get you, then the cocaine must . . .

For Derwent one of the abiding memories of Paris in the 1920s was 'the little *poules* sniffing away in the lavabos, in the days when *la came* was still cheap.' Other drugs abounded. 'Heroin seems to have been the source of sexual exploits that built up portentous Rabelaisian stories,' Derwent recalled. As for opium, Derwent pictured himself sitting 'on the floor of Princess M.'s white sitting-room down at Le Vésinet, watching through the dull-lit gloom the crackling pipes held to the flame, and drinking in through fascinated, guilty nostrils that unforgettable smell, both sweet and acrid, deterrent and cloying.' Vice was one of the lures of Paris: the arrest in March 1922 of a black-mailer, his mistress and a seventeen-year-old boy drew attention to the systematic entrapment of tourists. This trio had picked up a visitor in Montmartre, taken him to '"artistic spectacles" of a very special character' and had then demanded money – a common ploy. Parisians were almost proud of their city's repu-tation for crimes of jealousy and revenge: 'post-war Paris', it was said in 1922, 'would indeed hardly be Paris without a few Satur-day or Sunday volleys of revolver shots in the streets or parks.'

All this urban energy was monitored and used by Proust. Although there are no alcoholics in *Temps perdu* (nor, indeed, any bankrupts or dogs), there are a few habitual drug users. During the fraught period when Robert de Saint-Loup has mar-ried Gilberte Swann, but is infatuated with Morel, he resorts to cocaine. It contributes to his febrile, duplicitous behaviour; but after the outbreak of war, he finds the excitement of military heroism surpasses his pleasure in drugs. Vicomtesse de Saint-Fiacre, whom the narrator meets again at the Guermantes' masked ball which provides the climax of *Temps retrouvé*, mixes her cocaine, it seems, with heroin or morphine: 'her eyes, deeply ringed with black, looked almost crazed. Her mouth was fixed in a strange rictus. She had got up, I was told, especially for this party, having spent months without leaving her bed or chaise longue.' It is a dismal encounter for the narrator. 'Time,' he reflects, 'has its special express trains which hasten you to a premature old age.'

For the French commentator Ambroise Got, writing in 1923, the 'moral ruin' wrought by the war was 'disastrous'. The heightened tensions and emotions since 1914 had 'aroused and exalted all the passions, all the cravings . . . and by wrecking the boundaries of public morals it has opened out a vast field for lunatics, neurotics, drug addicts, all those who want oblivion.' Got felt that 'all social classes, to a more or less virulent degree, are participating in this madcap pleasure, in this savage onslaught of agitated glee.' Vicious post-war self-indulgence was typified, he lamented, by the new styles of 'dancing, in alcohol taken in all its forms, in the "artificial paradises" of opium eaters, cocainomania and sexual excess'. Parisian exuberance had always been expressed through dancing; but the music and dances of Proust's early manhood seemed archaic by the 1920s. In the 1890s the craze had been for musicians, brightly dressed with red-braided coats, called Tziganes, who had reached their peak when a Tzigane violinist at Maxim's eloped in 1896 with the Princesse de Caraman-Chimay: a scandal to which Charlus alludes in À l'ombre des jeunes filles en fleurs. The Tziganes had long since been superseded in Paris modes by Russian balalaika-players and knife-throwers. Square-shouldered, heavily moustached men, who had once seemed so attractive, found themselves less alluring after a war in which masculine aggression proved so unsuccessful.

The 1920s were the golden age of sleek-haired, wasp-waisted young gigolos who guided plump older ladies around the dance-floors and were rewarded with presents and petting. The waltz and the polka became obsolete in the decade of the tango. 'Glid-ing, swaying, hopping, tripping, vibrating from shoulder-blade to ankle, after-war Paris danced as not even the dance-inventors could have ever dreamed or hoped,' Derwent recorded. 'The dances were easy and not tiring; the music was cheap and anyone could dance to it; and so it has the charm of *la canaille* [vulgari-ty]; you dance to what the errand-boy not only whistles, but round the corner, steps to himself also; so I suppose the faults of jazz, as music, must be counted among the crimes committed in the name of Democracy.' Proust investigated the exotic or mod-ern dances that were captivating Parisians, and professed to be pleased by them. Djemil Amik, looking like a 'black pearl', danced at the New Year's Eve party at which he arrived on the stroke of midnight on 1 January 1922. Five weeks later, at Princesse Soutzo's soirée in February, Thérèse d'Hinnisdal, Mar-quise de Lévis, gave Proust a 'choreographic demonstration' of the latest modern dances. He was 'charmed' to see her perform 'dances *les plus 1922*' with a graceful peculiarity which made him think of unicorns; but the fact that the tango evoked in him images of heraldic beasts suggests that his eager receptivity to the modern was always idiosyncratic if not antiquarian.

James Joyce, who had moved from Trieste to Paris in 1920, found life there congenial: it was 'the last of the human cities', he told Wyndham Lewis. In the early years his most persistent difficulties were to find lady typists who were able, or permitted, to type out his manuscript – in 1921 one woman's husband read Joyce's text, tore it up indignantly and threw it in the fire – and to find suitable accommodation for his family: 'an entire month of flat-hunting, out every morning and back at night, in taxis, buses, trams, trains, lifts, agencies, newspaper offices,' he lamented to Ezra Pound. Even this problem was temporarily relieved during 1921 by the thoughtfulness of Valéry Larbaud, a writer who mostly guarded his domestic privacy with unusual vigilance, but lent his apartment for several months to the Joyces. Meanwhile the bookseller Sylvia Beach had been collecting subscribers to fund the publication of a private edition of *Ulysses* in book form, and in February 1922 she handed the first finished copy to its author. That night Joyce went out with a party of friends for a celebratory dinner at an Italian restaurant. During the meal Joyce kept his copy of the book in a package under his chair until, after dessert, he untied the parcel and put the book on the table. When his companions then toasted the book, two waiters approached, asked if he had written it, and if so, whether they could show it to the *padrone* of the restaurant. This was a period when for the citizens of Paris it felt an agreeable duty to show respectful interest in the arts: Paris where, as Stravinsky said at this time, the pulse of the world's creativity was throbbing most strongly.

The artistic strength of the city came from its lack of insularity: there were about 400,000 foreigners among a total population of about 3 million. Paris remained the world's cultural capital, where fashions were still set in the arts, in clothes and the pleasures of life, because it did not exclude or oppose young foreign talent. The leaders of fashionable Parisian society preferred to serve art rather than power. One of the most discriminating collectors had been Alexandre Berthier, the dashing Prince de Wagram, a soldier with a passion for the poetry of Mallarmé, whose pioneering ardour for Impressionists and motor-cars was commemorated by Proust in *Guermantes* after his death of war wounds, at the age of thirty-five, in the last months of the war. The prince had a tactile nature, striking looks, endearing laugh, and great susceptibility to beauty, which his kinswoman Elisabeth de Clermont-Tonnerre attributed to his Rothschild mother – the Princesse de Wagram who had welcomed the young Proust into her house when he was beginning his explorations of the Guermantes world. The Prince de Wagram's greatest accomplishments were in the visual arts: by 1908, aged only twenty-five, he owned thirty paintings by Courbet, fifty Renoirs, forty-seven van Goghs, twenty-eight Cézannes, forty Monets, twenty-six Sisleys, twenty Pissaros, ten Puvis de Chavannes, eleven Degas and twelve Manets. Around the time of Wagram's death Proust had made a foray with Gautier-Vignal to the Bernheim Gallery in Boulevard de la Madeleine to study paintings by Monet, Sisley, Pissaro, Renoir and other Impressionists. He looked at the pictures with sad intensity, Gautier-Vignal thought, as if he was taking leave of beautiful objects that he would never see again. Yet in 1922 there were still many new artistic wonders to be seen and heard in Paris every week. Raymond Mortimer, a young visitor avid for culture and later a renowned English Proustian, was awed in the spring of 1922 by the windows of Bernheim's Gallery, full of paintings by Derain and Matisse, and excited by watching flawless performances of three different plays on three successive nights at Jacques Copeau's Théâtre du Vieux-Colombier. In the week of the Schiffs' supper party, in May 1922, Galerie Paul Rosenberg was exhibiting ten Cézannes and works by Corot, Pisarro, Rodin, Ingres, Delacroix, Monet, Sisley, Gauguin and Toulouse-Lautrec.

'Modernism is almost dead – and I am glad of it!' trumpeted

Percy Scholes, music critic of the *Observer*, in January 1922, immediately after the Russian Ballet's disastrous winter season in London. Modernism, for him, was 'mere eccentricity for eccentricity's sake, a hope to obtain *réclame* by appearing publicly with one's clothes buttoned behind instead of in front.' It all seemed bogus or outlandish to Scholes. 'For "modernism",' he wrote in the ringing tones of obscurantism, 'we have largely been offered freaks – French freaks and Italian freaks.' In order to restore traditional no-nonsense English notions of beauty to their rightful sovereignty, 'let us clear all this musical-political, French-Italian-Russian rhetorical rubbish out of our path.' Yet Modernism was not moribund in 1922, and it was (at its best) not an expression of revolutionary infantilism but of the matured, disciplined resurrection of historic cultural riches. The Modernist guests of honour at the Schiffs' supper party – Proust, Diaghilev, Picasso, Stravinsky and Joyce – were conservatives as well as revolutionaries. They understood their national traditions, revered the past and were each of them engaged on schemes of creative revival. Their works were acts of heroic repudiation of sentimentality, gimcrackery and vapid good taste – the stuff that Percy Scholes customarily praised in the *Observer*. They rejected the tendency of nineteenth-century Western culture to try to educate, uplift and talk down to a wider public. Instead they tried to create a privileged domain in which artists could work beyond the levelling demands of the cultural marketplace. They resisted safe mediocrity and (with the partial exception of the future Communist, Picasso) had no political purposes in their art. They sought a select audience that was sufficiently sophisticated and informed to sympathise with their efforts. This élite could be joined by anyone who was sufficiently discriminating to care to do so. Western civilisation, the élitists all understood, is built upon discrimination: a culture that does not rest on discrimination, that penalises people who discriminate, or rewards the undiscriminating, is worth very little and has only callow, childish pleasures. Whereas Progressives saw universal suffrage, wider prosperity and foreign holidays as civilising and virtuous, and seldom regretted that cultural distinctions were blurred in the process, the great Modernists worked to restore, or invigorate, cultural distinctions, and fought the barbarous idea that either individuals or nations could emancipate themselves from their histories.

There was a natural, unforced affinity between the great Modernists' outlook and the cosmopolitanism of the avant-garde Princesse Edmond de Polignac, who first brandished a copy of *Swann* in London in 1914 and thus encouraged an early outbreak wave of Proustians in England. The concert parties held in the music-room of the Princess's house in Avenue Henry Martin have been pictured by one of her regular guests: 'the rostrum was at the far end, and the Princess's train of silver-grey satin would rustle as she moved up and down the aisle while her faithful clan assembled to the right and left to await the start of the sacred moments. Automatically the different groups went to their places: the first three rows for the American multi-millionairesses, with white hair and diamonds, and English duchesses, the next three rows for important Frenchwomen with their hair dyed, the heavenly young were grouped at the back whispering and jostling, while standing about, decorating the doorways, were always some old aesthetes, boon companions of the princess's youth.' The Princess was the only Paris hostess who never turned to scrutinise the doorway or her guests after the concert had begun: instead she sat rapt in intense concentration. Her demeanour resembled that of Charlus at the musical soirée he arranged to promote the reputations of Morel and Madame Verdurin in the Faubourg Saint-Germain. To indicate to the guests 'the religious silence that ought to be observed, the detachment from every worldly care, he displayed himself, as he raised to his fine brow his white-gloved hands, as a model (whom others should emulate) of gravity, almost of ecstasy, ignoring the greetings of late-comers, so indelicate as not to understand that it was now the moment for High Art. They were all hypnotised; no one dared to utter a sound or move a chair; all of a sudden, respect for the music – imposed by Palamède's prestige – had been inculcated into a crowd as ill-bred as it was elegant.' The behaviour of Charlus and his set is painfully self-conscious, no doubt, but disciplined; and without the pantomime of affectation described at another *soirée musicale*, given by Charlus's *bête noire* the Marquise de Saint-Euverte, at which the Princesse des Laumes beats time with her fan, to show that she is listening to a pianist playing Liszt; but so as not to forfeit her independence to a hired performer or to the other socially inferior guests, she beats a different time from the music being played.

The high social and creative stratosphere of a musical evening *chez* Polignac was characteristically Proustian – Proust had wanted to dedicate *À l'ombre* to the memory of the princess's husband – and was thought all the more detestable for that by Wyndham Lewis. This most angry and graceless Vorticist detested 'the art of this High-Bohemia of the "revolutionary" rich'. He condemned its 'glittering highly-intellectualist surface, and deep, sagacious, rich though bleak sensuality', although he conceded that it was 'a vast improvement on the fearful artlessness, ugliness and stupidity that preceded it'. He identified

Proust as 'the classic expression up-to-date of this millionaire-outcast, all-caste, star-cast world', and attacked the Russian Ballet as 'the perfect expression of the society Proust has immortalised'. Lewis accused Diaghilev of 'deliberately manufacturing a bastard "revolutionary" article to flatter the taste of his clientèle – the "revolutionary" High-Bohemia of the Ritzes and Rivieras', and never forgave the impresario for having ensnared Picasso as a stage designer or, in his words, 'to have associated in the mind of the great Public the work of the finest artists of this time with the vulgar life of the war-gilded rabble'. Lewis, too, denounced the sexuality of Diaghilev, and hence of Proust. Diaghilev, he raved, 'has used and degraded' splendid artists – a stab at his affair with Nijinsky – as well as first-class artistic ideas: 'with his high-brow loot from the Paris studios, he has toured the world, surrounded by an epicene circus'. During the 1920s, Lewis received several financial subsidies from Sydney Schiff, but he was a self-obsessed, perpetually aggrieved man, with an over-developed martyrdom complex, who resented Schiff's patronage, and pilloried his benefactor (and Proust) in his novel *Apes of God* (1930). Schiff is caricatured, in a chapter entitled 'Chez Lionel Kein Esq.', as a pampered, vain mediocrity. Volumes of Scott Moncrieff's translation of Proust are prominent in Kein's drawing room, for he and his wife are Proustian zealots: 'it is some combination of your *power-complex* and your appetite for gossip that makes you so pleased with . . . Proust,' she is told by an outspoken acquaintance. Lewis's literary portrait of the Schiffs, both as social figures and Proustians, showed 'awful treachery', Edith Sitwell thought, 'but he is evidently mad'.

Lewis's career was a financial calamity, and he seethed at the easy

access available to some great Modernists into the luxurious houses of those hospitable noblemen, ambitious *femmes du monde*, rich
avant-garde patrons and discerning collectors who comprised the
Ritz-Riviera or High-Bohemia sets. This was indeed the element
that had always sustained Diaghilev, whose first public success had
been as curator of an acclaimed exhibition of historic portraits
loaned from the country houses of Russian provincial noblemen.
'The end of a period is revealed here, in these gloomy dark palaces,
frightening in their dead splendour, and inhabited today by
charming, mediocre people,' Diaghilev announced in an astound-
ingly shrewd speech at the opening ceremony of this exhibition.
'We are living in a terrible period of transition. We are witnesses of
the greatest moment of summing-up in history, present at the creation of a new culture, which will be created by us, and which will
sweep us away.' His words might have served as the chief epigraph
of *À la recherche du temps perdu*. Diaghilev's career as an international impresario was launched with the support of a Grand Duke,
and until the disastrous revolution of 1917, he received a steady
income acting as a financial intermediary between pushy Russian
capitalists who wanted to acquire honours or titles, and the Grand
Dukes within whose influence the awarding of these gewgaws lay.
After his self-exile from Tsarist Russia, Diaghilev moved smoothly
between sumptuous hotels in Paris, Madrid, Rome, London,
Monte-Carlo and other fashionable resorts. These were precisely
the milieus and habits that aroused the envious loathing of Wyndham Lewis.

At this stage of his life Picasso, no less than Diaghilev,
enjoyed the *beau monde*. He was gratified when Cocteau began
introducing him into the smarter avant-garde Paris salons. He
did not squirm in this new environment – so different from the

Montmartre tenements where he had begun his Paris life – but revelled in it. He was proud of his own lineage, enjoyed having an aunt from the Malagueño nobility and justifiably felt, as an aristocrat of the arts, at ease among *grands seigneurs*. Picasso's introduction into the houses of the rich Modernist sympathisers was assisted by a highly constructive patron of the Ballets Russes called Eugenia Errazuriz (in whose apartment Proust once watched several of Picasso's cubist paintings being unpacked from their cases). She was a shrewd financial supporter of Stravinsky and Diaghilev, helped to assemble an art collection for Massine and commissioned Le Corbusier to design a villa for her in Chile: altogether she was a most discriminating and life-enhancing protector of Modernism. Lewis would never have had the wit or tact to cultivate her.

Everything that Wyndham Lewis, and puritan moralists like Got and Anquetil, hated about Modernism and Paris was concentrated in Le Boeuf sur Le Toit, a night-club that opened in January 1922 in Rue Boissy d'Anglas. From the outset *Tout-Paris* of High Society and High Bohemia had flocked to the club. It superceded a smaller establishment, the Gaya Bar, operated by the same club owner, Moysès, which had been frequented by Diaghilev, Picasso, Stravinsky, Marcelle Meyer, Misia Sert and Gide among others. The habitués of the new place included the Princesse Lucien Murat, Grand Duke Vladimir of Russia, Princesse Soutzo, Comte Étienne de Beaumont, Coco Chanel, Picasso, Picabia, Mauriac, the actor Jacques Porel, the retired courtesan Émilienne d'Alençon and even on one occasion Proust. Le Boeuf sur le Toit was particularly associated with Cocteau, who brought in his train a set of sophisticated young *littérateurs* and their friends. Indeed Moysès named his *boîte de nuit* after a musical extravaganza written by Cocteau in association with Erik Satie and Darius Milhaud. The establishment contained a boisterous – sometimes unpleasant – bar and an agreeable dining room with square black tables and a tiny central dance floor; on the central wall there was a big manifesto conceived by Picabia covered with signatures and graffiti while the other plainer walls were decorated with disorientating yet compelling photographs by Man Ray. Poulenc, Milhaud and Auric were among the composers who were constant habitués of Le Boeuf; there was a grand piano in a corner, on which a fat, black-haired Belgian would improvise parodies of Chopin or hammer out hypnotic tunes with silly lyrics, 'My sweetie went away', 'What'll I do when you are far away?', 'Venetian Moon' and 'Yes, we have no bananas'.

'The supreme advantage of the Boeuf was that from six in the evening until two in the morning Montparnasse and the Ritz and the Russian Ballet hangers-on and serious creative artists could all rub shoulders, eating and drinking what they chose in a somewhat champagne-ridden city,' one devoted regular wrote with nostalgia as world war loomed in 1939. 'I have always suspected huge, plump, smiling Moysé [sic] of adulterating the innumerable bottles that lined the back wall, and even the *oranges pressées*; but ten francs a glass was not an exaggerated price to pay for feeling slightly peculiar.' This was the testimony of Lord Derwent, the Yorkshire squire who so ardently turned Parisian, and for whom Le Boeuf, however motley its crowd, encapsulated the entrancing spirit of Paris in the early 1920s. 'The Boeuf had nothing to do with anything apparently serious,' Derwent admitted,

    no connection with Disarmament or Reparations or the

Ruhr, no link with the life of Paris proper, Paris out in the streets under the flickering green of its trees, Paris of the concierges, the bistros, the shops and buses; but it *was*, with all its art-flummery and dubious morality and second-rate hangers-on, a real meeting-ground of those curious of something else than their neighbours' private affairs in a home-town, curious of what Europe meeting the World over a gin-fizz could produce, of what Europe might be up to apart from thwarting President Wilson, those whose sense of intellectual adventure could find satisfaction in this erethism of novelties, this strange frontier between the Silly and the Sensible, easy to cross and to cross back again, with profit from both.

In Paris, during the early 1920s, while Modernism thrilled and Le Boeuf sur le Toit thrived, there also survived the redoubtable *puissance* of British ducal glory. 'The Duchess of Portland and the Duchess of Sutherland were certain of their omnipotence, knowing that they didn't belong to the secondary race of "Continental dukes",' an admiring French duchess wrote. During midsummer of 1921 Proust had a pleasant flirtation with one of this omnipotent breed of British dukes and attended his marriage to an American bride, Gladys Deacon, whose strange beauty and charm had been admired by select Parisians for years. Robert de Montesquiou had likened her to an archangel; and Proust – spasmodically at least – lavished attention on her. He was used by Elisabeth de Clermont-Tonnerre as an intermediary when she tried to arrange Deacon's marriage to Prince Léon Radziwill. When Deacon's mother died in 1918, Proust wrote a letter of condolence hoping that 'this terrible illness which is grief' would soon pass 'so that you can appreciate the divine sorrow of remembering'. During a dinner at the Ritz in 1919, Proust blew an 'adulatory kiss across the table' at her. She was introduced into his novel under the name of Miss Foster.

In 1921 Gladys Deacon finally settled to marry 'Sunny', the Duke of Marlborough, whose long, unhappy marriage to an American heiress had recently ended in divorce. Proust participated in the festivities of his second marriage, and basked in the amiable glow of the Marlboroughs. On 16 June he and the Princesse de Polignac were both guests at a dinner given by 'ravishing Madame Hennessy' to celebrate the Marlborough engagement. He also attended the subsequent wedding on 24 June at the British consulate-general in Paris: his urbane American devotee Walter Berry was one of the two witnesses, and perhaps ensured his invitation. There was a fierce heat-wave and drought that June and July, and the exertions of the wedding day coupled with *la canicule* afflicted Proust with an attack of migraine.

The Duke of Marlborough impressed Elisabeth de Clermont-Tonnerre by his defiant superiority to 'the vulgarity of democratic clamour'. He believed in his caste and held fast to his dynastic traditions: 'to be a duke, that is my trade,' he told her when she visited him at Blenheim (there are only two palaces in Britain, she was taught, Buckingham and Blenheim). Proust's meetings with the Duke gave him as much pleasure as his earlier conversations with the Earl of Derby. Marlborough tried to coax Proust out of his invalid existence by recommending the self-help techniques of Émile Coué, a French pharmacist turned popular-psychologist. Coué taught that people could improve themselves by conscious auto-suggestion, notably by repeating to themselves twenty times daily, 'Day by day, and hour by hour, I grow better and better.'

Patients who made the pilgrimage to his clinic at Nancy were told, 'Look into my eyes and believe; repeat the formula; you will be healed.' Marlborough shared Coué's certitude that one can cure oneself by convincing oneself that one is cured. 'If one believes one is well, one will be well,' the Duke advised Proust. 'Just repeat to yourself: "I feel marvellous".' This formula did not work for Proust, and was mocked by Sydney Schiff, who felt jealous of the Marlborough influence, insisted to Proust that Coué was an 'imbecile' and preferred to combat his own hypochondria by a special régime of Swedish keep-fit dancing. The duke held out to Proust the 'dream' of a visit to England and the comforts of his great palace outside Oxford. 'M. de Marlborough told me, I'll put you in a sleeper at the Gare du Nord, I'll tuck you up in a cabin on the boat and you can stay in bed at Blenheim,' Proust told Schiff.

The Duke's life was an Anglicised version of the Guermantes degeneration. Stylish, peremptory and spoilt, he had grown accustomed to the backing of his first wife's Vanderbilt fortune, and felt destitute without it. 'We are both awfully poor,' he replied when asked in 1921 about the wedding presents he had exchanged with his new bride. Whereas Proust's other English grandee, Lord Derby, was an optimistic *bon vivant*, Marlborough was oppressed by Proustian regrets and presentiments of historical decline. The pessimism of the Hapsburgs seemed to have been grafted onto him, and he 'always imagined the world against him,' said his kinsman Lord Londonderry. Marlborough's Proustian possibilities – his disappointed brilliance, his despondent discovery of his futility in a time of swift social evolution – were evoked with empathy by his cousin (and sometime heir-presumptive) Winston Churchill's compelling memoir of him: 'when in 1892 he became Duke of Marlborough life opened very brilliantly for him. The old world still existed in those days, and in the glittering and it seemed stable framework of an aristocratic society he had a place where few were his equals and none his betters. A famous name, a wonderful palace, great connexions, and an adequate fortune, youth and the world before him!' Yet in the ensuing decades there was a social transformation in Britain which deprived such men of their property and in some cases drove them from their homes. This process darkened the Duke of Marlborough's life. 'He was always conscious,' said his cousin, 'that he belonged to a system that had been destroyed, to a society which had passed away, and he foresaw with not ill-founded apprehension that the world tides which were flowing would remorselessly wash away all that was left. He resigned himself to this . . . but all the same it saddened and chilled him.' If Proust had somehow inherited a dukedom, then psychologically he would have been a duke like this Marlborough.

There was, however, one curb on the mutual sympathy between Proust and the head of the Spencer-Churchills: he 'could not talk at all of Sodom to the *duc de Marlborough*'. But then it was hard to talk easily with many men on this subject. Throughout Proust's Marlborough summer and the ensuing autumn of 1921, he was still coping with doubtful reactions to *Sodome et Gomorrhe*. Jacques Rivière, who as a prisoner-of-war in a German camp had prized his copy of *Swann* almost above everything, wrote on 6 September about the selection of an extract to be published in a forthcoming issue of *Nouvelle Revue Française*: 'I only ask you to avoid anecdotes in which M. de Charlus is the hero.' Ostensibly this was because the novelist

Paul Claudel had rebuked Rivière for the 'growing licentious-
ness of the review' and Rivière felt driven by commercial pressures to avoid giving any 'chance of attack' to his critics. But
perhaps the Charlusiens made Rivière himself a little queasy: 'If
I go back into that little hole,' he cried in delirium while he lay
dying of typhoid in 1925, 'a hole of the queers [*pédérasts*], I'll be
lost.' Rivière's request 'shocked' Proust who felt the 'recommendation to avoid indecency is really misplaced': ultimately,
though, he provided the *NRF* with an extract from *Sodome et
Gomorrhe II* which even the flying-squadrons of moral police-
men could only find innocuous. Similarly when Jacques
Boulenger understood Proust to propose that his *Revue de la
semaine* should publish an article to promote *Sodome et Gomorrhe*, he was aghast: 'I could not possibly do an article on *Sodome
et Gomorrhe* without risking mass cancellations of subscrip-
tions.' Proust was more conciliatory to Boulenger – 'I find it
absolutely understandable that one cannot talk of my *Sodome et
Gomorrhe*'– and felt consoled when Boulenger arranged for his
Revue to publish an interview with him instead. Proust's defensiveness about his personal reputation never abated during 1921.
In the autumn, when someone – describing the scene when
Charlus first encounters Jupien – declared that the eavesdropping narrator was thus 'initiated' into inversion, Proust was pre-
dictably upset. 'That's not right at all. In the afternoon I saw M.
de Charlus picking someone up. That could be described as a
discovery, or whatever. But "initiated" seems to mean that the
person who says I is inverted. It's quite to the contrary.'

In October 1921 Proust developed uraemia, and was accidentally poisoned by a pharmacist's error in making up a medicine,
but he recovered to finish his corrections to *Sodome et Gomorrhe*

II: 'the psychologically richest fiction that I have yet given,' he had promised Gallimard. In November 1921 Anatole France was awarded the Nobel Prize for Literature, which made it improbable that the prize would be awarded to another Frenchman the following year: the next Frenchman to receive it was Proust's cousin Henri Bergson. Nevertheless, Proust was delighted at this time by the growing international interest in *Temps perdu*. 'All the English, American, Swiss newspapers are doing studies of the Duchesse de Guermantes,' he wrote in September: 'a course is being taught in Sweden, and conferences are being held in Holland and Switzerland.' German and Italian periodicals sought his permission to publish fragmentary extracts from *Sodome et Gomorrhe II*, and in November he was visited by Bernard Fay, who lectured on French literature at Columbia University and whose students had started writing theses on *Temps perdu*. Another American, Ellen FitzGerald, published a laudatory essay in *The Nation* of 7 December. 'The French,' she concluded, 'are unafraid of their emotions and are artists; they are unafraid of their vices and are moralists; they are unafraid of their ideas and are real intellectuals. M. Proust in all three is French of the French.' Although, like most early American reviewers, FitzGerald avoided mentioning the Charlusiens, such plaudits delighted Proust. 'Your compatriots,' he told Walter Berry, 'are very kind to me and constantly request interviews about *Sodome et Gomorrhe*.' Berry's compatriots, though, were sometimes too tenacious in their attentiveness. During this same winter an American couple, who had come to Paris determined to pay homage to Proust, called almost daily at Rue Hamelin, where Céleste Albaret always told them that Monsieur Proust was too ill to receive visitors. The indefatigable but self-defeating duo sent Proust enormous sheaves of expensive winter roses, which caused him such violent sneezing fits that they were quickly thrown away. After Montesquiou's death in December, hearing that American editors paid generously, Proust considered writing an 'anecdotal, high-society' memoir of his friend to satisfy the American public's supposed avidity for tales of the French nobility. This project was discarded; but he soon realised that Montesquiou's death permitted him to 'enrich' his portrayal of Charlus, and to enlarge on his traits, in the remaining volumes of *Temps perdu*.

On New Year's Eve Proust attended a lavish celebration given by the art connoisseur Comte Étienne de Beaumont: 'He amuses me,' Proust told Céleste Albaret, 'but he is one of those men who borrow what little wit they have from those around them.' He sent Beaumont a message beforehand: 'from fear of being unable otherwise to come to you I have taken drugs in such profusion that it will be a man half-aphasic and especially wobbly on his legs, from vertigo, that you behold.' He asked two favours of Beaumont: to be given a cup of scalding tea on arrival; and 'not to be introduced to too many wearisome intellectual ladies'. On the night of the 31st Céleste Albaret telephoned the Beaumonts ten times before Proust's arrival to check that the scalding tea was prepared and that there were no draughts. There was a stir among the Beaumonts' guests when he finally arrived, at precisely midnight, his face looking pallid and puffy. 'Look at him,' said Picasso, 'he's in his element', as Proust toured the party talking to no one except dukes. The painter Jean Hugo, who had last seen Proust in 1917, was taken over to speak to him. 'Proust turned away for a moment from the duke to whom he was talking,' recalled Hugo, and exchanged a few commonplaces about the prettiness of country living, before turning back and resuming his attentions to the duke.

The next day he was sent an affectionate, solicitous letter by Jacques Rivière hoping that 'this new year will see the culmination of your admirable work and a decisive improvement in your health'. In fact, the coming year was to be dominated by Proust's fight to finish his work before a final, fatal collapse of health. By January 1922 he was convinced that he was dying. He complained of 'infinite mental distress combined with physical suffering. It's useless for the doctors to be clever . . . because my awful clairvoyance sees right through their contradictions and deprives me of any hope. How unfortunate that doctors must be conscientious and that instead of "treat me" you cannot say to them "kill me" since they are unable to cure you.' Despite dosing himself with a combination of the barbiturate soporific Veronal and the hypnotic sedatives Dial and Luminal, he claimed in mid-March that he had not 'slept a minute for six days'. He was so fearful of contamination that he had his morning post steamed in disinfectant. When asthma attacks prevented him from talking, he communicated with Céleste Albaret by scrawled messages on small, square pieces of paper. His nerves were tautened by his doubts about the honesty of his publisher Gallimard and his recurrent alarm that the printer would ruin *Sodome et Gomorrhe II*. Notwithstanding Proust's premonitions of death and his self-starvation (the staple of his diet at this time was *café au lait*), he ventured out one evening in January to a ball at the Ritz, where unusually he ate some lamb; and soon afterwards he went to the eighteenth-birthday celebration of his niece Suzy and to parties given by Jacques Porel and Princesse Soutzo. On 27 February he again visited the Ritz, and in March he attended a soirée given by Comtesse Joachim Murat. These rationed but vital contacts with Paris life sustained his exterior interests as, throughout early 1922, he worked with relentless fury on the third and fourth volumes of *Sodome et Gomorrhe*: volumes ultimately published as *La Prisonnière* – a title devised in mid-May – and *Albertine disparue*.

Erudition, the sedentary life of libraries, museums and lecture-halls, time spent browsing in bookshops and bookstalls on the *quais* were supremely valued in Paris. The zestful respect accorded to all affairs of the intellect was splendidly manifest in the fashionable furore over Relativity that was erupting in Paris as Proust toiled with frantic, distraught ferocity. French academicians had boycotted their German counterparts for eight years; but Albert Einstein, heartened by the success of a tour in the USA, had agreed to visit Paris in an attempt to restore scholarly contacts between the two countries. Initially there were fears of chauvinist demonstrations. While Einstein was travelling south by train, on 28 March, the French police warned that a hostile group of nationalist students were waiting to mob him at the Gare du Nord. In fact the students were admirers, but he alighted at a suburban station, and was driven discreetly away. His first lecture, on 31 March, in the Collège de France, was tightly policed: only ticket-holders were admitted, and Paul Painlevé, who had been wartime Minister of War, was among the stewards who excluded hostile demonstrators. Einstein's fluent, attractively-accented French, and pensive, confidential manner ensured that he became the darling of the Paris press. 'Everyone had the impression of being in the presence of a sublime genius,' reported *L'Humanité*. 'As we saw Einstein's noble face and heard his slow, soft speech, it seemed as if the purest and most subtle thought was unfolding before us. A noble shudder shook us and raised us above the mediocrity and stubbornness of everyday life.' English observers were sardonic about the Relativity craze sweeping Paris: 'The visit of M. Einstein to Paris has given the *précieuses ridicules* a new battle-cry. "Relativity" is the word with which they conjure at their tea parties, and as they flocked to M. Einstein's conferences, so now they invite their friends to hear other lecturers develop his theories, in the abstruseness of which they appear to delight.' Parisians were inveterate in their pursuit of intellectual distractions. 'The fashionable woman and the busy middle-class housewife, as well as the student, attend with regularity the lectures at the Sorbonne and other centres of learning. They find pleasure in intellectual pursuits and bring intellect to bear on what are known as amusements.'

The names of Einstein and Proust were often coupled together in 1922. It was a joke between Wyndham Lewis and Sydney Schiff to refer to Proust as Einstein even before the mathematician and literary critic Camille Vettard published his article 'Proust et Einstein' in the *Nouvelle Revue Française* of 1 August. 'Your magnificent article,' Proust told Vettard, 'is the greatest honour that I could possibly receive', for he relished being compared to the German physicist, and was pleased to be told that he, his cousin Bergson and Einstein had independently of one another discovered the essence of Time. Proust hankered to understand Relativity. 'How I should like to talk to you about Einstein!' he exclaimed to his scientifically-informed friend Armand de Guiche. 'They may write that I derive from him, or he from me, but I don't understand a single word of his theories, as I do not know algebra. I doubt that for his part he has read my novels. We have, though, it seems, a similar way of distorting Time.'

Einstein's visit was punctuated by tension, racial prejudice and touching gestures of French breeding and sensibility. Although thirty members of the French Academy declared that if he was invited to participate in a session, they would leave the room at the moment he entered, when Einstein visited the battlefields of Northern France, and lunched in a restaurant at Rheims, two senior French army officers, who were seated nearby, recognised him, stood and bowed. Overall, so the German Embassy in Paris reported on 29 April, 'Einstein created a personal sensation – one on which the intellectual snobbery of the capital certainly did not want to miss out.' Best of all, the Théâtre des Champs-Élysées, emboldened by Einstein's success, and by the ebbing of anti-German sentiment, on 19 May announced the first post-war season of Wagner. Proust, the old Dreyfusard, welcomed these rebuffs to French chauvinism. In an article published at this time in the *Nouvelle Revue Française*, he praised Wagner's genius, extolled *Tristan* and *Die Meistersinger* as masterpieces and deplored the intrusion of angry nationalism into matters of aesthetics and philosophy.

It was just before – or during – the publicity storm of Einstein's visit to Paris that a great moment happened quietly at 44 Rue Hamelin. One spring afternoon Proust called Céleste Albaret to his room. She found him in an exultant, mysterious mood. 'A great thing happened during the night,' he told her. 'It is great news. Last night I wrote the word "Fin". Now I can die.' There were innumerable additions and emendations to be made – almost to Proust's final breaths – but his novel's structure was in place. For Proustians the victorious pride of the exhausted novelist, coupled with the privileged confidences received by his servant-woman, created an emotive, momentous scene: Proust

and Céleste, at that moment, both represented a vocation fulfilled; and 'The End' represented the apogee of a heroic creative
commitment. It was Sydney Schiff who gave the first published
version of this incident in his pen-portrait, 'Céleste', published
in 1924 in T. S. Eliot's periodical the *Criterion*. 'Then, suddenly,
one afternoon, "Look, Céleste," he said, holding up the green
copy-book: FIN.'

CHAPTER 8

Rich Amateurs

Violet and Sydney Schiff oozed through Proust's life during the
early summer of 1922 like pigment colouring a fabric. For two
months they seemed to commandeer his social energies.
Although he kept his address at 44 Rue Hamelin 'quasi-confidential', he told Elisabeth de Clermont-Tonnerre, to deter visitors, he nevertheless had repeated rendezvous with the Schiffs
from April to June 1922 – almost to the exclusion of others.
When Geneviève Straus, 'the only person,' Céleste Albaret
thought, 'for whom he kept, right up to his death, the sort of
affection and admiration that's closest to friendship,' sent him a
delicate, touching letter early in May 1922, hinting that they
should arrange a final meeting before one of them died, he did
not make time for her. All his generosity with his most precious
asset, time, was lavished on the Schiffs. It was a privilege that
they worked hard to obtain and for which (once he was dead)
they both felt a lifetime of gratitude. In a self-serving memoir
published in 1924, Schiff suggested that Proust's meetings with
Violet and himself had re-invigorated the ailing novelist: 'they
were the best friends for him now, because they were the newest
ones. There was no old experience, happy or the reverse, associated with them.' Actually they were too possessive: Proust felt
'weary' because they behaved like monopolists, and Céleste

Albaret thought they were egotistical in their demands. As Proust wrote in July 1922, reproaching Sydney for yet another claim for special attention, during the period that he had seen the Schiffs 'exclusively' he had received 'fifty or more telegrams' from Prince Antoine Bibesco, who was visiting Paris on furlough from his diplomatic posting at Washington DC, all asking '"Could you dine with us here tonight or wherever you like with whomever you like?" and I didn't go once.' For their part, the Schiffs talked Proust, thought Proust and planned for Proust during the last eighteen months of his life, and after 1922 they talked, thought and lauded him for the rest of their days.

In London, between the wars, the Schiffs were known as gracious if persistent lionisers; but in Paris their fixation with Proust became obsessive, raw and unveneered. It is too extreme to say that Sydney Schiff's obsession with Proust resembled, at times, that of Marcel for Albertine or Swann for Odette de Crécy. The better, if less dignified, parallel is with another Jewish financier, Nissim Bernard, who in a jokey interlude in *Sodome et Gomorrhe* falls for one of a pair of identical twin brothers, ruddy farm-boys with heads like tomatoes. 'Tomato No. 2,' says Proust, 'took frenetic pleasure in giving delight exclusively to the ladies, Tomato No. 1 was nothing loath to condescend to the tastes of certain gentlemen.' But because Bernard cannot tell them apart, he keeps propositioning the wrong brother and receiving indignant thrashings; and in time develops an aversion to tomatoes, about which he pesters strangers in restaurants. Sydney Schiff adored Proust, and desired that each of them should be at the centre of the other's life; but he often made the wrong approach, like Nissim Bernard mistaking recalcitrant Tomato No. 2 for compliant Tomato No. 1, and duly got his punishment. The Schiffs' pursuit of Proust was not the common enough tale of social-climbers hunting a literary lion or cornering a beleaguered celebrity. Proust was an active participant in the trio's relations. He was Tomato No. 1 who welcomed, indeed courted, Nissim Bernard's overtures. Any account of him is incomplete if it does not stress that he needed and desired the Schiffs' slavish devotion. It is what he had craved as a boy from Madame Proust, as a young man from Reynaldo Hahn, in early middle age from Agostinelli; and cannot have expected to receive at the end from a pair of rich avant-garde hypochondriacs living in a square in Bayswater.

The Schiffs were demanding, but they offered Proust their servitude. Their marriage, indeed, was dedicated to honouring and serving the creative élite. Sydney Schiff was rich and privileged, but had lived in a temper of frustrated discontent until, in middle age, he found fulfilment in a contented second marriage. In an atmosphere of ostentatious marital devotion, he launched himself as an experimental novelist, became a patron of painters, sculptors, authors and musicians, and hosted a salon where creative schemes were hatched, literary magazines projected and reputations bolstered. The Schiffs' gift for friendship was evident in the intellectual sympathy, emotional succour and practical support that they gave T. S. Eliot. The first letter of congratulation received by him after publishing *The Waste Land* was from Schiff, who acted as his intermediary with Proust. Eliot called Violet his 'beloved friend'. His enduring, affectionate gratitude belies the late twentieth-century depictions of him as an implacable anti-Semite. The Schiffs protected or helped other talents, including Frederick Delius and the Futurist Emilio Marinetti, who addressed Schiff as '*Mon très cher ami*' just as the singer Paolo Tosti addressed Violet as '*Amica carissima*'.

Edith Sitwell told 'Dearest Sydney' that she counted Violet and him as 'among my dearest and best friends'. Katherine Mansfield wrote to Violet in 1921: 'I love you and Sydney deeply, warmly, and I always wish you happiness and freedom from all those things that interfere with your beautiful *understanding* of Life.' Even misanthropic Richard Aldington was moved to write: 'I don't know how to acknowledge your sweetness and generosity properly. They always leave me surprised and rather dumbfounded.'

Sydney Schiff disarmed people with his sympathetic, even obsequious attention but could tire them with his own clamorous need of admiration. He was a perceptive reader, a shrewd if sometimes laborious critic, with an earnest desire to help creative processes, but he was vain, and craved the gratitude, trust and respect of fellow authors: his correspondence with them was intended to impose and enforce intimate personal affinities. Sacheverell Sitwell was irrepressibly touched by one of Schiff's typically careful letters: 'its sympathy and understanding seem to mark an important stage in my life and I must frankly tell you that I was moved to tears on reading it.' Schiff's advice to literary friends about their work in progress was apt and flattering. The poet Edwin Muir burst with gratitude for the 'heartening letters' sent by Schiff. 'I have been walking on air! Your suggestions are all just.' Schiff's need to be ingratiating led him into half-truths or insincerity. The congratulations he sent to Middleton Murry for his Proust essay made Murry's wife Katherine Mansfield fulsome in her thanks. 'There is a moment which is the perfect moment,' she responded. 'One of those moments marvellously realised, marvellously fulfilled was when you wrote to Murry. He *needed* your letter and you gave it to him . . . the simple truth is, Sydney, that your comprehension and your generosity are beautiful. One loves you for your gifts.' Yet Schiff described Murry to Proust as 'a gifted man, without convictions or principles, a mediocre poet, more or less learned, superficial, not over sincere, a man who reacts always to his passing emotions'. It is not surprising that the Schiffs failed to attract universally. Ezra Pound, for one, was relieved to have avoided them during their visit to Paris in 1922.

Schiff's messages to Proust were effusive or even idolatrous, usually self-centred, and intermittently rambling or tactless; but they impressed their recipient as if they were rare *objets d'art* crafted from the crooked timber of humanity. 'Your letters,' Proust wrote gratefully in 1921, 'are filled with more faces than a museum and more human beings than a town.' Although Schiff buttered his compliments to Proust, there is no reason to believe he was insincere: 'marvellously true like all you say,' he trilled after reading a pre-publication extract from *Sodome et Gomorrhe II* printed in the *Nouvelle Revue Française* of December 1921. 'Your books are inexhaustible mines: I find in them an inde-scribable solace.'

Although Schiff and Proust had many temperamental affini-ties, the Londoner's antecedents were more cosmopolitan and prosperous than the Parisian's. His Frankfurt-born grandfather Leopold Schiff had been a banker in Trieste, that teeming poly-glot port of the Austro-Hungarian Empire where James Joyce settled in 1904 as a language teacher: its dialect Triestino mar-vellously enriched the vocabulary of *Ulysses*. In 1860, after Leopold's death, the eldest of his three sons, Alfred, then aged twenty, shifted to London, where he subsequently became a stockbroker in partnership with his brother Ernest. Despite their studied imitation of English manners and gestures, Alfred and Ernest Schiff exuded cosmopolitanism and regarded all of Europe as an undifferentiated realm of operations. Like all good Triestines, they were fluent in several languages: although based in London, their financial connections in Trieste, Vienna and Bonn were extensive and ramified. Sydney Schiff wrote that his father, although 'generally considered a very rich man . . . was rather a man who made a great deal of money.' Alfred was a compulsive gambler who played for high stakes and chased his losses. This destructive habit gained on him during the 1890s when his wife's failing health forced him to spend several months of each year at their Riviera villa. He sometimes visited the casino in Monte Carlo three times daily: before lunch, before dinner and again in the late evening until the tables closed. Sydney Schiff felt that worry over the gambling short-ened his mother's life: 'no one can stand it,' he wrote, 'that sort of thing kills in the end.' Certainly, at Alfred Schiff's funeral in Brookwood cemetery, his ship-owner client Lord Furness declared that he would have lived ten years longer and have left another quarter of a million if he hadn't liked the tables too much.

Alfred Schiff became involved during the 1860s with Caro-line Mary Ann Eliza Scales. At the age of about seventeen, in 1861, she had married John Scott Cavell, but they had separated two years later when she became pregnant by another man: the child, Louise, later married Sir Sidney Alexander. In 1865 the disgraced Mrs Cavell met Alfred Schiff who provided her with a discreet villa at Putney. She again became pregnant while her husband was seeking a divorce in which he cited Alfred Schiff as co-respondent. The legal quandaries caused by these illicit

intrigues were such that the birth of her second child, Sydney
Alfred Schiff, was never registered: the boy was later assured that
he had been born in London on 12 December 1868. Only after
the Cavells' divorce was finalised in 1869 were the lovers finally
able to marry. Subsequently a second son, Ernest, and then
three sisters, Edith, Rose and Marie, were born to the family,
who lived in opulence at 30 de Vere Gardens, Kensington until
the 1880s and then at 40 Upper Brook Street in Mayfair. Mrs
Schiff was a woman of daunting beauty who suffused her surroundings with an air of luxury: in time she took further lovers
while her husband kept mistresses in separate establishments.

Sydney Schiff's first marriage was equally louche in origins
and development. As a young man, while touring in America,
he met Marion Fulton Canine, a dentist's daughter from
Louisville, Kentucky. She set out to catch him for his fortune,
allowed herself to be seduced, worked on his lust and guilt, and
hustled him into an elopement. Eventually, in August 1889, they
married in Algoma, Ontario, after lying about their ages. Marion Schiff soon proved to be a grasping, shrewish, jealous yet
adulterous wife. Her busy social life during their twenty years of
marriage was, by his account, insincere, sybaritic, snobbish and
predatory; and his own seemed banal, passive, ineffectual and
useless. The young Schiffs wasted years touring European
resorts where he collected works of art and she collected male
admirers. After his mother's death in 1896, his father established
them in a villa with several acres of mountainside and foreshore
on Lake Como. He and his wife fastidiously restored and sump-
tuously furnished the dilapidated house, and created wonderful
grounds; yet Sydney Schiff was almost metabolically dissatisfied, and his pleasure in the villa was transient.

By the death of his father in 1908 Schiff became independently rich: with money of his own he found the confidence to live separately from his wife. One evening in 1909, accompanying his sister Edith to a performance of *La Bohème* at Covent Garden, he met her friend Sybil Seligman, who kept a musical salon and had fallen in love with Puccini five years earlier. In the box with Mrs Seligman was her equally musical spinster sister Violet Beddington (1875–1962), who had been taught to sing by Paolo Tosti. From the outset he adored 'her courage, her determination, her unusual maleness of character' and her 'exceedingly human, sweet and lovable disposition'. In contrast to his irritable, bullying wife, who was 'one great lump of *Schadenfreude*', Violet 'was gay and light-hearted, frivolous even, enjoyed Life and loved others to enjoy it'. Proust's description of his ideal woman – 'a woman of genius who leads a private life' – is an apt summary of Violet. She was determined, even dominant, with a playful sense of humour and a rich woman's caprices. *L'Ange Violet*, the 'Angel Violet', Proust called her, and indeed she had a Proustian preciousness. 'The most essential thing is to preserve your own atmosphere, whomever you associate with, and on no account allow it to be diluted or swamped,' she wrote. 'Your own personal individual world is your uniqueness and your power, and others gain by coming into it and you lose by leaving it for theirs.'

Marion Schiff was induced by the offer of a generous settlement to sue for divorce in 1910, and received her decree absolute on 8 May 1911. Two days later Sydney Schiff and Violet Beddington were married. Immediately, with her encouragement, he began his transformation into a virtuoso of the arts. He attuned himself to the most daring creative innovators of the epoch: big names crowded into his house and into his life. He sought out Epstein, Guadier-Brzeska, Rosenberg and Bomberg. He bought paintings by Picasso, de Chirico, Wyndham Lewis and Mark Gertler. It was in the Schiffs' London house that Marinetti tried to convert English painters and poets to Futurism while another Italian guest, the great Italian tenor Enrico Caruso, put on a false nose and threw himself on the floor under the piano to tease Marinetti's earnestness.

Whereas Marion Schiff had derided her husband's literary tastes, Violet fostered them; and never more decisively than in 1915 when she introduced him to Proust's novel in the French original. '*Du côté de chez Swann* was a chance discovery,' Sydney wrote. 'Her enthusiasm for it was kindled from the first line she read, and so far from waning when she finished it, the book grew into the fabric of her being.' His reaction when she first recommended Proust as 'my newest and best friend' seems to have been, 'Damn Proust. What's the good of Proust with the world in this state? Proust belongs to the past.' Initially *Swann* seemed to him a long, meandering and inconclusive novel; but ultimately his life was transformed by it. 'Once Proust got you, there was no escape from him and his interminable discourse,' he later wrote. 'Here was an end, once and for all, to plot and pretence and subterfuge. Hereafter, for the finer minds, there could be no return to the pseudo-realism of the past. This amazing conversationalist had given a new impetus to psychological research and, by exposing the hollowness of a culture which rested upon social attitudes, had given a new twist to history.' Schiff found it 'difficult to believe that any pure-bred Frenchman could have evolved a style so exotic and anti-classical, still more that he would have selected a typical cosmopolitan Jew as one of the principal personages of a novel in which all the social values of pre-war France are reviewed and assessed.' The Jewish sensibility that Sydney Schiff felt he detected in *Temps perdu* fired his enthusiasm; and Proust's susceptibility to the Schiffs reflected his philo-Semitism which derived from his veneration of his mother. Violet Schiff convinced her young cavalier Julian Fane that she resembled old Madame Proust while her husband suggested that her facial expressions were similar to Proust's and imagined her being described by Proust as 'our kind'.

The Schiffs' pose as the earliest committed English Proustians was spurious. Henri Bernstein, the French playwright who appears in Sydney's novel about Violet, *Myrtle* (1925), as her suitor Bloch, recommended *Du côté de chez Swann* in 1913 to the London drama critic A. B. Walkley, who thereupon procured a copy and converted himself into an ardent devotee. Schiff was jealous of the pretensions of that 'idiot Walkley' as a Proustian: 'he is an old journalist who for many long years has written banal and boring articles on the theatre,' he advised Proust. 'He has no literary status. George Bernard Shaw has written several lampoons about him.' Princesse Edmond de Polignac, who like Bernstein read *Swann* on its publication in 1913, also promoted the Proustian cult in London. In August 1914, as Europe's armies mobilised, she dined at Lady Randolph Churchill's house in Brook Street and enthused about Proust to the man-of-letters Edward Marsh, to whom she lent her copy of *Swann*. Although the princess was probably invited by Diaghilev to the Schiffs' Ballets Russes supper at the Majestic, her early support of Proust in London may have been resented by them just as they resented Walkley: Sydney once annoyed Proust by saying he found the princess tedious. Her dinner companion Eddie

Marsh became another pioneering English Proustian, and like Schiff later advised Charles Scott Moncrieff in his translation of *Temps perdu* into English.

As part of the revitalisation of his aesthetics by Proust, Schiff became part owner of an illustrated quarterly magazine, *Art and Letters* (of which the art critic Herbert Read and poet Osbert Sitwell were co-editors). He contributed an essay on Proust to the magazine as well as a ponderous imaginary conversation between Lenin, Trotsky and Kerensky. This appeared in the summer 1919 issue which also included the first publication of Eliot's 'Burbank with a Baedeker' and 'Sweeney Erect' as well as Firbank's 'Fantasia in F Sharp Minor'. Despite the magazine's quality and modernity, Schiff became bored with his responsibilities, and in 1920 (the year of its closure) told Katherine Mansfield that *Art and Letters* was a 'beastly little rag'. Next Schiff funded Wyndham Lewis's magazine *The Tyro*, and then helped to revive *Art and Letters* with Lady Rothermere's money. The magazine resumed publication in 1922 under a new name, the *Criterion*, and with a new editor, T. S. Eliot. Schiff was an early contributor under his *nom de plume* Stephen Hudson.

Several early London Proustians were members of the Schiffs' coterie, and one can trace in Sydney Schiff's correspondence his efforts to initiate fellow writers into Proustian marvels. He discussed Proust's novel with them, and encouraged their public affirmation of Proust's genius. Like a huckster handing out free samples, he sent Proust's volumes to Stella Benson in China. 'Proust really was an angel of understanding,' she replied from her husband's outpost in Yunnan. 'Everything human and spontaneous was worthwhile to him, everything, as long as it was true.' Zeal in the Proustian crusade was always rewarded by the Schiffs. Richard Aldington was recruited as one of their pet writers after publishing in 1921 an essay that proved formative of Proust's English reputation. Aldington was writing when several volumes of Proust's novel had yet to be completed – *Guermantes* was the latest part of the sequence to be entirely available to him – and this coloured his sense of the novelist as a social historian. 'The complicated but perfectly controlled knowledge, the enthusiasm for a "situation" which Saint-Simon put into the discussion of some problem of precedence, some Court manoeuvre, are devoted by M. Proust to the modern interests of psychological analysis, a nuance of sentiment, a delicate relationship, an appreciation of some fine distinction.'

Schiff admired the 'elemental truthfulness' of *Temps perdu* and was puzzled by Edmund Gosse's complaint that Proust's subject matter was 'infinitely insignificant'. He prized the fact that dazzling flashes of insight and rapturous moments of discovery occur in Proust's world as the result of chance occurrences and sudden associations, such as the narrator dipping his biscuit in tea or Charlus visiting Madame de Villeparisis at an unwonted time and discovering Jupien. 'He possessed,' wrote Schiff, 'that rarest gift of touching everyday people, things and concerns with gold, imparting to them a vital and abiding interest. Anything and everything served as a starting point, nothing was too minute to kindle an idea.' *Temps perdu* convinced Schiff that it was in the aimless acts and inconsequent remarks of negligible people that the real human truths were to be found. Excited by Proust's ideas and techniques, Schiff (under his Hudson pseudonym) published a sequence of autobiographical novels centred on a single character, Richard Kurt. The vision of life offered in these books was based on a sense that mundane incidents, acts and impulses have irrevocable consequences. The banality of Hudson's fiction was purposive and carefully constructed, but for many readers it has proved dreary, and the books never achieved more than a recondite readership. The trouble is that the detail can seem too realistic for the books to be credible as novels. 'He says,' Stella Benson reported after a long talk in 1925, 'that out of a hundred thousand words he destroys about sixty thousand – and that very often good work, only not in the direct path to the narrow goal he has set himself. He says he doesn't get any joy out of writing. I cannot feel that he is a very real artist – if he is, it is in some way that is antipathetic to me.' The first of the Hudson sequence to be published, *Richard Kurt* (1919), was dedicated, enigmatically, 'To M. P'. A decade later Scott Moncrieff dedicated the English translation of *Sodome et Gomorrhe* 'To Richard and Myrtle Kurt and Their Creator.'

In the third Hudson novel, *Prince Hempseed* (1922), which was dedicated to Proust's memory, Schiff recreated his own childhood in that of his alter ego Richard Kurt. Several scenes seem saturated with Proustian feeling: Schiff even vied with the great traumatic moment in *Swann* when the narrator is sent to bed without his mother's customary goodnight kiss. Having absconded from school, Richard Kurt is returned in disgrace by his father, who insists on visiting his son's boarding-house cubicle.

When we got there, he took darling mamma's picture off the bracket in the middle of the partition over my bed and said, 'When you prove that you deserve such a mother, you shall have it back.' It was a lovely hand-painted photograph she had given me in a black ebony carved frame, in a ball dress, standing up. Pater knew how I loved that picture. I

asked him to take the big photo of the phaeton and cobs
with mother sitting with the reins in her hand and Frank
standing at their head instead but he wouldn't do that. Then
I said there was one thing he could do anyhow and when he
asked what that was I said 'Go away and never let me see
your face again.' He said 'You'll be sorry you said that one
day.' But I haven't been sorry yet.

It was on the basis of such passages that Thomas Mann wrote in
1926 that *Prince Hempseed* was 'without doubt one of the best,
truest and freshest boy stories in all English literature, and that
means a great deal, because England is the classical land of the
Boy, and has the best Boys' stories of the world.'

The Schiffs' cultivation of Proust was run in tandem with
their nurturing of Katherine Mansfield. The young New
Zealand writer first met them in April 1920, while she was
enduring an invalid's life at Menton and they, with 'their Gauguins and Picassos', were occupying Villa Violet at Roquebrune.
Their friendship quickly soared to a high level of emotional
intensity. Sydney Schiff had recovered years earlier from mild
tuberculosis: Mansfield was dying, slowly but visibly, of the
same disease. 'You're such a lovely little thing I want to cry,' Violet told her in the first days of their acquaintance. Within a few
weeks Mansfield was writing to Middleton Murry:

Mr Schiff is a kind of literary fairy godfather to me. He
looks after me so perfectly and so gently & Violet Schiff
seemed to me the last time far more beautiful and more fascinating than before. She will *fascinate* you – the movement
of her lips, her eyes, her colour, all her beauty. And their
house is always for me the house where *lovers* dwell. He

loves her perfectly. And her quick 'darling' and hand out-
stretched . . . They are so real & dear & beautiful to me and
they understand one's work.

Sydney was soon urging Mansfield to read Proust, and was
delighted by Murry's essay on Proust published in 1921. 'We
lived Proust, breathed him, talked and thought of little else for
two weeks,' Mansfield told Schiff. 'The marvel is that those
books go on breathing after you have put them away; one is
never at an end with them. But they spoil one – they spoil one
fearfully for other things.' Mansfield's involvement with the
Schiffs was punctuated by suppressed irritation and phases of
seething distaste: at times she became like Tomato No 2, and
struck out at them – so much so that Violet withheld clearance
for the publication of disparaging references to her in an edition
of Mansfield's *Letters to John Middleton Murry* of 1951.

Both Schiffs, but Sydney especially, could be tactless or self-
obsessed. Typically, at a meeting with Valéry Larbaud, he made
a bad start by declaring that he was 'too tired to speak in
French'. Larbaud, who was altogether offended by his manner,
reported that he received Schiff's 'compliments with excessive
coldness, and neglected to ask on what he was working, and . . .
let him lead the conversation.' Larbaud sensed that Schiff was 'a
littérateur of the same type as myself, that's to say a "rich amateur", and who like me . . . has never been *compelled* to work,
has never written anything except for his pleasure, repelling all
projects that don't seem to offer him the intensity of an ardent
love affair.' Larbaud cited Proust, Gide and himself as examples
of rich amateurs 'who were told in childhood by their family
servants, "With all the money you are going to have, you won't

need to work". And that prospect, which can be so dangerous and which without doubt is fatal in the majority of cases, has been for us a blessing. Our response, "Yes, I'm a rich kid, I work for the satisfaction of it", was our first coherent affirmation of our vocation.' Rich amateurs, Larbaud believed, were privileged with 'a larger vision, a broader horizon, a carelessness about future prospects, the habit of preferring pleasure to material gain, choosing a life freedom on limited resources to the social servitude of affluence.' He and Schiff shared an identical 'superiority complex', derived from their privileged background, but he did not like the Englishman.

It was very different with that other rich amateur, Proust. By the summer of 1919, within a few months of their first meeting at the Ritz, he was on confidential terms with Violet Schiff, and praising her for being 'marvellously well versed in French literature'. His epistolary friendship with her husband flourished in affectionate intimacy. '*Cher Monsieur* (do we add "*et Ami*"?) ,' he began a letter of 1920. '"Friend" would be both pleasant and true.' His gratitude for Schiff's most recent letter was fulsome: 'it enchants me, shocks me . . . enchants me because of the gallery of portraits you draw, which is splendid, and also for your profound views on humanity, so savoury and so sharp . . . Your remarks on people in general, their boringness, makes me die laughing. They are so like me!' Schiff was always shameless in soliciting compliments, reassurance and promises of fidelity: on this occasion Proust obliged. 'How could you have thought I didn't like you right away? There is no one else I should have taken so much trouble to see as I did during your Paris visit.' As to the Angel Violet, 'I adore the enchanting tenderness with which you refer to her.' From early in the friendship, one suspects, the Schiffs yearned to be immortalised as characters in their favourite novel. Lionel Kein, Wyndham Lewis's spiteful version of Sydney Schiff in *Apes of God*, is asked if he would have liked to have been one of the prominent social figures whom Proust used as models for his protagonists – however disobliging or unceremonious the characterisation. 'I should consider it *well worth the privilege*,' Kein replies with a 'deep tremolo of emotion' and Schiff's abject sham-humility, 'of having known Proust to be treated in *any* way by him that he thought fit.'

It is hard to tell if Sydney Schiff emulated his idol or if they shared long-entrenched tendencies. They both had, for example, an intrusive, apparently undiscriminating inquisitiveness about other people's personal details. 'Marcel Proust revelled in the private lives of people he scarcely knew or didn't know at all, but when he spoke of them he was more vivid than reality,' Elizabeth de Clermont-Tonnerre noted. An illustration of his avidity for gratuitous but minute details occurs in Harold Nicolson's account of his first meeting with Proust at a dinner given by Princesse Soutzo at the Ritz in 1919. Proust quizzed Nicolson about his diplomatic duties at the Peace Conference. Nicolson started to explain that the negotiating sub-committees convened at ten in the morning, but was interrupted by Proust. 'But no, but no, you are going too fast. Start again. You take your official car. You alight at the Quai d'Orsay. You climb the stairs. You enter the conference room. And then? Tell me precisely, my dear sir, precisely.' So Nicolson supplied every detail: 'the sham cordiality of it all: the handshakes: the maps: the rustle of papers: the tea in the next room: the macaroons'. Proust was enthralled yet still interrupted. 'But be precise, my dear sir, don't go too fast.' The Schiffs, as representatives of the easily bored rich, thrived on this fast, urgent, insatiable appetite for pointless details, which 'Stephen Hudson' likened to the brilliant naïveté of a child prodigy. Proust, so Hudson-Schiff wrote in 1923, 'was penetrated with boyish eagerness and curiosity, asked endless questions, always wanted to know more. What had you heard, what did you think, what did they say or do, whatever *it* was and whoever *they* were. And there was no denying him this or anything he wanted; he always must have his way – he always did have it until the end of his life.' This Proustian trait became so pronounced in Sydney Schiff as to irritate others. At a dinner party in 1925 Stella Benson found him importunate and inquisitive (as well as – like Proust – a fussy eater). He 'must have all details about everything – I don't know what he does with such information as he demands about the temperament of my brother George, the upbringing of my husband, etc, etc. He says Good – good – at certain details, as though he felt he was getting somewhere.'

Testy self-pity was another trait shared by Proust and Schiff. 'You tell me,' the Frenchman had once retorted to his mother, who thought he was dramatising minor worries, 'that there are people who have as many problems as me but have to work to support their families.' But, he insisted, a professional or working man 'having problems, even much bigger problems, infinitely greater problems, doesn't necessarily signify the same amount of suffering' as an author might experience: 'literary work makes perpetual calls on those feelings most connected with suffering.' Twenty years later, in 1922, Schiff recounted to Proust that he had written to his sister Edith Gautier-Vignal begging her to ask her stepson Louis, Proust's nocturnal companion in the war years, if he could recommend 'a young friend

. . . who could serve us, so to say, as a sort of guide in Paris'. His sister had replied with brisk callousness that Louis Gautier-Vignal had no such friend. 'She is content that I have no one to help and inform me,' Schiff complained, 'and when I told her that I'm suffering a lot from my nerves, she told me that I take myself too seriously and that I would feel better if I played golf or went dancing – treatment, I suppose, to cure me from being different from her. Isn't it curious to encounter in precisely the people closest to one the least sympathy and understanding?' Neurasthenia was one of Schiff's preferred devices for claiming Proust's trust: ragged nerves, he felt, were an enticement. 'I am a nervous, moody creature but I understand the nerves of others,' he told Proust in 1919, when he was soliciting a contribution for *Art and Letters*.

Both Schiffs were sympathetic to Proust's erotic imagination. Violet felt 'sorry about his homosexuality for his sake, because it caused him much suffering, as . . . it was always bound to'; but was not dismayed. Her redoubtable novelist sister, Ada Leverson, nicknamed 'The Sphinx', had long before proven a steadfast friend to Oscar Wilde after his arrest; Sydney Schiff, too, had openly taken up cudgels on behalf of Wilde during the trials of 1895, and always tried to be ingratiating or confiding when alluding to these subjects to the author of *Sodome et Gomorrhe*. 'Mon cher,' he wrote to Proust on 30 April 1922, from the Villa Majestic,

> Ali, my valet, being homosexual, everyone here has concluded that I am an invert. And it's just the opposite. Being excessively masculine, masculine to such an extent that I can't bear to be shaved, scarcely even to have my hair arranged, by a man, I don't like to have any man near to me.

Ali, who is like a young girl, is exactly what suits me. Only he imitates me too much. I've told him that he should copy those of my mannerisms that derive from my intelligence, not those that result from my temperament. I told him, for example, that he should cultivate feline, suave and steady gestures in contrast to nervous, abrupt, jerky motions . . . Violet has delicious gestures.

During Ali's appearance as a minor character called Hassan in *Apes of God* Wyndham Lewis attributed to him 'feminine haunches', 'a limp hand', 'red lips', 'eyes of great traditional feminine docility', 'fans of lashes', a 'tripping fairy-footfall' and a lisp 'in the grating deep cockney of the levantine ghetto' – epithets that bore the usual pejorative tone of inter-war fiction. With some courage, Schiff in his novels was more subtle. Emboldened, perhaps, by Proust's example, but also keen to display his easy acceptance of homosexuality, he included a congenial Sodomite among the characters in what was arguably his most successful novel, *Tony* (although Schiff thought it a failure). *Tony* is narrated by a character based on Schiff's younger brother Ernest, 'the worst of profligates from the West End of London' as a real-life barrister called him, who had been killed in 1919 by a furious Cornish miner whose daughter he had seduced. In one passage Tony Kurt, who is a confirmed womaniser, meets a cheerful, cultivated Austrian who teaches music at a Capuchin monastery in Italy. 'I knew his sort the moment he came in and began speaking,' Tony says in his bluff way. 'I'm not down on them, I always rather like them. They're generally cleverer and more sympathetic and easier to get on with than other men, especially when they're foreigners.'

Schiff also tried to impress Proust with his friendship with Robert Kitson, an engineer whose family manufactured locomotives in Yorkshire but who had in 1903 settled at Casa Cuseni, a property near Taormina, commanding panoramic views of Mount Etna. 'Kitson has been my friend for twenty years,' Schiff wrote.

> Violet finds him insupportable. He's a man of 48, desiccated, formal, a homosexual of the type who likes little boys, terribly miserly. I met him at Taormina where he had a villa which he had built in a very beautiful garden which he had laid out and planted himself. He paints well in watercolours in the old style, that's to say by modifying and copying Nature living and dead. He is miserly but once, long ago, he lent me without security a very large sum of which I had an urgent need and never mentioned it again until the day I repaid him – a service which I have never forgotten. Besides, I like his sly, independent spirit because he is very conventional and bourgeois at heart, loving the young Prince of Wales and other handsome types.

By June 1922 Schiff was trying to gratify Proust with more broad-minded gossip: 'Kitson (the homosexual who lives in Sicily), who was again here today, flirted abominably with Ali, who, ever since, has been more stupid than ever and does nothing but irritate me.' Other manly confidences were at times extended by Schiff: '*Tutoyer* does not come to me easily. Formerly the tarts used to find it elegant that I called them *vous*.'

The Schiffs' determined incursion into Proust's life in 1922 began with a premonitory letter on 6 April. 'Recently I have suffered from nervous exhaustion, as I do periodically,' Schiff wrote to Proust. 'I can neither read nor write without a sustained effort nor take any decision whatsoever nor occupy myself with practical affairs.' As a result of this 'nervous irritability my adorable wife has repeatedly been obliged to submit to kaleidoscopic changes of plan. We are going, by turns every day, to the Riviera, to Paris, to the country.' He had prescribed himself a prolonged rest in bed; and as his nerves recovered, resolved to visit Paris for a month or six weeks: 'we will see you where, how and when you want. I have an immense desire, an urgent need, to see you.' Although meetings with Proust were the main purpose of Schiff's Paris visit of 1922, he also hoped to arrange for his novel *Elizabeth Colhouse* to be translated into French and for extracts of his work to be published by the *Nouvelle Revue Française*. Proust was enlisted to approach Jacques Rivière, who decided not to publish on the basis of a reader's report. When Schiff, always in need of reassurance, started fretting that Proust's opinion of him would be lowered by Rivière's rejection, Proust insisted that his publishers had indifferent judgement: 'There are some remarkable personalities at the *NRF*, but these are neutralised by the rest and make in totality a mediocre average.' Rivière's offer to find a competent French translator for several autobiographical Hudson stories assumed 'enormous importance' for Schiff, who felt that it was only through the medium of French translation that Proust could read his work with full comprehension and thus understand him. Proust was businesslike and realistic throughout these negotiations. Schiff's later recommendation of T. S. Eliot to him ('possibly our best critic and certainly our best poet') and Eliot's request for an extract from *Temps perdu* to publish in the *Criterion* made Proust feel wary if not oppressed by possible complications: 'this Eliot question is all mixed up with the more delicate Schiff question.'

The Schiffs reached Paris on 7 April, and were immediately pitched at distressing cross-purposes with Proust. 'Despite a high temperature,' Proust recounted, he took fortifying shots of the stimulant adrenalin 'so as to be able to get up and visit you at the Ritz, where you told me you were going to stay.' The Ritz, indeed, was the Schiffs' usual hotel in Paris; but on this occasion, they had taken rooms in the Villa Majestic, an annexe of the hotel set further back from the noise of Avenue Kléber. It can hardly be doubted that they chose this location because it was less than a minute's walk from Proust's apartment in Rue Hamelin, and that they cherished hopes that when they were in such close proximity to Proust, he would yield to sudden loving impulses and summon them for intimate conversation, or else yield to their hints and appear in their rooms on unheralded but deliciously confidential visits. Reaching the Ritz, Proust discovered after long frustrating enquiries that the Schiffs were staying elsewhere – indeed virtually on his doorstep. He claimed to be too exhausted by this abortive outing to see them for some time – partly a device to muster and protect his strength before the publication of *Sodome et Gomorrhe II* – but nevertheless affectionate letters began to be exchanged between the Villa Majestic and 44 Rue Hamelin. Schiff emerges from their correspondence as possessive, neurotic and manipulative; Proust by contrast seems tender, resolute and able to defend himself against Schiff's presumption.

From April until November 1922 Sydney Schiff, sometimes incited by Violet, made repeated incursions into Proust's time. He badgered him for meetings and begged for letters which, he claimed, calmed his neurasthenia. He cavilled at Proust's Paris friends and denigrated his London admirers. He tried to insinuate his way into every corner of Proust's most intimate existence. He hoped Violet's nephew might marry Proust's niece, and sought introductions to the most confidential of Proust's friends whom he could interrogate about Proust's motives and desires. He became a dogged, fanatical disciple, but a disciple with a self-aggrandising streak. For him the corrected proofs of *Temps perdu* were like holy relics, and he wanted to acquire pieces. For him the published volumes were like books of the Old Testament, and he must be anointed as the member of the sect who was trusted to translate the prophet's words into English. He sent artists with instructions to capture the great man's image: at times his idolatrous preference for the prophet's company rather than submission to his creed showed that he was a disciple who did not understand the faith. It is an important clue to the state of Proust in 1922 that he let the Schiffs figure so prominently in his life. The Schiffs, of course, satisfied his insatiable craving for admiration; but the decisive fact is that Proust recognised in Sydney Schiff a version of himself. It is a possibility that if Marcel Proust's sexual preferences had been for women, and he had married a capable, managing *bourgeoise*, his life would have been very much like Schiff's – and *À la recherche du temps perdu* would never have been written. Many of Proust's unprepossessing traits were evident in Schiff, as were several of his virtues, but Schiff had no trace of inspirational genius.

Proust's will-power and self-defensive wiliness were evident when he foiled the Schiffs' plot to become his relations by marriage. Early in April, stretched on a chaise longue in his chilly living room, Proust held a tea party to introduce his sister-in-law Marthe Proust and her eighteen-year-old daughter Suzy to his English friends. Violet professed to be taken with Suzy, and set out to win her trust. Proust had not been keen for his niece (the only child of his brother Robert) to read *À l'ombre des jeunes filles en fleurs*, and confided to Violet Schiff his anxiety that *Sodome et Gomorrhe III – La Prisonnière* as it was renamed – would be too terribly corrupting for an innocent young girl. There was a sly sequel to the tea-party, though. A few weeks later, on 27 April, Violet's brother-in-law Walter Behrens (the widower of her sister Evelyn) died at Valescure Saint-Raphaël. Behrens was a neighbour of Princesse Edmond de Polignac in Avenue Henry-Martin, a former President of the British Chamber of Commerce in Paris, a promoter of Anglo-French postal, telegraphic and trademarks reform, and an advocate of the Anglo-French tunnel under La Manche. He was also an amateur violinist who had re-married in 1914, as Schiff told Proust, 'a Dreyfus, a very rich, good and boring woman who is now going to inflict us with her sadness.' Walter's bereaved son Edward (afterwards Sir Edward Beddington-Behrens and like his father a pioneer of European economic unity) visited the Schiffs in Paris on 30 April.

Violet Schiff, like Proust, preferred vicarious pleasures. 'The contradiction between her feeling for life and her fear of active participation in it she resolved by living through other people,' according to Julian Fane. 'She was fascinated by the adventure of love, she chiefly talked and read and thought about love affairs, yet to all intents and purposes she had been tied emotionally to her father for the first half of her life and to Sydney for the second.' As a result, she was an incorrigible but not infallible matchmaker. After Walter Behrens's death, it occurred to her to push Suzy Proust and Edward Behrens together. Exploiting the success of the April tea-party, Violet invited Suzy to visit them in London and at their country house during the summer. Proust outwitted this manoeuvre deftly but with inner irritation; and Edward Behrens instead married the daughter of Sir Montague Burton, the Lithuanian-born high-street tailor. Schiff nephews, indeed, were not such a catch: Stella Benson, meeting one of them with the Schiffs at the Gargoyle club in 1928 thought him 'a bounder' with 'a leering face'; Julian Fane described another nephew as 'a peculiar man, large and bald, shrewd, uneasy, complacent and dissatisfied with himself, a tough financial tycoon who was disconcertingly apt to assume the manner of an innocent child'.

On 22 April, shortly after the Suzy tea-party, Proust wrote to Schiff praising his 'magnificent powers of expression' and 'gifts of intellect'. They were in such close agreement that their friendship now seemed 'the sole example of exact reciprocity that I have perhaps ever known'. Proust and Schiff however both felt that their conversations were becoming too earnest and intense. 'Of course you are right,' Proust continued, 'we speak a great deal too much of serious things, serious conversations are for people who haven't an intellectual life. People like the three of us who have an intellectual life need, to the contrary, frivolity when they escape from themselves and from their hard inner labour. We should, as you say, speak of all our minor concerns and leave philosophy for our solitude.' On 26 April Schiff dutifully responded with a stream of incoherent family gossip and social trivia. Evidently his style of letter-writing was relished by Proust even if it does not seem beguiling to outsiders. 'My sisters have been very hostile to me since I began to gain a little reputation as a writer,' he explained as the prelude to discursive family malice. His sister called Rose Morley 'is very snobbish in a despotic, stupid way. She has never succeeded in achieving the fashionable position to which she has aspired and which she could easily have obtained if she had not been so disagreeable to everyone who was more or less of this world that she envied. She is a pretty woman, well off without being rich . . . but she is totally without tact and says things intended to wound. Superficially she seems intelligent because she speaks with pointed emphasis. But actually is unreflective and never listens.' Schiff rambled on about a Mrs Cohen, whom he had recently seen in a restaurant, and a half-Jewish peer called Lord Ludlow: 'he married, some time ago, the inordinately rich widow of Sir Julius Wernher, whose son has married the daughter of Grand Duke Michael of Russia, who hasn't got a sou, I believe, and depends entirely on his son-in-law.' His letter was full of complaints about a 'wearisome' operetta *Dédé aux Bouffes Parisiens*, the cost of beer at the Café de Paris, and the nasty writing paper provided at the Villa Majestic. This final cause for dissatisfaction he turned into an opportunity for grovelling. 'Mlle Céleste must let me know where she buys your paper. I would love to have the same as yours in the same way that I would provide myself with the same scent as that of a woman whom I loved. Only in your case it's a great deal more serious. Violet and you represent my world. You are my world because you are the sole person who has given me all that I want, all that I expect of life.'

Violet Schiff was one of those society ladies who spent much of their time in bed retreating or recuperating from human contact. She pampered herself in a calm, complacent way: her lying-down days resembled those of Proust without the creative stress or grief at wasted time. 'Violet has had to rest in bed again today,' her husband wrote from the Villa Majestic in late April. 'This angel is not the slightest bit depressed. She approaches everything with the same perfect serenity.' These retreats from the world left Sydney to venture out in Paris alone, but he seems to have been timid on his own, and seldom dared more than to take solitary meals at the Ritz, during which he often drank too much champagne. More than ever, when abandoned to his own resources, he dropped hints intended to obtain meetings with his idol: a letter to Proust of 30 April, for example, concluded, '*I am going to lunch now at the Ritz – alone and I am going to dine there also – alone.* Tenderly, S.'

Ultimately, Proust submitted to this pressure and on 1 May sent Schiff a stream of directions setting out his terms for a rendezvous: 'I don't understand why you want to see someone who has not switched off his electric light nor closed his eyes for eight days, and who has today had the very worst possible day, both shapeless and overwhelming, but really, we can't go on like this and I will do my best to see you within the next four days.' He rejected Schiff's false solicitude: 'don't say to me "don't tire yourself" etc.' Instead Schiff was instructed to book 'a very hot room' at the Ritz or a table in the restaurant if he could ensure that all the restaurant windows were closed: 'I don't want any other place than the Ritz.' He apologised for 'the rather imperative tone of this letter but it's because after such a day I don't know what's to become of me, and my tenderness dissolves into despair.' Schiff, who received this message at 4 o'clock, immediately arranged everything as Proust wished, and told his idol not to apologise for issuing imperative orders: 'I love your tone which requires me to understand and provide exactly what you want.' Alas, while preparing for his night out, Proust accidentally took an undiluted dose of adrenalin, which scorched his throat and stomach as if it was vitriol. When the Schiffs arrived to collect him at eight, he was howling and weeping with pain, and for a month afterwards survived on a diet of ice-cream and chilled beer which Céleste Albaret brought daily from the Ritz. Despite his pain, Proust's behaviour in the Ritz restaurant was, so his hostess recalled, 'charming and gentle all the time. No one could suspect that a few hours before he had nearly killed himself. He objected to my husband drinking too much champagne, although he himself drank an enormous quantity of iced beer supplied exclusively by the Ritz people.' Proust's throat was so badly scorched that for three weeks he could not swallow solids: when, around 27 May, he managed to eat some asparagus, he crowed about it in all his letters. His visit to the Schiffs' Diaghilevien supper party at the Majestic was his first excursion after this accident.

'My very dear Marcel,' Schiff wrote to Proust on 8 May, 'even though each meeting is a wasted opportunity, caused in part by my deafness and my stupidity, in part by the infernal, ubiquitous, destructive noise, for nothing wrecks me more than noise, each of our meetings adds something. For my part, I see you, I touch you, I savour you, and you are also able to familiarise yourself with my demeanour, my habits, my way of speaking and of operating: to know me fully, it's a cardinal need that you should have me before you in person to judge and analyse – to form an idea of what I think, of what I am and why I shut myself up in my secret garden.'

Had Schiff been toping champagne before he wrote this needy, self-centred effusion? 'I would so much like to know what you are doing today. It's terrible to think that possibly a week will pass without my seeing you.' The letter closes – perhaps tipsily, certainly excessively – 'I love you with my heart, chosen friend, *ami rêvé* [dream friend: perfect friend].' Proust replied to this importunate screed on 14 May explaining that he had a persistent violent fever since his adrenalin accident. 'I have not been able to quit my bed. When I can, if you have not already left, my first visit will be to you.' He signed off, '*Tendresses de votre Marcel.*'

Schiff always tended to confound Proust with his narrator – 'as he shows himself in his books, so he was in life' – yet Proust had waged war against biographical exegesis in his essays in *Contre Sainte-Beuve* and according to Léon Pierre-Quint 'expressed violent scorn for those of his worldly admirers who had not actually read his books': Pierre-Quint's phrase for them is 'pretentious idiots'. Certainly Proust was vexed by Schiff's reductive frivolity in reading *Temps perdu* through the personality of its creator and in expressly preferring the man to the book. The banality of matching Proust's characters with living originals is often a refuge from thinking about his big ideas yet Schiff persisted in trawling *Temps perdu* in search of personal keys or intimate clues. On 15 May he reported that he had only read *Sodome et Gomorrhe II* (published a fortnight earlier) once he had accepted that it was

> useless to continue to hope every day that I was going to see you. Like Violet, I find this last book more personal again (if possible) than any of the others save perhaps a part of *Swann*. You are the most marvellous of men. With you the

novel has reached its highest altitude, after you it will go into decline because there is nothing left to do. I can never say more than a small part of what I think of your books. But you who understand everything, you understand me too, it's unnecessary for me to say any more.

Proust can hardly have been happy to be told how personal to him *Sodome et Gomorrhe* seemed: Schiff compounded this tactlessness with a yet more intrusive letter enquiring the name of one of Proust's intimate friends to whom he could go for a talk. There was so much, Schiff protested, that he wanted to ask about Proust personally and creatively, but on the rare occasions when they met there was never enough time. In these few careless sentences he became Nissim Bernard making advances to the wrong Tomato. Proust's rebuke for this inquisitive vulgarity, which seemed so defective in true friendship, was immediate. 'Once before,' he replied, 'you acted in my view in a way that was altogether friendly yet seemed unnatural, for in a true friendship one does not thwart one's friend.' Proust forced himself to extenuate Schiff's asinine intrusiveness: the Englishman had shown such 'immense kindness, even if not in accordance with my theory and practice, that it would be churlish of me not to adore you for what you are'. He landed a hard blow, though, to punish Schiff's bad manners. 'If you wish to interrogate someone who understands me, it's very simple, ask me. I don't have a single friend who understands me entirely. And if there were such a person, I trust he would be worthy of the name of a friend, and in consequence not answer any questions at all.'

After Proust's death, the Schiffs claimed that he had not wished to know the date of their departure from Paris, because the thought of their absence so upset him; but this was make-believe, as shown by a letter from Proust, dated 29 May, in which he assured them that he had only one current preoccupation: 'Will I be in a state to get up before Thursday when my great friends (the Schiffs) leave?' Once they had returned to London, Proust allowed himself some social outings that were not Schiff-centred; and Sydney Schiff did not like it. In mid-June Proust went to a party given by Madame Hennessy to whom he afterwards sent a hilarious letter imitating the fatuous chatter on which he had eavesdropped. As he talked to Boniface, Marquis de Castellane, two other guests discussed him audibly – 'I can tell immediately he isn't our sort of person' – and after various inanities agreed on his identity: 'It's the famous Marcel Prévost, author of *Don Juanes*.' Proust mentioned this party in a message to Schiff on 14 June: 'I am suddenly getting better,' he wrote, and 'went out the day before yesterday to a party where, sad reminder, were Madame de Polignac and Castellane.' Schiff's reply was unpleasantly self-promoting with a shocking strain of envy: 'marvellous that you feel suddenly better,' he declared. 'I know that you are getting better because of our visit. I knew, when we were with you, that we were making you improve. I think that the effort that you made out of your immense goodness of heart to prove your affection for us, this effort benefited you more than it tired you.' This part of the message was egocentric enough; but then Schiff began to sound like Madame Verdurin venting her bile on the Guermantes. 'The memory of Mme de Polignac is more tedious than that of Castellane but I have no interest in either one of them. Everything that is purely worldly seems tiring to me. I don't see any sense in this way of living. The instant one leaves such people one forgets them. I have often remarked that only those people of whom one still thinks as much or more after one has quit them than when one is with them, are genuine.'

Proust reacted like Tomato No 2 to Schiff's self-centred impertinence.

> You have written me a revolting letter, purely and simply to revolt me, so that I, horrified, should feel obliged to write back. That's what I'm doing, asking myself if I'm not wrong to submit to such blackmail. You know well enough that I see no one: except for attending one soirée about which I told you, I have not seen a living soul except you and Mme Schiff for many months . . . You know that you yourself pursue exactly the kind of life for which you reproach me, but which I do not lead. If you would read my book, you would discover in it the stupid capriciousness of fashionable society, which I discarded at the age of twenty [sic]. Though that did not prevent the *Nouvelle Revue Française* twenty years later from rejecting *Swann* as the work of a mere society amateur. But you don't read my book because, in common with all the other Society people who dislike it, you are too nervous in Paris, too busy in London, and in the country you hold too many house-parties . . . Yet from the day it appeared, the real friends of the book have been reading it in the Métro, in their carriages, in trains, oblivious of their neighbours, forgetting their stops.

Schiff on more than one occasion, perhaps as an attempt to force himself into further meetings with Proust, insisted that reading a book written by a friend rather than seeing him was as futile as listening to a gramophone record of a singer who was still alive. 'I ignore your theory that you prefer the man to his work. I would refute that sophism in two minutes if I was less weary . . . One thing revolted me more than all the rest put together. That you should think I claimed to feel better after you had left. Your departure could only have reduced me to tears. It's just as absurd for you to believe that I felt better because you were here.'

Later in June Schiff devised a new means of involving himself in Proust's existence: portraiture. 'Violet has sat today for Wyndham Lewis,' he wrote from London on 21 June in one of his stream-of-consciousness screeds that Proust so appreciated.

> He is going to make a drawing of me too. If they are successful I will send them to you. W. L. is our Picasso, but a difficult fellow, hard and charmless. He is very intelligent, possibly the most intelligent man (after you) whom I know, but not at all scholarly . . . I don't like him but he interests me enormously. Of the rest, I love no man except you and don't want to love anyone else. Lewis is a stronger spirit than Picasso but doesn't yet paint as well; perhaps he will never manage it. His sketching is better with more verve.

He proposed asking Picasso to sketch Proust: 'as I know him to speak to, he would reply.' (When a few years later Picasso was asked by some prominent Americans-in-Paris to undertake a portrait of James Joyce, he replied that he never did portraits to order, and they had to be content with commissioning a sketch of Joyce by Brancusi.) Shortly afterwards, Lewis went over to Paris, and contacted Proust, who on 7 July acknowledged 'the letter which you have done me the honour of writing to me and which will remain for me a precious autograph' (perhaps an ironic remark, as

Lewis had a peculiarly smudgy handwriting and ugly signature). 'Unfortunately I've caught cold this evening and if you are leaving on Monday I am very much afraid that on Saturday and Sunday I will still be suffering too much to receive you [but] if by any chance I get better, I will send for you.' Proust tried to mitigate this disappointment: 'To be sketched by you may be my only chance of being remembered by posterity! Because of that, and because of the pleasure I would have had in seeing you, thank my great friend Monsieur Sydney Schiff, when you see him, for such a delicate, noble thought.'

After the projected portraits came to naught, Schiff started negotiations to buy Proust's corrected proofs of *Sodome et Gomorrhe*. 'For a long time I have dreamt of owning them but I have a horror of money matters between friends, above all a friend like you.' Paragraphs on the subject were exchanged by the two men throughout the summer. But more important to Schiff, he outlined his claims to be the authorised or monopolist English interpreter of Proust. A letter, sent from his house in Cambridge Square on 23 June, opened with slighting references to the English Proustian Walkley, who had worked in the Post Office until his appointment as drama critic of *The Times* in 1899, and to another London admirer of Proust, Aldous Huxley.

'No-one here has yet written a proper serious critique of your works,' Schiff continued.

> For a long time I have wanted to do it if I could, but I wouldn't be able to do anything adequate, lacking the critical training, the knowledge, the technique . . . It's a shame because there's no-one who understands you as we understand you, who appreciates all the nuances as we do, who

senses what has been left unsaid as well as what has been said, who responds like us from the fibres of our being to your intimate thoughts.

But if Schiff disqualified himself as a critical interpreter, he was confident that he was the ideal translator of *Temps perdu* into English. 'There is no-one but me to make this translation. You wouldn't know it from listening to my execrable spoken French, but I understand it better, and in any case that's not the main question, it's a question of my sympathetic intuition, of my literary taste and my intellectual faculties. I often think: would I not do better to put aside my own work and undertake the translation of all *La Recherche*?' A self-promoting, pushy letter but not insincere: the Schiffs *did* adulate Proust. 'I believe,' Violet wrote, 'Marcel Proust to have been one of the most angelic human beings that ever lived. His first impulse was always to try and make everyone who came near him happier than they had been before, to help them in any way, possible or impossible, regardless of whether or not they deserved it, or in fact even needed help. He was completely disinterested, un-self-protective, fantastically generous, loving and loveable.'

Schiff was too late. Charles Scott Moncrieff had already been selected as translator, possibly through the intervention of Schiff's bugbear Walkley, who was Scott Moncrieff's colleague on the staff of *The Times* and was publicly complimented by Scott Moncrieff as the doyen of English Proustians. An accomplished translator of Stendhal, Pirandello and the letters of Abelard and Héloïse, Scott Moncrieff had worked as private secretary to the lunatic proprietor of *The Times*, Lord Northcliffe, before joining the newspaper's staff from July 1921 until

May 1923. His deplorable weakness for writing sneering squibs had earned him the loathing, for one, of Osbert Sitwell, Schiff's former editor of *Arts and Letters*. Scott Moncrieff, wrote Sitwell, was 'a sad, twisted creature with an Anglican mind gone Catholic and an Academic mind struggling after modernity, but only really happy in the pages of *Punch*'. Sitwell, who regarded Scott Moncrieff as his 'virulent enemy', deplored his 'ghoulish' effort to invade 'the dead body of a great mind' by having the temerity to translate Proust. The brief correspondence between Proust and Scott Moncrieff was civil if stilted; but Proust, who in his last years cultivated a regular visitor to the Paris Ritz, an immaculate, homosexual baronet and MP, with a princely fortune, called Sir Philip Sassoon, would have been aghast at the inferior verses beginning 'Sir Philip Sassoon is a member for Hythe', describing him as a 'lackey' and a 'dunce', which Scott Moncrieff wasted his time writing in 1923. Schiff, more accurately, assessed Sassoon as 'intelligent but very highly strung'.

When, in early September of 1922, announcements began to appear in London literary papers about the imminent publication of the first instalment of Scott Moncrieff's translation, Schiff warned Proust against the titles both for the projected series, *Remembrance of Things Past*, and for the opening volume, *Swann's Way*. He evidently did not recognise the derivation of the first title from Shakespeare's Sonnet 30, and maliciously represented to Proust that 'Swann's way' meant 'In the manner of Swann' or 'Swann's method'. This mischief-making succeeded in disquieting Proust, who challenged these supposed distortions in an excited letter to his publisher Gaston Gallimard: 'I refuse to let the English destroy my book.' Schiff's mood at this time of anxious discontent partly originated, one can suppose, from his chagrin at being supplanted by Scott Moncrieff as Proust's interpreter to the English-speaking world. After *Swann's Way* was published in the third week of September, Schiff told Proust that he felt 'really very depressed'. He had collected newspaper cuttings of all the 'banal and unintelligent' reviews: 'I want to vomit each time I read a new piece of effusive praise heaped on your translator.' The fact is that the Schiffs were possessive and jealous about the genius in Rue Hamelin whom they reckoned was peculiarly their own: they remained keen all their lives to proclaim their own privileged status among the 'Happy Few' and the exclusivity of true Proustians. 'There are many,' Violet declared, 'who write and talk so much and so admiringly of Proust and unconsciously hate him. No one is any good to him who does not love and understand him.' Her doting husband similarly suggested that true Proustians 'can with safety be estimated at the merest handful'. It was a very 'select' group: those who truly understood Proust were united by a common bond, 'the bond being, of course, himself'.

Proust would have been aghast to realise that there was a splinter of truth in Schiff's claims about the selectness of his readership. Evidently people who knew Proust *did* read the novel differently from those who had not met him. Edmond Jaloux, reviewing *La Prisonnière* on its publication in 1923, judged that in its final section, 'the principal incident is the *coup de théâtre* in which Morel, catechised by the Verdurins, publicly insults M. de Charlus at the end of a musical party organised by the Baron to establish Morel as a star performer.' For many readers this pivotal scene is one of ineffable malice and repulsive cruelty; but for Jaloux the scene was 'powerful comedy'. Most commentators, Jaloux continued, cannot fully appreciate the novel's humour because they never had 'the luck of knowing Marcel Proust personally'. Morel's repudiation of Charlus irresistibly reminded Jaloux of his comic late-night companion at the Ritz who 'told such funny stories, with so much verve, hiding his hand behind his mouth as he tittered'. Proust, says Jaloux, had 'a bitter humour, born from his observation of humanity and the ridiculous discrepancy between men's enormous pretensions and their actual worth.' One must accept Jaloux's assurance; but it is impossible now to see the joke in the tragic scene of Morel's spurning of Charlus, which diverts the course of the Baron's life towards miserable straits.

Although Scott Moncrieff's *Remembrance of Things Past* made Proust available to a new segment of English readers, the novel remained the pleasure of a small, discriminating élite. Readers who could not master the French text were able to savour Scott Moncrieff's version, and to submit to the wonderful rhythms of its language, but the difficulties of Proust's style did not relent in English. E. M. Forster, for example, regretted that as the volumes of *Remembrance of Things Past* appeared through the 1920s, he did not find the novel easier to read in translation.

A sentence begins quite simply, then it undulates and expands, parentheses intervene like quick-set hedges, the flowers of comparison bloom, and three fields off, like a wounded partridge, crouches the principal verb, making one wonder as one picks it up, poor little thing, whether after all it was worth such a tramp, so many guns, and such expensive dogs, and what, after all, is its relation to the main subject, potted so gaily half a page back, and proving finally to have been in the accusative case.

This was not the makings of a best-seller. The first edition of *Swann's Way*, printed in 1922, totalled only 1,000 copies. 1,600 copies – some destined for the United States – were reprinted in 1923, and 1,250 copies in 1924. *Swann's Way* continued to sell at this level for over thirty years. Chatto & Windus moreover found that sales for this first volume were about seven times as high as for the subsequent volumes: most readers did not persevere. English sales only began to rise after the publication in 1959 of the first volume of George Painter's biography, which was detested and even opposed by some crucial French Proustians. *Swann's Way* was not published as an English paperback until 1966 in response to the success of Painter's delayed second volume.

Six out of seven readers of *Swann's Way* never bought its sequels with such prettified titles as *Within a Budding Grove* or *The Sweet Cheat Gone*; but the exceptional seventh readers were vanquished by the power and beauty of the sequence. A typical Proustian acolyte of the 1920s was the Oxford undergraduate and aspirant author, Cyril Connolly, who bought each Scott Moncrieff volume as it was published, and was 'intoxicated' by them for years. 'I tried to talk like Proust, think like Proust, and write like Proust, and had to destroy it all later.' After Scott Moncrieff succumbed to a painful cancer in Rome in 1930, leaving the final volume untranslated, Schiff finally obtained his perceived rights as Proust's chief English friend and interpreter; but his rendering of *Temps retrouvé* into *Time Regained* – published under his alias of 'Stephen Hudson' – was inferior to Scott Moncrieff's: unadorned, even unpolished, and sometimes clumsily obscure. As one example, a Hudson sentence about Charlus's pro-German sympathies during the war reads: 'Great as his admiration had been for England, that impeccable Eng-

land incapable of lies preventing corn and milk from entering
Germany was in a way a nation of chartered gentlemen, of
licensed witnesses and arbiters of honour, whilst to his mind
some of Dostoevski's disreputable rascals were better.' Yet Schiff
could not have worked harder, and for the sake of his Proust
translation, he forfeited the friendship of Sir John Rothenstein
whom he had invited for the summer to Switzerland. Schiff had
flattered Rothenstein in London, but when, as the art historian
later remonstrated, he and his wife reached the Schiffs' chalet at
Glion, 'the worse for our long uncomfortable railway journey,
and our walk up the mountain side in midsummer's heat, Mrs
Schiff met us as if we were importunate strangers, explaining
that Sydney was translating Proust and must not be disturbed.
It was five hours before he stopped translating Proust, and
emerged, radiating friendliness, which from that moment was
reciprocated in ever diminishing measure.'

The fulsome Proust-Schiff exchanges continued through the
summer of 1922: from Paris to London – 'Dear Madame Violet,
hidden flower, fragrant and marvellous like those Léonardo de
Vinci has sketched' – and from London to Paris: 'My dear Marcel, I love you with all my heart.' Although Schiff was incessant
in his praise of the book as well as his love of the author, he did
not scruple at distracting Proust from novel-writing to letter-
writing. 'Your delicious eighteen page letter has done me a great
deal of good,' he wrote in late July. 'I have been very exhausted
and very depressed recently and your dear unhoped-for letter
helped me to bear my woes, which naturally are totally imaginary.' And twice in early September he made the same refrain:
'your letters are the delight and reward of my life'; and again a
week later begging to be sent a few lines: 'I've been very

depressed lately, and I need your news.' Out of the great goodness of his heart the invalid Proust replied on 14 September. He
stated that he was feeling very ill, perhaps because he was being
asphyxiated by noxious seepages from his chimney. 'Whatever
the cause, the result is a despair that's worse than death.' He
professed to be too weary to concern himself with the niceties of
Scott Moncrieff's translation, and did not respond to Schiff's
request for permission to dedicate his forthcoming novel about
childhood, *Prince Hempseed*, to Proust.

The last letter in the correspondence was written by Schiff
when (unknown to him) Proust was beyond recovery, and it
reached Paris when Proust was almost dead. It is plaintive,
needy, and pathetically sad. Schiff, one feels, had briefly fixed
himself onto Proust's life, but realised that his hold was weaken-
ing. He was puzzled whether Proust was now too ill to be interested in him, or vexed with him; and he sensed that the glorious
moment was over. Schiff had been wholeheartedly attentive to
the sick potentate in Rue Hamelin – deferential, adoring, glad
to be of use – but he had become too insinuating and too
importunate with his requests for favours. The balance of power
at Proust's court had shifted.

Schiff's last message to Proust, on 14 November, read like
this: 'It's hard to write to you. I feel very far away from you and
I don't know how much you really love me. Your last letter
greatly saddened me, and I've written to you twice since then
without getting a response. And I'm suffering, really very
depressed.' He was correcting the proofs of *Prince Hempseed*,
which he again asked Proust's permission to dedicate to him,
but felt 'unbearably bored'. As a restorative to his spirits, he was
thinking of visiting Paris for a few days just to see his idol. 'A let-

ter from you would be for me the answer to a prayer which my lips never stop sighing for, the tears that my eyes shed. But the letter never comes, and I don't know if you are better or worse, if you think of me or not, if I can continue to reassure myself: he is there, he is there, or if, like everyone else except one, he has flown away.'

CHAPTER 9

18 November 1922

The dead season in Paris began in mid-July when its inhabitants started retiring to *la campagne* for the summer. The grand boulevards, though, always largely international, were crowded with provincial and foreign visitors gazing at the expensive shops and resplendent hotels, and there were some Parisians left – those with professional responsibilities and those who were too poor or ill to travel – among the jostling crowds.

For many years, now, Proust had felt too weak to leave Paris in summer; and the busy men who delayed their departures included his 'dear, close friend' of the moment, the novelist Edmond Jaloux, and a young writer called Paul Brach. In June Brach had sent Proust a reproduction of a Tissot painting, then being exhibited in a Second Empire art show in the Louvre, showing Charles Haas (the model for Swann) and other Society swells standing on a club balcony. This prompted the insertion of another late addition to *Sodome et Gomorrhe III*: a passage addressed to Haas, 'whom I scarcely knew when I was still so young and you so near your grave', indicative of Proust's constant, urgent preoccupation with mortality and memory.

> It is because someone whom you must have regarded as a little fool has made you the hero of one of his volumes, that

people are beginning to speak of you again and that your name will perhaps endure. If people always mention you now, looking at Tissot's painting of the balcony of the Rue Royale club, where you stand with Gallifet, Edmond de Polignac and Saint-Maurice, if people are always drawing attention to your figure, it is because they know that there are some of your traits in the character of Swann.

Proust's faith that his Art would make the memory of his name imperishable was, as he moved towards death, embracing some of his contemporaries too; and indeed no one, nowadays, would think of Haas or Montesquiou if it was not for Swann and Charlus.

On 15 July, immediately after Bastille Day, Brach took Proust and Jaloux to the most fashionable of Paris nightclubs, Le Boeuf sur le Toit in Rue Boissy d'Anglas, which had opened in January under Cocteau's auspices. At the end of their meal there, when it was time to leave their tips for the waiters, Proust's manner became typically 'royal'. Even after his companions protested – 'You're going to *ruin* this place: we can never dare to return if you're so madly generous' – he wanted to leave a *pourboire* for a servant who, as Brach pointed out, had not waited on their table at all. 'Oh, but I can see in his eyes such wistful sadness at the thought of not receiving anything,' Proust retorted. In other ways this evening was full of incident: indeed Jaloux thought 'this Boeuf sur Le Toit frightened him a bit'. At one stage Comte de Maleissye-Melun and some other drunken revellers got involved in a brawl with several men whom Proust characterised as 'unspeakable pimps'. In the scuffle Proust was nearly struck by an ice-bucket and by a roast chicken. 'I thought my delight-ful duelling days were back again, but it seems that our assailants were not the sort of people with whom one fights,' Proust wrote next day. At another moment in the evening, Jacques Delgado, a young habitué of Le Boeuf who was (according to Brach) 'blind-drunk', got up and stumbled over from his table to theirs, 'astounded by Proust's appearance, by his shawl and his bowler hat', and accosted the novelist without knowing who he was. Delgado's drunken sallies were so insolent that Proust wanted to send his seconds to call, and the two men exchanged addresses. At dawn Odilon Albaret presented himself at Delgado's address, but Proust's intended antagonist, who had presumably discovered the identity of the man in the bowler and *pelisse*, rendered a handsome apology. Proust, in turn, returned a cordial answer which showed that he still half-hoped, as he admitted amiably to Delgado, that Le Boeuf would provide 'an opportunity for something I used to enjoy very much and which my health is no bar to my enjoying again: a duel'.

There were other dark pleasures in July: wondering, for example, if he could sue Montesquiou's executor if he was attacked in the count's memoirs, which were being prepared for publication. In August, thanking Elizabeth de Clermont-Tonnerre for the present of a book which would provide, he said, 'a thousand reasons to think of you with melancholy yet grateful pleasure', he was still preoccupied by readers' reactions to *Sodome*: 'the twofold but contradictory indignation of those who believe that my book is an indictment and those who imagine it is an encouragement'. But overall he was in physical decline and making necessary mental adjustments. He felt ill and could only 'think with horror of my life,' he told Brach on 27 July. It was hard to rouse himself to correct the proofs of *La Prisonnière*, and he was tired by the lessons in French history that he was giving to Odilon Albaret. His misanthropic self-sufficiency was moving to a new level. 'One thinks of people yet one can so easily do without them,' he warned Brach on 9 August; but he was feeling less persecuted by demands for his attention from those exasperating time-wasters at whom he had often wanted to hurl the threat, 'I'll drown you in an ocean of shit.' He was retreating further than ever from social contacts as the need to fight for life became more urgent.

In the late summer Proust's admirable physician brother went on a provincial tour. 'At every station,' Robert reported, 'I asked for *Sodome* and didn't find a single copy.' He thought this suggested the feeblest promotion by the publisher Gallimard: 'considering your sad life, which costs you so much, I wonder that you don't complain.' Little Marcel's life was getting sicker if not sadder. He was 'once again very bothered by my health,' he informed Armand de Guiche in early September. He was either being asphyxiated by leakages from a cracked chimney in his apartment or it was 'the approach of death' which would be 'annoying with my book still unfinished.' In his room that month he had several falls caused by dizziness or fainting, and took an accidental overdose of opiates and barbiturates in quantities that might have finished a less hardened drug user. During late September he suffered three days of severe asthma attacks and in early October he contracted a chill after venturing out on a foggy night to a soirée at Comte Étienne de Beaumont's. The chill turned to bronchitis which made it painful for Proust to speak: by mid-October he was bombarding Céleste Albaret with plaintive little written messages. 'The acrid smell of your laundry causes unnecessary coughing fits,' he scribbled on one occasion. 'I have just coughed over 3,000 times.' There were

many other notes to Céleste. Will she come and stand comfort-
ingly at the end of his bed? Will she send someone to fetch
aspirin? Has a letter not arrived from Madame Schiff? Can he
have – immediately – a salad of green beans with a spoonful of
vinegar? 'Of all the great people who cared for him, who regarded his friendship as a prize, not one was really necessary to him,'
Schiff thought – except Céleste who consecrated her life to serve
his domestic tyranny. And all this time, despite his growing
weakness, Proust (said Schiff) 'was working, working, correcting, changing, adding'. Dr Maurice Bize, whom Proust consulted at this time, had other words to describe what his patient was
doing: Proust was killing himself by overwork.

As Proust's condition deteriorated, Bize feared that he would
contract pneumonia, and shared his forebodings with Robert
Proust, who tried to coax his little Marcel into admitting himself into a nearby clinic. The stubborn patient decided that he
was being bullied by his brother whom he refused to see again
for some time. It must have been excruciating for Robert Proust
to recall that their father too had overworked to death and that
their mother had died because she also had refused treatment or
medicines. At Robert Proust's instigation, Reynaldo Hahn sent
a touching letter beseeching his ex-lover to let himself be nursed
and doctored properly; but it had no effect.

On 24 October, so Proust told Rivière, he finished his efforts
to perfect La Prisonnière, but ten days later he wanted to re-read
and check it a final time. By then he had stopped eating, and
would only consume iced beer, herbal tea and his usual café au
lait. Viral pneumonia now seized him, but he refused camphor-
ated oil and other medicines prescribed by Maurice Bize,
because he would not let drugs befuddle him as he fought to

make his last improvements to his manuscripts. In consequence
he developed an abscess on the lung. He had been warning
throughout 1922 that he was dying, and it seems that he was
convinced that nothing could now cure him; but his fatalism,
his refusal of care, anguished those who loved him, his brother,
Céleste Albaret, Reynaldo Hahn and other friends, as it has generations of his readers. Throughout these dismal scenes Céleste
Albaret remained formidable and dedicated: the same Céleste
who, with her sister Marie Gineste, he had lately described to
the world in *Sodome et Gomorrhe*. Born in a village in the Lozère
foothills of the mountainous Cévennes, reared in a mill-house
that was often damaged by river torrents passing beneath it,
Céleste (wrote Proust) was usually 'slack like the waters of a
calm lake, but with outbreaks of terrible recurrent seething in
which her fury recalled the peril of flash-floods and whirlpools
that carry away everything before them.' She could be, at times,
'quivering, furious, destroying everything, detestable', but at
other moments she was 'truly celestial'.

By the end of October Proust's body was worn out; but he did
not allow himself, or Céleste, to rest. Still correcting and amend-
ing the proofs of *La Prisonnière*, 'he was always ringing the bell,
either for a hot-water bottle, or a woollen, a book, a *cahier*, a scrap
of paper to stick in,' she records. She contested many later
accounts of Proust's decline in September and his infections in
October, but conceded that he was incontestably ill in November:
it was nightmarish for her to minister to that 'poor body under
the sheets, martyred with coughing and choking, and tortured by
the longing to finish his work'. In these last atrocious weeks of
suffering, she was 'probably the only one still under the illusion
that he would recover. It wasn't that I rejected the idea of his

dying – it simply didn't enter my head.' This was despite Proust's instructions to her in the event of his death: 'Send for the good Abbé Mugnier half an hour after I die – you'll see how he'll pray for me'; 'When I am dead, have them call in Helleu to do my portrait'; and other remarks that should have showed her that he was expecting death. At midnight, on the night of 17–18 November, Monsieur Proust sent for her to sit with him. 'At first we talked a bit; then he started adding material to and correcting the proofs. He started by dictating to me – until about two in the morning. But I couldn't have gone very fast, because I was reaching the end of my tether, and the room was terribly cold.' He worked at the proofs, making additions on little strips of paper to amplify the death of Bergotte, and jotted down a phrase about 'the unbelievable frivolity of the dying' which he had adapted from Emerson when long ago translating Ruskin. Work continued until half past three in the morning when, it seems, the abscess burst. Septicaemia began to poison him.

Around dawn on 18 November Proust hallucinated that a horrible fat woman dressed in black was plucking at the sheets of his bed and moving the papers with which it was strewn. A few hours later Maurice Bize came to administer an injection, and Robert Proust fed his brother oxygen from a cylinder, asking 'Is that a bit better, my little Marcel?' In the late afternoon, the neurologist Professor Joseph Babinski, who had attended Proust in the past, arrived for a consultation. He advised against heroic but futile measures to prolong the patient's life. 'No, my dear Robert,' he said, 'don't make him suffer: it's pointless.' Afterwards, as Babinski was leaving the apartment, Céleste Albaret stopped him at the door. 'Professor, you *are* going to save him, aren't you?' she demanded. He took her hands and, visibly moved, replied, 'Madame, I know all you have done for him. You must be brave. It is all over.'

She went into the sickroom, and joined Robert Proust. The dying man, now speechless, gazed fixedly at them. At half-past four Robert Proust signalled the end to Céleste: he got up, bent over his brother, and closed his eyes. Brother and housekeeper together laid him out, and each took away a lock of his hair. Then Reynaldo Hahn came, and began telephoning or sending notes to Proust's intimate friends. He stayed the night in the apartment, sometimes keeping a vigil by the bedside, and sometimes writing music in another room. The poet Fernand Gregh, who had been a fellow pupil at the Lycée Condorcet, came at midnight to sit with Proust while Hahn rested; the diplomat Paul Morand and Gabriel Astruc, an impresario who had promoted the first Ballets Russes season in Paris, also went to the apartment that evening. Early on Sunday morning Léon Daudet came and wept. A stream of grieving visitors followed: Anna de Noailles, Lucien Daudet, Georges de Lauris, Cocteau, Jaloux, Jacques Porel, Maurice Martin du Gard, Jacques Rivière, Robert Dreyfus, Princesse Lucien Murat, the banker Henri Gans, the diplomat Robert de Billy, the art dealer René Gimpel, who had first met Proust at Cabourg before the war, and countless others. As Gimpel signed the book of condolence, he overheard the reminiscences of an elderly man, who forty years earlier had given Greek lessons to Proust during family holidays at Houlgate. 'At thirteen, he really loved Greek, did little Marcel, and already his dream was to become a writer,' said the old teacher. 'He didn't care for playing on the beach. He was always trying to draw my wife aside, far from the animation, into quieter spots to discuss literature, and he would ask both of us: "Do you think that one day my play will be performed at the Comédie Française?"'

Gimpel asked the classicist, who was so proud of the pupil he had not seen since the Houlgate holiday, what he thought of *À la recherche du temps perdu*. 'The old professor of Greek, stooped and quavering, replied: "Ah, monsieur, Proust's books are a bit difficult for me!"'

As Proust had requested, Paul Helleu (one of the models for the artist Elstir in *Temps perdu*) made an etching of him laid out in death; then André Dunoyer de Segonzac made a charcoal drawing; the sculptor Robert Wlérick studied the dead man's immobile face, gaunt with illness and lightly bearded; and (at Cocteau's suggestion) Man Ray photographed the corpse. Proust has the look, in Man Ray's photograph, of a Jewish prophet, with his fringe of beard and a nose that suddenly seems, like Charles Swann's, more prominent. There is no hint that he had ever been an aesthete, a diner-out, a duellist or the financier of a male brothel.

'If one is not "somebody", the absence of a well-known title speeds up the process of decomposition after death,' Proust had recently written in *La Prisonnière*. And in *Temps retrouvé* he was dismissive of the perfunctory feelings of mourners. 'Every death is a simplification of life for the survivors; it relieves them of being grateful and of being obliged to make visits.' Proust's death proved, once and for all, that he was a Somebody, but it brought no simplification of life for his survivors. The news of his death rippled across Paris, spread out from the capital, and became, to adapt Ezra Pound's maxim, News that stayed News. The reactions of Parisians proved Proust to be among the most privileged of the city's inhabitants: when he died, Paris paused; and when he was buried, the traffic stopped. The days from Sunday 19th until his burial on the 22nd were unparalleled in the capital since the death of Victor Hugo in 1885. His friends paid their tributes, his readers gathered for the funeral and his books assumed their new significance for posterity. 'Here are the paper volumes,' wrote an admirer in early December, 'seven or eight of them, distinguished-looking yet paper volumes all the same, which henceforth will be what most people call Marcel Proust.' In fact, there were three more volumes to come: *La Prisonnière* (published in November 1923); *Albertine disparue* (then entitled *La fugitive*) in November 1925; and *Le Temps retrouvé* in September 1927. The commentaries proliferated too. 'Faced with the enormous body of Proust-criticism in five languages,' wrote an essayist in 1930, 'one thinks of the many hundreds of True Crosses which might be recovered from the treasured fragments scattered over the Christian world.'

The American poet John Peale Bishop remembered being in a group with Valéry Larbaud, Elisabeth de Clermont-Tonnerre and Ford Madox Ford, when a young woman appeared with an expression that betokened calamity, and interrupted their talk of Henry James: '*Proust est mort*,' she announced. The Duchess was incredulous. 'When they heard of his death, everyone felt that Marcel Proust was playing a trick,' she recorded. 'He had oscillated between life and death for so long that the choice that he took one day of death seemed to overturn everything.' The Duchess's brother Armand de Guiche had received a telephone call from Céleste Albaret only three days before Proust's death asking on her employer's behalf for the name of a physician whom the duke had once recommended. So many of Guiche's meetings with

Proust had been cancelled at the last moment because of illness that he was not worried by the call: he had no thought of his friend's imminent death. Afterwards, though, Céleste's message from Proust came to seem 'a call for help that I did not understand'. In a mood of self-reproach Guiche asked himself, 'Did he want me to know he was very ill? Did he long for a friend's visit?' The duke felt guilty for surviving Proust.

Ford Madox Ford testified that when the young woman made her announcement to Peale Bishop and himself, 'the death of Proust came to me like the dull blow of a softened club'. Later that same Sunday, in the evening, he went to a drinks party given by a French writer with an American wife. 'That party was like death. People sat about with panic-stricken faces, silent. You would have thought that everyone there had lost all his relations and all their fortunes in a war.' Like Elisabeth de Clermont-Tonnerre, Paul Brach, the dead man's host at Le Boeuf sur le Toit, could not believe that Proust was dead. 'He had so often risked going into that zone between life and death, and had always returned rich with impressions captured at the very limit of the Unknown', wrote Brach a few days later, that his admirers had come to expect him to continue playing 'this dangerous game' indefinitely. Instead, Brach felt, Proust had succumbed to his own intrepid researches into Death. Brach's other companion at Le Boeuf, Jaloux, had thought Proust 'so powerful, so total, so invincible' that his death seemed impossibly tragic. But for Misia Sert Proust's death was insufficiently artistic: 'The same God who ordained that Molière should breathe his last on the stage should have ensured that Marcel Proust died at a ball.'

News of Proust's death was carried across Paris that Sunday morning by word of mouth and only later by the press. As a

Proustian recorded at the time, 'November 19th, a Sunday, a typical November Sunday, with a threat of rain in the air that was less a threat than the absent-minded recollection of a threat of bad weather the day before . . . was made more like a November Sunday by the announcement in the evening papers that Marcel Proust had passed away full twenty-four hours before. The morning papers had not said a word about it.' It was not just the intelligentsia who reacted to the death in Rue Hamelin. The crowds, largely composed of working men, to be seen at the Louvre and other Paris museums on Sundays demonstrated the respect for intelligence and enthusiasm for the arts that characterised most Parisians. 'It seems that he is dead: it was very unexpected,' a taxi-driver said to Madox Ford, who was eloquent about the impact that Sunday and Monday of Proust's death. 'Paris was a stricken city. In every house, in every café, on all the sidewalks people said continually: "It seems that he is dead. It was very unexpected."' Ford had seen similar reactions in London only five weeks earlier after the music-hall entertainer Marie Lloyd died. 'London traffic stopped for half a minute, whilst the paper boys ran down the streets shouting: "Ma-*rie* dies! Ma-*rie*'s dead!" But Paris was hushed for three days – and not for a music-hall singer. At that time, if you said to a waiter: "Where's the funeral?" he told you, or if, being in deep black, you hailed a taxi, the man, without orders, drove you straight to where Proust lay in state.' Camille Wixler, one of Proust's favourite young waiters, never forgot the moment on that Sunday when Olivier, the maître d'hôtel at the Ritz, came up to him to say, 'Camille, you know, Monsieur Proust has just died.' Fifty years later Wixler still felt the grief and regret: 'I cried in front of everyone. Oh! if only I could remember everything that Monsieur told me.'

Parisians' response to Proust's death is not surprising: his characters had become part of the social coinage of Paris. 'Each month the vogue for M. Proust makes further progress,' the critic Fernand Vandérem had recently written. 'There are few people, in Society, who do not know his characters and who do not speak of them like old friends.' Françoise, the Duc and Duchesse de Guermantes, M. de Norpois, the Verdurin clan and others were talked about as representative types, and in some cases treated like leaders of fashion, by the *beau monde* of Paris. Vandérem had recently been quizzed at a dinner party about the standing of the visitors to a certain salon. When he replied vaguely, his interlocutor cut him short with an allusion to the Guermantes. 'In a word,' she demanded with a smile, 'do Oriane and Basin go there?' Generally, Vandérem had declared in June, Proust should be the happiest of men. 'What greater joy for a writer, what finer reward, than to see the characters whom he has counterfeited from humanity start to live as if they are real beings?' In time, too, some of Proust's real-life friends and readers grew to resemble his characters. A quarter of a century after his death, Elisabeth de Clermont-Tonnerre, who had re-read his books constantly in the intervening years, had come to seem like 'the *Ancien Monde* personified,' said someone who met her in old age: 'with yellow satin ribbons on her hat and a goitre, quite enchanting, amiable and secure, and so victorious over World and Time that she had long ceased to trouble herself about them.'

On 19 November François Mauriac went to the 'sordidly furnished apartment', as he called it, to pay homage in 'the room where Marcel Proust lay and where he finished his suffering.'

Like the other mourners assembled there, he was awed by the extent of Proust's self-sacrifice. Proust had renounced his life, and forfeited his creative spirit, in order to fulfil his vocation, they all agreed. 'You don't create so many people without having to yield up your own life,' Paul Morand said to Mauriac. It was Morand who first likened Proust's final physical collapse to the death agony of Pascal 260 years earlier, and in the days that followed Anna de Noailles, François le Grix, Mauriac and Maurice Martin du Gard all took up this comparison with Pascal when they spoke or wrote of Proust's death. The details of the last days were retold among the callers at 44 Rue Hamelin: how Proust had refused to eat, had sent away his doctors and had promised Céleste, 'only when I have finished my work, will I start looking after myself.' Everyone endorsed the verdicts of Proust's old friend Gabriel de la Rochefoucauld, who exclaimed when he had heard the stories of Proust's last dealings with Céleste, 'what will-power, what perseverance, what love of truth!'; and of Claudel, who thought Proust's life and death were 'a type of martyrdom'.

There was a bunch of violets on Proust's chest; nearby, a sprig of box and holy water. Jacques Porel slipped onto Proust's finger a cameo ring that had been given to his late mother Réjane by Anatole France. Mauriac, as a Catholic, was offended by the secular arrangements of the corpse: 'His hands were not clasped together as in prayer, there was no crucifix resting on his chest – all signs of his renunciation of God.' (In fact Céleste Albaret had forgotten that Proust had asked for a rosary to be placed in his fingers after death.) Edmond Jaloux, his companion at Le Boeuf sur le Toit, was amongst the visitors who called in homage and grief at Rue Hamelin. 'The last time I saw Proust, he was laid out on his death-bed,' Jaloux recalled. The din of the city reverberated outside, and Proust's 'miserable little under-furnished room that testified to his indifference to comfort' looked as if its occupant had never finished moving in, with wallpaper that had not been hung, and the doors all scraped and in need of paint. On the chimney mantelpiece, an array of notebooks was laid out in tribute to the departed genius. 'I had the impression that Marcel Proust, lying there lifeless, was more dead than other corpses,' Jaloux wrote. 'He was totally absent . . . In the same way that he hadn't been alive like other people, he wasn't dead like other people.' The notebooks were what Cocteau remembered best about the room of death: the *cahiers* seemed alive, he said, like a wrist-watch still ticking on a dead soldier.

Maurice Martin du Gard, too, never forgot the sight of the notebooks displayed on the chimney-shelf. He was one of the earliest callers – arriving just as Hahn and Lucien Daudet left in great distress – and felt awed by the experience. 'I crossed a rather provincial drawing-room where the sofas and chairs were swathed in dust-covers; I entered the bedroom, which was very simple, almost bare,' he described. 'On a brass bed-stead, stripped of its usual blankets, sheets, bed-shawl, notebooks, penholders, books and newspapers, Marcel Proust lay motion-less in a peace that enhanced his nobility, his hair and mous-tache looking waxed, with immensely dark rings around his eyes, his hands nearly as white as the bed-sheet.' Gide was another caller. 'I saw him again,' Gide wrote on the Monday, 'all gaunt and already turning blue from the cold of the grave. My heart felt very heavy.' Others shared Jaloux's feeling that Proust in death was awesome and distinctive. 'Oh, it was horrible, but how handsome he was!' Paul Helleu exclaimed on the day of the funeral when he was talking about his drawing of Proust's corpse. 'I have done him dead as dead. He hadn't eaten for five months, except for *café au lait*. You can't imagine how beautiful it can be, the corpse of a man who hasn't eaten for such a long time; everything superfluous is dissolved away.' Mauriac agreed with Helleu that Proust looked handsome in death: 'Laid out on his bed, one would not have thought that he was fifty years old, but scarcely thirty, as if Time didn't dare to touch him who had tamed and vanquished it,' he wrote.

Many of Proust's acquaintances, in the days after his death, wrote grieving tributes for the press: Léon Daudet's 'La mort de Marcel Proust' in *Action Française* (20 November), Paul Souday's 'Marcel Proust' in *Le Temps* (20 November), the Comtesse de Noailles's 'Adieu à Marcel Proust' in *L'Intransigeant* (21 November), Paul Brach's 'Souvenir de Marcel Proust' in *L'Opinion* (24 November), Princesse Elizabeth Bibesco's 'Marcel Proust' in the *New Statesman* (25 November), Robert de Flers' 'Marcel Proust' in *Le Figaro* (25 November), Paul Morand's 'Une Agonie' in *Les Nouvelles Littéraires* (25 November), Jacques Rivière's 'Marcel Proust' in the *Nouvelle Revue Française* (1 December) and Albert Flament's 'Marcel Proust' in *Revue de Paris* (15 December). All these obsequies displayed insight and skill, some had grace and humour, and others analytical power; but one tribute above all others was a classic: François Mauriac's meditation 'Sur la tombe de Marcel Proust' published in *La Revue Hebdomadaire* on 2 December. It was crucial in creating the posthumous legends of Proust's commitment to his vocation and self-immolation for the sake of his art. 'We must reflect on the extraordinary fate of a creator who was devoured by his own creation,' Mauriac began. 'Marcel Proust gave up his life so that his work could live,

and that is unprecedented.' It was the logical, if extreme, conclusion to his pre-war decision to become a recluse living chiefly in
a domain of his imaginative creation: 'Proust only quitted the
world in order to construct another world . . . Now that he is
walled up in his tomb, we finally can understand this strange
asceticism, this total repudiation of everything that did not bear
on his work, that went so far as to refuse all food because he
thought that fasting would aid his recovery, or at least give him a
respite in which to achieve his heroic yet insane pursuit of *temps
perdu*.' Mauriac told his readers of the final creative surge, hours
from death, sitting up with Céleste Albaret in that icy, sordid
bedroom. 'On his last night he dictated some final reflections on
Death saying, "That will serve for the death of Bergotte." And
we have seen ourselves on an envelope stained by herbal tea the
last illegible words that he scrawled, of which the only decipher-
able one is the name of Forcheville: in this way, right to the end,
his characters fed on his vital substance, and exhausted what little was left to him of life.' Mauriac, like Morand, recalled Pascal's
death agonies in 1662, and especially 'the prayer in which Pascal
asked God to what good use he could put illness and bodily
infirmity. Marcel Proust, who was as much debilitated by pain as
Pascal, like him asked the same question, and responded like
him by giving his all.'

Accounts of Proust's last hours began to circulate in Paris and
beyond: in their vivid unreliability they vied with the contradictory versions of his conversation with James Joyce six months
earlier at the Majestic. These apocryphal stories romanticised
the bleak and uncompromising facts of death: they tried to
ward off Time from swallowing Proust whole. Mauriac, for
example, came to simplify the 18 November 1922 into an event

that was neat and fit: a self-willed death by someone whose life work was finished. 'Proust wrote "Fin" on the last page of *Le temps retrouvé*, and then he died,' Mauriac believed, in old age. 'When the creator has within him, as Proust had, a completed monument, on no matter how vast a scale, with its proportions, its balance, its harmony duly established, then, once the work is finished, there is nothing for him to do except take refuge in silence.' The expatriate community in Paris was full of tales. 'They say he greeted death as a sort of importunate and expected guest,' wrote the young American-in-Paris Malcolm Cowley. 'A few days before he died, his novel was finished, as nearly finished as such a work can ever be; it lacked a final adornment, but the great fleshed skeleton was complete. He asked that all his eight books be brought to him. "Find the passages where I have spoken about death. It seems to me that I should know it better now. I want to rewrite the death of Bergotte."' Clive Bell, in London, heard that a few hours from death Proust revised his account of the death of the narrator's *grandmère* saying, '*J'ai plusieurs retouches à y faire.*' 'Art was Proust's last illusion,' said Bell. 'Love he had seen through.' Across the Atlantic a more dramatic death-bed scene was enacted in Harvey Wickham's imagination: 'His brother, Dr Robert Proust, finally forced his way to the bedside of the dying man, but it was too late. The novelist, on the last night of all, dictated a few notes completing his description of the death of Bergotte. It was the night of November 18, 1922. The bottle of ink upset. Proust was dead.' Princesse Marthe Bibesco, a good Catholic, provided yet another version. 'Just before the insomniac abandoned himself completely to his final rest,' she claimed, 'he woke up for an instant and demanded . . . that Abbé Mugnier should come and pray alone for an hour, by the bed where Proust was lying surrounded by his last papers, and make his general and public confession. Abbé Mugnier came, and he prayed.'

Travellers, letters and telegrams took forth the news from Rue Hamelin. The artist Jean Hugo had gone to visit his grandmother near Lunel, a southern town between the foothills of the Cévennes and the Mediterranean coast. 'One morning, I was sitting under a bower of passionflowers, in a coppice of bamboo. Jean Godebski, who had arrived from Paris by the night-train, said: "Thingummy is dead! It's idiotic, but I can't bring myself to say his name. O, all right, it's Proust!"' Ever afterwards Hugo associated passionflowers with the death of Proust. The flow of letters told contradictory stories. 'Ah, Proust!' Dorothy Bussy wrote to Gide on 22 November. 'Without having known him, one has felt his departure like the loss of an intimate friend. What an event he has been in all our lives!' The sense of loss was palpable. The young writer Roger Martin du Gard similarly told Rivière that his brain was 'paralysed by the news of Proust's death', although they had never met. 'Proust's death,' Madox Ford wrote from Paris on 25 November, 'has cast an extraordinary gloom on literary parties – though he was pretty generally disliked personally.'

In London the news dazed the cognoscenti. There was a palpable sense of loss among his dedicated readers when, on Monday, *The Times* announced that Marcel Proust was dead. 'It seemed,' wrote the Englishwoman Elizabeth Bibesco, 'like a breach of confidence to read it in a newspaper. It is the price you pay for loving public characters, suddenly to see in cold, hard print a name that you have murmured and cherished and wrapped up in warm folds of intimacy. Out they walk of the

fire-lit room you have known them in, suddenly dispossessed, a
foundling, a pauper on the public rates of admiration.' Walkley's reaction, too, was visceral.

> To judge from the newspapers, there have been tremendous
> 'crises' in public affairs lately: the triumph of Fascismo in
> Italy, the Lausanne Conference, the English elections. But
> to many of us the great events are merely spectacular; they
> pass rapidly across the screen, while the band plays irrele-
> vant scraps of syncopated music, and seem no more real
> than any other of the adventures, avowedly fictitious, that
> are 'filmed' for our idle hours. They don't come home to our
> business and bosoms. But one announcement in *The Times*
> of last Monday week shocked many of us with a sudden,
> absurdly indignant bewilderment like a foul blow: I mean
> the death of Marcel Proust.

Of course, as a reader commented shortly afterwards, the vast
majority of the English had never heard of Proust; but to the select
few 'his death came as a shock so great that it was as if one of their
most intimate acquaintances had suddenly passed from them.'

Apart from *The Times*, where Walkley and Scott Moncrieff
worked, British journalists did not know how to interpret
Proust to their readers: most London newspapers reported his
death under such vague captions as 'the French George Mered-
ith'. We have no record of the Schiffs' immediate grief; but a
year later Sydney wrote a sentence that says more about him
than about his idol: 'the great comfort to those who loved him
is that till the last he was a glorious spoilt child.' Schiff also composed a measured tribute for publication in the special Proust
issue of the *Nouvelle Revue Française* of January 1923. In this

essay he finally renounced his personal fixation with the primacy of Swann: 'it is the portrait of Charlus, in my opinion, which
is the very greatest triumph of Proust: first among equals in a
gallery of masterpieces.'

Proust himself had been fictionalising his death until the last
hours of his life. The final dictation that Proust gave to Céleste
Albaret, in the early hours of 18 November, was still attempting
to improve his description of the death of his character
Bergotte. 'I didn't yet know what it's like to die when I wrote it,'
he supposedly told her. 'I know it more now.' These last scraps
are incoherent, as Mauriac said, but even without them, the
death scene of Bergotte remains magnificent. Proust had written it after visiting an exhibition of Dutch paintings at the Jeu
de Paume in May 1921. There he had studied Vermeer's 'View of
Delft' which he had last seen on his visit to The Hague in 1902.
As a result, he created a death scene that provides his own
apotheosis. Bergotte, Proust writes, has long adored Vermeer's
View of Delft, a picture which he thinks he has memorised well;
but a critic has just praised the perfection of 'a little patch of yellow wall' that Bergotte cannot remember. So, already ill, he goes
to the exhibition. He passes other pictures that look dead; then
at last reaches the Vermeer. It is a painting that he

> remembered as more brilliant, more distinctive than any-
> thing else he knew, but in which, thanks to the critic's article,
> he remarked for the first time little human figures in blue,
> the pinkness of the sand, and finally the precious tiny patch
> of yellow on the wall. His giddiness increased; he fixed his
> eyes, like a child on a yellow butterfly which it wants to
> catch, upon the precious little patch of wall. 'That is how I

ought to have written,' he said. 'My last books are too dry, I should have kept overlaying them with more colour, made my sentences more finely-wrought, like this little patch of yellow wall.' Meanwhile he realised the gravity of his physical faintness. It appeared to him that on the heavenly scales were balanced, on one side, his own life, on the other the little patch of wall so beautifully painted in yellow. He felt that he had rashly surrendered the former for the latter . . . He repeated to himself: 'Little patch of yellow wall, little patch of yellow wall'. While doing so he sank down upon a circular settee; then at once ceased to think that his life was in jeopardy and reassured himself, 'It's just simple indigestion from those potatoes that were insufficiently cooked; it's nothing.' A new stroke beat him down, he rolled off the settee to the floor, as visitors and attendants rushed towards him. He was dead. Dead for ever? Who shall say?

Six months to the day before Proust's death, at the Schiffs' supper party for the Ballets Russes, James Joyce had thought he looked 'ten years younger than his age' and had felt no presentiment of his rival's death. That May night at the Majestic, though, signalled the close of an epoch as well as marking the start of Proust's final deterioration in strength. The party had brought together a set of cliques that were mutually exclusive and even mutually insulting; and yet individuals in each coterie were eaten by curiosity and envy, or teased by nostalgia, about what was happening in the other sets. Overall the mood of the diners was frivolous and eager: though sensitive about their own feelings and bedevilled by their own hopes, they were callous, for the most part, about others. Diaghilev played to perfection his role as the evening's great controlling impresario: Sydney Schiff, fretful and probably full of champagne, played with more modesty the part of a diligent host. Proust was effusive, Stravinsky nervous and touchy after the première of *Le Renard*, Joyce brooding and maladept, and Picasso (one can suppose) felt ruthless and unassailable as he sat among the more vulnerable bit-players in the social comedy. Larionov boomed, Fitelberg glowered and looked around for the main chance, Tchernicheva looked utterly beautiful, and Nijinska was as plain as ever but full of self-respect and integrity. Clive Bell, representing the Bloomsbury set, watched the Paris masters of Modernism with the keenness of an affable hawk. Music-lovers quarrelled about Beethoven's quartets, and Marcelle Meyer grew bored by the noisy egos. Some of the Russian *émigrés* badly needed feeding; other guests like Charles Mendl kept tables that were among the best in Paris. James Joyce felt overwhelmed by the lavish feast, and unsettled by the material comforts enjoyed by Picasso and Proust. Delafosse, one suspects, winced inwardly when he saw Proust, but unlike the fashionable lady who thought her parsimony had been derided in *Temps perdu*, he did not make an outward show of hostility. This was the Ritz-Riviera world so hated by Wyndham Lewis, populated by the chic rather than the great, where heraldic quarterings still sometimes counted, but where aesthetic discrimination mattered most. The next time many of the guests were together was for the funeral of Proust and the procession that carried his coffin to the cemetery. Whether he was dead for ever – or whether his little patches of yellow paint would ensure that his memory lived – was for his readers to decide.

That night at the Majestic encapsulated the quandary about

Proust's posthumous reputation. Did he belong to the past or was he a great innovator? Was the party, with all its expensive elegance, its *belle époque* décor and its noblewomen and *haut bourgeois*, essentially nineteenth-century in its style and temper? Or were the stateless and precariously situated Russians, the rich cosmopolitan Jews, the representative from the Groupe des Six, and those unlikely Communist sympathisers, Elisabeth de Clermont-Tonnerre and Picasso, all proof that the Schiffs' party was a twentieth-century *mélange*? The weeks after Proust's death were rich with tributes from Poles, Spaniards, Germans, Italians, Englishmen and Americans. 'I don't think,' Joseph Conrad mused in December 1922, 'there ever has been in the whole of literature such power of analysis, and I feel pretty safe in saying that there will never be another.' But throughout the tributes there was disagreement about the Modernity of Proust. Malcolm Cowley, from Pennsylvania, was categorical: 'the nineteenth is Proust's century: all the congregation of his friends and imitators cannot advance him into the twentieth.' From Spain, however, Ortega y Gasset hailed Proust as the 'inventor' of 'a new way of seeing': without his work, 'literary evolution since the nineteenth century would contain a huge hole'. Proust's German champion, Ernst Robert Curtius, averred that *Temps perdu* had ushered in 'a new era in the history of the great French novel'. Proust, declared Curtius, 'surpasses Flaubert in intelligence as he surpasses Balzac in literary qualities and Stendhal in understanding of life and of beauty.' From Italy came gratitude for the example that Proust's work had so 'fruitfully' given to an ambitious new generation of novelists. On the issue of modernity, the English temporised between the views of Europeans, who hailed Proust's twentieth-century innovativeness, and the Americans, who treated him as a figure already historic. John Middleton Murry posed the question, 'Is he an end or a beginning?', and concluded, 'More an end than a beginning, perhaps.' Certainly Proust's name was sacrosanct in London during the eighteen months after his death. 'The most elegant conspiracies of our literary drawing-rooms centre on that odd king over the water, M. Proust,' wrote a leading English man-of-letters in 1924. 'The vogue has risen into a cult; and the cult, embracing the cultured masses, has deepened into a wave; until the whole of our literary taste is threatened by the towering line of this tidal, this positively Marcel, wave.'

On Tuesday 21 November 1922 Proust was put in his coffin by the undertakers. Next day he was taken for a noon service in the small, architecturally nondescript seventeenth-century church of Saint-Pierre-de-Chaillot, which served the prosperous residents of the *quartier* Chaillot in the sixteenth *arrondissement*. The church was only a short distance from Proust's apartment: Rue Hamelin is on the east and Rue de Chaillot on the west of Avenue d'Iéna which runs up to the Étoile. (In the 1930s the old building was demolished and a magnificent new church was inaugurated on the site in 1936: it is all the more imposing for opening onto spacious Avenue Marceau rather than narrow Rue de Chaillot, where the houses rise up high like the walls of a gorge.) As a Chevalier of the Légion d'Honneur, Proust was accorded a military escort; and at his request Ravel's *Pavane for a Dead Infanta* was played during the ceremony instead of the customary liturgical music. There were family mourners as well as the Albarets and *Tout Paris*. Friends and acquaintances represented every phase of his fifty-one years: Fernand Gregh from

his schooldays; Comte Greffulhe from his days as a young
social-climber; Comte Étienne de Beaumont and Princesse
Lucien Murat from his nights as a Ritz celebrity; Jean Girau-
doux and Maurice Rostand among the multitude of authors.
Only Gide's absence was notable. Maurice Martin du Gard felt
that the diversity of the congregation turned the funeral into a
rare spectacle as well as an occasion for grief: 'Dukes, princes,
ambassadors, members of the Jockey and the Union, in buttoned boots, in monocles, with brilliantined hair (even the bald
ones), patrons of the Turf, high Russian Jewry and the leading
Parisian homosexuals, with their varnished nails . . . and all the
writers who mattered, or were going to matter in the future.'

Once Abbé Delepouve had pronounced absolution, and the
mourners had streamed out of the church to the sound of
tolling bells, the funeral procession left Saint-Pierre-de-Chaillot
for the cemetery of Père Lachaise. Gathered again in the church
and the streets were guests from the Schiffs' night at the Majestic: Diaghilev accompanied Reynaldo Hahn's sister to the funeral mass; outside the church the multitude of spectators waiting
in Rue de Chaillot and Avenue Marceau included James Joyce.
Vladimir Mayakovsky, the Russian Futurist émigré, who had
just been admitted into France on a visa obtained for him by
Diaghilev, was among the street crowd too. So, also, was Ford
Madox Ford, who thought the funeral 'a tremendous affair'.
Mourners who had known Proust long before, but had been
excluded from his later life, felt saddened and estranged by the
crowd of Proustians who had only known him through his
books or by recent visits to the sickroom in Rue Hamelin. On
that sunny November day, as the choristers of Saint-Pierre-de-
Chaillot sang their requiem, Albert Flament, who had first met

Proust as a teenager, felt distanced from 'the Marcel Proust of recent years, during which so many admirers visited him although his friends could no longer ever see him.' As Flament gazed at the coffin of his boyhood friend, he was flooded by powerful, even violent memories of *le temps perdu*. He did not weep 'for the Marcel Proust of great fame and literary glory', but instead for the intense, vulnerable eighteen-year-old boy whom he had known living with his parents in Boulevard Malesherbes.

After the service Gabriel Astruc and Léon Daudet, who had been bitter enemies for over thirty years, came face to face after climbing through opposite doors of the same taxi. Astruc apologised, Daudet smiled, and they were reconciled: indeed, wrote Astruc, they later separated that day '*avec un grand salut à la française*'. There were final leave-takings as well as reconciliations. Both Martin du Gard and Mauriac glimpsed Barrès for the last time as he left the church after Proust's funeral with his bowler tilted over his eyes and his umbrella hooked over his arm. 'I always thought him Jewish, little Marcel, but what a beautiful funeral,' he said to Martin du Gard as they faced the crowds (including Joyce, Madox Ford and Mayakovsky) on the opposite pavement. Barrès, said Mauriac, 'was astonished by the blaze of glory aroused by the death of someone whom he had known so well, and even loved, without ever a suspicion of his greatness. "So, this, at last, is what's happened to our young man," he repeated to me.'

The long funeral procession led by black horses drawing the ebony-coloured hearse moved slowly eastwards from church to cemetery. It traversed Avenue Marceau and Avenue George V – halting the traffic on those great urban arteries – and turned right into the Champs-Élysées, which Proust's narrator had thought such a melancholy district when Charles Swann lived there. Indeed Paris, throughout Proust's final journey, had never seemed richer in Proustian associations, although its street cries, which he had been so proud of evoking in the novel, were temporarily stilled as the catafalque passed by. When the cortège reached the gardens of the Champs-Élysées, which had been laid out by Colbert, and were bounded by Avenue Gabriel and Avenue de Marigny, Cocteau pointed at the spot where Proust's fictional self had frolicked in adolescence with Gilberte Swann and discovered the joys of *frottage*. It was in this garden also that another of his characters, the young Duke of Châtellerault, posing as an Englishman, had enjoyed a steamy encounter with the *aboyeur*, or usher, who announced the names of visitors at the Prince de Guermantes's house. In answer to the satiated *aboyeur*'s grateful questions the duke had stubbornly replied, from one end of Avenue Gabriel to the other, 'I do not speak French.' Fittingly, near the close of the twentieth-century, the gravel footpath that bisects this garden was renamed Allée Marcel Proust by the Paris authorities.

At Place de la Concorde (where in a scene in *Sodome et Gomorrhe* a summer sunset had given the Luxor obelisk the appearance of pink nougat and where later the moon resembled a golden scimitar in the sky) the procession turned north towards the Opéra, where Proust had seen and celebrated the Ballets Russes, and where his narrator had watched Berma perform an act from *Phèdre* while it seemed to his fancy that the aristocrats in their theatre boxes resembled sea-goddesses, nereids and tritons. It was at this moment that Maurice Martin du Gard, Cocteau, de Lauris, Jaloux and the young prodigy Raymond Radiguet discreetly peeled away from the procession: they were hungry, and as Rue Boissy d'Anglas runs north out of the Place from the corner with Avenue Gabriel, they hastened up the narrow street to Le Boeuf sur le Toit, where they fortified themselves with pancakes. Afterwards, they took taxis to the cemetery, which they reached while the convoy was still trudging with slow solemnity along Avenue de la République.

Indeed the funeral march through the Paris streets was so prolonged, and the cortège inched so gently up through the lines of tombs towards the summit of Père-Lachaise, where Proust was laid in a grave beside those of his parents, that the mourners only began to disperse from the cemetery towards dusk. Some of them flung flowers on the newly covered grave. It would have pleased Proust that his funeral made such an impression on his city; and pleased him too that so many mourners, although anguished by his death, were also thinking of his books, which would preserve his name in perpetuity. Maurice Martin du Gard, as he descended from the summit of the graveyard to the city streets, walked behind Rostand and Léon Daudet, whose distress was painful to watch. After an unwontedly sunny morning, it had become a grey day, which made the stones of the cemetery seem all the drabber. Martin du Gard felt especially desolate when, for a moment, he contrasted this dismal, muddy November scene with the flowering orchards and joyous May blossom of À l'ombre des jeunes filles en fleurs – part of that visible and invisible universe that Proust had created, and which would be what most people would remember him for.

In the heavenly scales Bergotte's life had been balanced against Vermeer's artistic perfection: for Proust in his final illness the countervailing weights had been personal survival and the impulse to perfect his book. When, a year after Proust's death, the scene of Bergotte's death was published in *La Prisonnière*, so many people – Jaloux and Elisabeth de Clermont-Tonnerre among them – were inexpressibly moved by this passage with its sublime consolation. The scene ends with two sentences of tentative yet transfiguring hope:

> The idea that Bergotte was not wholly and permanently
> dead is by no means improbable.
> They buried him, but all through the night of mourning,
> in lighted bookshop windows, his books arranged three
> by three kept watch like angels with outstretched wings
> and seemed, for him who was no more, the symbol of his
> resurrection.

Céleste Albaret recalled that as she returned to the empty Rue Hamelin apartment after the funeral, a bookshop in the vicinity had done exactly that: decked its illuminated windows with Proust's volumes, arranged three by three, as if promising his resurrection.

Acknowledgements

To judge by the dates written in my worn copies of the Scott Moncrieff/Schiff translation of *Remembrance of Things Past* I bought my first volumes of Proust with money given as a birthday present in June 1969, but did not succeed in reading *Swann's Way* until a holiday at Gracefield in Quebec in August 1970 when I was trying to impress my friend John Sherwood. Like many readers I did not get past this first volume at my initial attempt; but next year, I returned to *Swann*, and evidently made serious headway during the summer of 1971 when I started to buy the later volumes at short intervals. Alain de Botton has famously written a book entitled *How Proust Can Change Your Life*. Proust changed my life when, as a borderline candidate for university entrance, I went for an interview at Selwyn College, Cambridge in September 1971. I was interview by Harry Porter, a historian of Tudor Cambridge and of Puritanism, the Treasurer of Cambridge Footlights theatre-club and an ardent Proustian. In those happier days it was still permissible for dons and undergraduates to flirt during interviews. 'Mmmmm,' he said as he handed me a glass of sherry, 'what have *you* got in *your* pocket?', and deftly plucked out a little volume of Proust in its merry blue-and-white jacket. Harry, as many husbands and grandfathers will remember with gratitude, was adept at getting his hands into the pockets of other men's trousers. Most of my interview, as I have often recalled, was spent discussing how gloriously Greta Garbo might play the Queen of Naples in a film version of *À la recherche du temps perdu*. I was offered a place at Cambridge, and if it was not due to Garbo, it must certainly have been due to Proust.

Harry Porter died in Cambridge in December 2003, and it was not until September 2004, when I was completing this book in Ardèche, that I realised quite how much was owed to him. When my Editor at Faber commissioned me to write *A Night at the Majestic*, I had purposely put aside the two finest Proust biographies, by George Painter and Jean-Yves Tadie, and tried not to refer to them. But finally picking up a copy of Painter, and reading some faded pencilled marginalia that I had made in 1971, I learnt something that startled me. I had always remembered talking about Garbo at my interview; but I had utterly forgotten that Harry also told me about Violet Schiff, whom as a young man he had visited at her house in Ilchester Place, that Harry had told me about her veneration of Proust's memory and had described to me her great party at the Majestic.*
This discovery in the blurred margin of an old book was a

*On 3 August 1944, the tenth anniversary of the Schiffs moving into Abinger Manor in Surrey, their house, together with the nearby church and a cottage they had lent to Max Beerbohm in exile from Italy, was damaged by a German bomb. They were taken, with slight injuries, by ambulance to Brighton: there, on 29 October, Schiff died of heart failure at the Sackville Court Hotel. As Richard Aldington wrote to Violet, 'Knowing how sensitive and highly strung Sydney was I cannot help thinking that he was really killed by that explosion – delayed shock.' Following the war Mrs Schiff moved into a square modern house in Ilchester Place, on the edge of Holland Park, where she received visitors keen to hear her reminiscences of Proust, although she preferred not to leave the house. Her death in 1962 was marked by T. S. Eliot's memorial tribute published in *The Times*.

minor revelation. It was nothing so momentous as Proust's fictional impersonator dipping a biscuit in his tea, or stumbling over the cobbles in the Prince de Guermantes' courtyard: I was not stunned by waves of rapture, but I realised with astonishment that I had for thirty years carried an unconscious memory of Harry Porter's account of Violet Schiff before I came to write this book. I wish I could thank him in person.

Amongst the living, my chief debt is to David Gelber, whose meticulous reading of my preliminary drafts, intensive criticism of my prose and ideas, and inspired discoveries on the open shelves of the London Library have immeasurably improved *A Night at the Majestic*. His challenges to my tired prejudices, his testing of my facts and the gentle, irresistible firmness with which he offered me his own ideas make it unthinkable that he should not be one of the dedicatees. How delighted Proust would have been to meet, in David Gelber, a Prince of the Holy Roman Empire; and how disappointed he would have been that David cares so little about his own quarterings.

Early versions of this book have also been read and criticised by Jenny Davenport and Christopher Phipps: both have saved me from errors of grammar, taste and judgement; both have reproached me when I have been inept and goaded me for self-indulgence. It is a pleasure to thank Professor Jennifer Greenleaves, Irina Kronrod, Giles Milton, Professor Luciano Segreto, Esther Selsdon and her husband Alex Games for providing references or helping with Italian and German translations. My friend and agent Bill Hamilton of A. M. Heath has given indispensable advice and generous support at every stage of my work. Julian Loose has been the most discreet but effective of Editors. Cosmo Davenport-Hines helped in the final preparation of this book for publication. During the final revisions of my manuscript I have been much influenced by the narrative power and thematic organisation in the histories and biographies written by Philip Mansel. Robert Noel, Lancaster Herald, has not been much help in answering my questions about the French peerage, but has consoled me with his jaunty assurances that the answers do not matter, and in other ways has given me more encouragement than he can possibly realise.

Other debts are an equal pleasure to acknowledge. George Painter's biography of Proust captivated me when I first read it thirty years ago, and encouraged me to make my earliest Proustian research trip, to Illiers-Combray and Paris, in the company of Rolfe Kentish in 1974. The scholarship and imaginative power of Jean-Yves Tadié's more recent biography of Proust fill me with admiration and gratitude.

The resources and staff of the matchless London Library have been as indispensable in the research of this book as they were to Violet Hunt, Sir Osbert Sitwell and so many other early Proustians. Much of my text has been written in the Library's Reading Room, which since 1999 has become (under the superintendence of Christopher Phipps) the most congenial clerisy on earth. On the few occasions when the London Library's resources failed me, I have been helped by the staff and facilities of the Athenæum, of Cambridge University Library, the Wellcome Library and the British Library.

For copies of Violet Schiff's correspondence with Richard Ellmann I thank the Department of Special Collections, McFarlin Library, University of Tulsa. Lorni N. Curtis, Head of Special Collections and Archives at the McFarlin Library, was singularly helpful and friendly. For permission to quote from the unpublished diaries of Stella Benson I thank Cambridge University Library. I am grateful to Faber and Faber, as publishers of Robert Lowell's *Collected Poems* (2003), for permission to quote from Lowell's poem 'F. O. Matthiessen 1902–1950'.

Excerpts from *CORRESPONDANCE de Marcel Proust 1880–1922*, volumes I–XXI, selected, presented and annotated by Philip KOLB. © Librarie PLON, 1973–1993.

Most translations in this book from French to English – from Proust's novel, from his correspondence and from the memoirs and essays of his contemporaries – are my own work. The chief exception to this rule is that I have often preferred, when making shorter quotations from *Temps retrouvé*, to use the words in the first edition of *Time Regained* over which Sydney Schiff laboured in 1930. Although I feel awed respect and resounding gratitude for the efforts of most of Proust's translators, and will always remember with pleasure my (largely non-Proustian) contacts with the late Dennis Enright and with John Sturrock, I have been affronted while researching this book by the high-handed re-writing or slipshod approximations to which several other translators have resorted. Some English-language writers render Proust's sentences in ways that suit their arguments rather than represent his meaning. Other translators have sought to improve on the memories or to re-devise the insights of Proust's contemporaries who knew him intimately: still others seem confident that they have a surer mastery of words than Proust, or of other literary figures of twentieth-century France, and produce sentences that for all their flourishes are faithless, complacent and false. My versions of French texts may dissatisfy some readers, but I have tried throughout to make them exact, complete and unembellished.

Sources

CHAPTER I: 18 MAY

1 All the. 'Paris Crowds Enjoy the Sun,' *The Times*, 8 May 1922, 10e.

1 As if. *SetG*, 170; *S&G*, 175.

2 The Hotel. Sir Maurice Hankey to Adeline Hankey, 18 & 22 January 1919, Churchill College Archives, Cambridge, HNKY 3/24; Sisley Huddleston, *In and About Paris* (1927), 174–5.

2 The dance. A. J. P. Taylor ed., *Lloyd George, a Diary* by Frances Stevenson (1971), 175.

3 Pretty elderly. Diary of Stella Benson, 3 August 1925, Add. 6792, CUL.

3 Very human. Diary of Stella Benson, 24 May 1928, Add. 6796, CUL.

3 Earnest mask. Wyndham Lewis, *Apes of God* (1930), 242–3.

3 Rather frosty. Benson diary, 24 May 1928.

3 Her Jewish. Julian Fane, *Memoir in the Middle of the Journey* (1971), 49.

4 Great point. Valerie Eliot ed., *The Letters of T. S. Eliot*, I (1988), 411.

4 Resourceful dextrous. Hudson, *RMI*, 108–9.

5 The first. 'Ballets Russes given at Opera', *New York Herald* (Paris edition), 20 May 1922, 2.

6 Truly embarrassed. André Messager, 'Les premières', *Figaro*, 21 May 1922, 5.

6 Kind Mr. Clive Bell, *Old Friends* (1956), 179.

9 His linen. Cyril Beaumont, *The Diaghilev Ballet in London* (1951), 231–2.

9 He was. Bronislava Nijinska, *Early Memoirs* (1981), 253.

9 Air of. Sir Osbert Sitwell, *Great Morning* (1948), 246–7.

9 The most. Ernest Ansermet, *Écrits sur la musique* (1971), 27.

10 Performed by. Diaghilev, 'The Russian Ballet', *The Times*, 13 July 1929, 10c.

10 Slender stooping. Beaumont, *Diaghilev Ballet*, 193.

11 Exhibited his. V.Z., 'Una cena geniale', *Paralleli*, no. 7 (May 1992), 15. 'Dal segreto animo di dandy, esibisce la rivincita dello smoking con una lunga faixa catalana avvolta intorno alla vita.' I owe this translation to the kindness of Professor Jennifer Greenleaves.

12 Not merely. D. Paige ed., *The Letters of Ezra Pound 1907–1941* (1951), 122.

12 Not certain. Clermont-Tonnerre, IV, 108–9.

12 Picasso finished. Ansermet, *Écrits*, 25.

12 A racket. François Garnier ed., *Correspondance Max Jacob*, I (1953), 160.

13 The first. Jean Crespelle, *Picasso and his Women* (1969), 124.

13 Je ne. John Richardson, *A Life of Picasso*, II (1996), 432.

13 Has eyes. Nathalie Blondel ed., *The Journals of Mary Butts* (2002), 223.

14 She has. Arnold Haskell, *Balletomania* (1934), 86.

14 Poor Bronia. Igor Stravinsky and Robert Craft, *Memories and Commentaries* (2002), 99–100.

14 An artist. Alexandre Benois, *Reminiscences of the Russian Ballet* (1942), 380.

15 He put. Artur Rubinstein, *My Young Years* (1973), 208, 279.

15 Like a. 'Les premières', *Le Gaulois*, 21 May 1922, 3.

15 Tall and. Beaumont, *Diaghilev Ballet*, 133.

15 Always very. John Drummond, *Speaking of Diaghilev* (1997), 216.

15 Write in. Ansermet, *Écrits*, 11.

16 A huge. Stravinsky and Craft, *Memories and Commentaries*, 152.

16 A very. Benois, *Reminiscences*, 378.

16 The greatest. Stravinsky and Craft, *Memories and Commentaries*, 102.

16 Idzikowsky's thin. Beaumont, *Diaghilev Ballet*, 169.

17 Trefilova is. Haskell, *Balletomania*, 91.

17 A beautiful. Stravinsky and Craft, *Memories and Commentaries*, 102.

17 What is. Ansermet, *Écrits*, 23.

18 The Ballets Russes dancers on 18 May were Bronislava Nijinska, Vera Trefilova, Lubov Tchernicheva, Lubov Egorova, Vera Nemchinova, Ludmilla Schollar, Doubrovska, and Oghinska; together with Stanislas Idzikowsky, Pierre Vladimirov, Viltzak, Kremow [Nicolas Kremnev?], Zverow [Nicolas Zverev?], Jasvinsky, Michel Feoderov. The singers were Messieurs Fabert, Dubois, Narcon and Mahieux. See 'Les Théâtres', *Le Gaulois*, 18 May 1922, p. 3.

19 Great pianist. Francis Poulenc, *My Friends and Myself* (1978), 37.

20 A dolmen. Comte Robert de Montesquiou, *Les Pas Effacés*, II (1923), 288, 290–1.

20 *Arrivistes* not. Philippe Jullian, *Robert de Montesquiou* (1967), 172.

21 I must. Margherita, Lady Howard de Walden, *Pages from My Life* (1965), 200.

22 Too far. Lord Derwent, *Return Ticket* (1940), 110–11.

22 Clive has. Nigel Nicolson ed., *The Question of Things Happening: the Letters of Virginia Woolf, II* (1976), 554.

23 She looked. Stravinsky and Craft, *Memories and Commentaries*, 119.

23 Combined the. Clermont-Tonnerre, IV, 148.

23 Munificent Princess. Jean Marnold, 'Revue de la Quinzaine: Musique', *Mercure de France*, 159, 1 December 1922, 234.

24 The duchess. Liane de Pougy, *Mes Cahiers Bleus* (1978), 180.

25 A jewel. Pougy, *Cahiers Bleus*, 169.

26 Warm contralto. Beatrice, Lady Glenavy, *Today We Will Only Gossip* (1964), 177.

26 I should. Wyndham Lewis to Violet Schiff, 22 [?] May 1922, Add. ms. 52919, BL.

28 He seemed. Bell, *Old Friends*, 179–80.

28 At half-past. Clive Bell, *Proust* (1928), 9.

30 Proust of. Duc de Gramont, 'Proust as I knew him', *London Magazine*, II (November 1955), 24.

30 Like the. Mary and Padraic Colum, *Our Friend James Joyce* (1959), 151.

30 He entered. Clermont-Tonnerre, II, 56.

31 An abundance. Gerard Hopkins trans., *Letters of Marcel Proust to Antoine Bibesco* (1953), 16.

31 As I. Corr., XI, 69.

31 Nothing amuses. Princess Marthe Bibesco, *The Veiled Wanderer* (1949), 58; Corr., XXI, 461.

31 Horrible hovel. Corr., XXI, 132.

32 I can. Poulenc, *My Friends*, 79.

32 Young man. Stravinsky and Craft, *Memories and Commentaries*, 101.

32 Slow freeze-up. Charles Chaplin, *My Autobiography* (1964), 349.

33 Every piece. Léon Daudet, *Memoirs* (1926), 267.

34 She had. Clive Bell, *Proust* (1928), 5–6, 8.

34 Most of. Stravinsky and Craft, *Memories and Commentaries*, 157.

35 Infinitely gracious. Bell, *Proust*, 9.

35 Doubtless you. Bell, *Old Friends*, 180.

35 Musical snob. Michael de Cossart. *The Food of Love: Princesse Edmond de* Polignac (1865–1943) and her salon (1978), 144.

35 Rich impressions. Georges de Lauris, *À un ami* (1948), 36–7.

36 Prodigious efflorescence. SetG, 140; S&G, 145; Cities, I, 198.

36 The Russian. Misia Sert, *Two or Three Muses* (1953), 95.

36 Exquisite supper. LaP, 226; P, 217; Captive, II, 42–3.

36 Charming invasion. *Recherche*, V, 314. Captive, II, 42.

37 How handsome. Corr., XVI, 143.

38 Whatever happened. Fernand Gregh, *Mon amitié avec Marcel Proust* (1958), 36.

38 Joyce began. Bell, *Old Friends*, 180.

39 Yes I. Richard Ellmann, *James Joyce* (1959), 523.

39 A bad. Clermont-Tonnerre, IV, 225.

39 I have. Richard Ellmann, *Selected Letters of James Joyce* (1976), 273.

39 What should. Wyndham Lewis, *Blasting and Bombardiering* (1937), 271–2.

40 Our talk. Frank Budgen, *Further Recollections of James Joyce* (1955), 10–11.

40 Create a. Colum, *Our Friend Joyce*, 151–2.

40 Two stiff. Ford Madox Ford, *It was the Nightingale* (1934), 270–1.

42 I've headaches. William Carlos Williams, *Autobiography* (1951), 218.

42 If we. Ellmann, *Joyce*, 524.

42 I hate flowers. Ellmann, *Joyce*, 635.

42 The next twenty. Dwight MacDonald, *Against the American Grain* (1963), 124–5.

43 Those poor / talked incessantly. Violet Schiff, 'Proust Meets Joyce', *Adam*, no. 260 (1957), 65.

44 Comfortable place. Ellmann, *Joyce*, 524.

44 Picasso is. Ellmann, *Joyce*, 606.

44 So eager. Hudson, 'Céleste', 343.

45 It is. Albert Thibaudet, 'A Letter from France', *London Mercury*, II (May 1920), 111.

45 He is. Middleton Murry to Schiff, 8 January 1922, Add 52919, BL.

45 I observe. Ellmann, *Joyce*, 506.

45 M. Proust. Richard Aldington, *Literary Studies and Reviews* (1924), 179.

46 The glory. *Times Literary Supplement*, 9 June 1921, 368.

46 One reads. T. S. Eliot ed., *Literary Essays of Ezra Pound* (1954), 405.

46 The French. Ellmann, *Joyce*, 524.

46 From the. Corr., XXI, 432.

46 Immense psychological. 'Les livres de demain,' *Le Figaro*, 30 April 1922, p.1.

47 Proust is. Louis Vauxcelles, 'La vie artistique', *L'Éclair*, 18 May 1922, 3; Corr., XXI, 217.

47 Not being. A. B. Walkley, 'More Proust: aristocrats real and romantic', *The Times*, 17 May 1922, 12a; A. B. Walkley, *More Prejudice* (1923), 37.

47 I was. Sylvia Beach, *Shakespeare and Company* (1960), 93.

48 All men. Ezra Pound, 'Paris Letter', *The Dial*, 72 (1922), 623.

48 Literary Bolshevism. Sir Shane Leslie, 'Ulysses', *Quarterly Review*, 238 (1922), 220, 233–4.

48 A turgid. R. W. B. Lewis and N. Lewis eds., *The Letters of Edith Wharton* (1988), 461.

48 The intelligent. T. S. Eliot, 'London Letter', *The Dial*, 73 (1922), 329.

48 There is. Wyndham Lewis to Schiff, 26 May 1922, Add 52919, BL.

49 La recherche. Corr., XXI, 391

CHAPTER 2: IT'S THE LITTLE PROUST

50 An extraordinary. Julian Fane, *Memoir in the Middle*, 65.

50 He wasted. Violet Schiff, 'A Night With Proust', *London Magazine*, 3 (September 1956), 20–22.

52 People who. *Fugitive*, 500; *Sweet Cheat*, 163.

53 Energetic, well-balanced. Adrien Proust, *The Treatment of Neurasthenia* (1902), 103–4.

53 The young. Proust, *Neurasthenia*, 105.

53 Child that. Proust, *Neurasthenia*, 107, 108.

54 The child. Proust, *Neurasthenia*, 106.

54 The miracle. Albaret, 65.

55 Marcel Proust. Lucien Daudet, *Autour de soixante lettres de Marcel Proust* (1929), 35–6.

55 Still a. Corr., V, 349.

55 I'm not. Léon Daudet, *Salons et journaux* (1917), 299.

55 My book. Roger Shattuck, *Proust* (1974), 169.

55 Especially evil. Proust, *Neurasthenia*, 95.

56 Great Oriental. Daniel Halévy, *Pays Parisien* (1932), 122–3.

56 Detested by. Corr., XXI, 137.

56 When someone. Corr., IV, 32.

57 No one can. SetG, 25; S&G, 27; Cities, I, 33.

57 Excellent lunches. Corr., XXI, 117.

58 He was. Colette, 'Marcel Proust', *Le Point*, vol. 39 (1951), 43.

58 Astonished I. Duchesse de Clermont-Tonnerre, *Robert de Montesquiou et Marcel Proust* (1925), 10.

59 The weather. Corr., I, 115.

60 Arrogantly humble. *Côté G*, 414; *GW*, 425; *GW*, 164–5.

61 Why is. Duchesse de Clermont-Tonnerre, *Marcel Proust* (1948), 29; Mina Curtiss ed., *Letters of Marcel Proust* (1949), 17.

61 Society men. Proust, *Neurasthenia*, 21–22.

62 He had. Clermont-Tonnerre, *Montesquiou et Proust*, 10–11.

63 What horror. Corr., VII, 45.

63 Despite being. Corr., II, 66.

64 A number. Corr., V, 180–1.

64 The Jews. Corr., I, 442.

65 A Conscience. Corr., IX, 138.

65 Swann belonged. *SetG*, 103; *S&G*, 108-9; *Cities*, I, 145.

65 Brutal fool. Corr., II, 323.

66 The accusation. Sir Henry Channon, 'How I met Proust', *Adam*, no. 260 (1957), 69–70.

66 Parisian Jewess. Clermont-Tonnerre, I, 198.

66 Very Hebrew. Sir Harold Nicolson, *Peacemaking 1919* (1934), 318.

66 A remarkable. Sir Harold Nicolson, *Some People* (1927), 103.

66 Concentrated Jewishness. Paul Claudel, *Journal*, II (1969), 715.

66 A splash. Clermont-Tonnerre, *Mémoires*, II, 247.

67 Une Israélite. Edmond Jaloux, *Avec Marcel Proust* (1953), 30.

67 Edmund Wilson, *Axel's Castle* (1931), 119–20, 121.

67 The difference. Edmund Wilson, *The Thirties* (1980), 328.

67 Artificial Jew. Robert M. Adams, 'A Clear View of Combray', *Times Literary Supplement*, 12 June 1981, 667.

68 What a. Corr. VIII, 193.

68 Young madmen. *SetG*, 24; *S&G*, 26; *Cities*, I, 32.

68 The Jews. *SetG*, 18; *S&G*, 20; *Cities*, I, 22.

69 I had. *LeTR*, 258-9; *FTA*, 261, 276; *TR*, 287–8.

69 The loyal. *TR*, 303.

70 As soon. *SetG*, 490–1; *S&G*, 497–8; *Cities, II*, 347–9.

70 Foreign machination. *LaP*, 224; *P*, 215; *Captive, II*, 40.

71 I was. Corr., XVIII, 535–6.

71 Us. Corr., III, 382.

71 I shall. Corr., VI, 159.

72 Around 7.30. Daudet, *Salons*, 298.

72 The writer. *TR*, 252.

73 Once we. *SetG*, 481; *S&G*, 488; *Cities, II*, 334.

74 He stayed. Daudet, *Salons*, 301.

CHAPTER 3: AN ARK OF MY OWN

75 Their emotionalism. Proust, *Neurasthenia*, 54–5.

76 There were. Lucien Daudet, *Soixante Lettres*, 45.

76 A snob. Alan Sheridan, *André Gide* (1998), 268.

77 How very. Corr., III, 447.

77 No child. Corr., IV, 108.

77 Ours was. Painter, II, 12–13.

78 Never knew. Daudet, *Salons*, 299.

79 Mon petit. Corr., IV, 240–1.

79 Do not. Bibesco, 'Heartlessness', 424.

80 It's a pity. Céleste Albaret, *Monsieur Proust* (1976), 245–6.

80 To think. Corr., V, 313.

81 Intolerably sad. Corr., V, 314.

81 I am. Corr., V, 341.

81 Madame trembled. Painter, II, 49.

81 My life. Corr., V, 348–9.

82 My ravaged. Corr., VI, 307.

82 Sons without. *SetG*, 16-17; *S&G*, 19; *Cities, I*, 20.

82 Nothing is. Proust, *Neurasthenia*, 54.

82 In withdrawing. Proust, *Neurasthenia*, 120.

83 When I. 'À Mon Ami Willie Heath', *Les Plaisirs et les jours* (1924), 13.

83 Better dream. Proust, 'Regrets et Reveries', *Les Plaisirs*, 185.

83 This life. Corr., III, 432.

84 Reclusiveness profoundly. Leighton Hodson, *Marcel Proust* (1989), 98.

84 Neuropathic case. Bibesco, 'Heartlessness', 421.

84 Guided by. Miron Grindea, 'Proust après Painter', *Adam*, 310 (1966), 11.

84 Rubber stocks. Corr., X, 80.

85 Someone advised. Corr., XX, 571.

85 Aesthetic pleasure. Marcel Plantevignes, *Avec Marcel Proust* (1966), 416–7.

86 Subtle, profound. Corr., VIII, 111–3.

86 Devotion to. Fane, *Memoir*, 66–7.

87 One can. TR, 428.

87 The final. Corr., XVIII, 536.

88 Melancholy nuance. Corr., XXI, 469.

88 I am ill. Corr., XI, 251.

89 Reflecting that. *SetG*, 401; *S&G*, 407; *Cities*, II, 218.

89 An hour. TR, 238.

89 Acquaintance with. *Le TR*, 37–8; *FTA*, 38; *TR*, 44.

90 A man. Serge Lifar, *Serge Diaghilev*, x.

90 Unreality. *TR*, 221.

91 Sham tiffs. Clermont-Tonnerre, *Montesquiou et Proust*, 98.

91 The work. TR, 247–8.

91 He never. Hudson, 'Céleste', 336.

92 Not having. Corr., XX, 502.

92 Proust received. Cocteau, *Adam*, 57.

93 Men often. *TR*, 245.

93 Perpetual vivisection. Bibesco, 'Heartlessness', 423.

93 Happiness serves. TR, 261.

94 Healthy sadness. Corr., II, 384.

94 You are. Corr., XVI, 211.

94 Something may. *AD*, 141; *F*, 489; *SCG*, 149.

94 If art. *Captive*, II, 66.

95 Proust was. Middleton Murry, 'Proust and the Modern Unconscious', *Times Literary Supplement*, 8 January 1923.

95 Marcel Proust. Painter, II, 340.

95 The acuteness. A. L. Rowse, *Homosexuals in History* (1977), 181.

95 The last. Edmund Wilson, *Axel's Castle* (1931), 154.

95 Reflect in. John Strachey, *The Coming Struggle for Power* (1932), 206, 208.

96 No banishment. *Captive*, II, 6.

96 The world. Corr., XVIII, 364.

96 I'm already. Clermont-Tonnerre, *Montesquiou and Proust*, 19.

97 With success. LaP, 175; P, 168; *Captive*, I, 248.

97 Unique need. Corr., XII, 254.

98 This modern. John Middleton Murry, 'Proust and Modern Consciousness', *TLS*, Jan 1923, 9b.

98 A deep. *TR*, 210.

99 Sudden chance. *TR*, 212.

99 Now in. *TR*, 221.

100 A name. *TR*, 232–3.

100 Vulgar temptation. *TR*, 230.

CHAPTER 4: FOOTMEN ARE BETTER EDUCATED THAN DUKES

102 His snobbishness. Sir Harold Nicolson, *Diaries*, I (1966), 150.

103 Historically-condemned. Adorno, *Minima Moralia*, 167.

104 In place. Wyndham Lewis, *Apes of God*, 260.

104 Cruelty infests. Elizabeth Bowen in Peter Quennell ed., *Marcel Proust* (1971), 72.

105 Often when. Bibesco, 'Heartlessness', 427.

105 Spent a. Hudson, *Richard, Myrtle and I*, 220.

106 Marcel regarded. Georges de Lauris, *À un ami* (1948), 20–1.

106 Succulently. Sir Harold Nicolson, *Diaries*, I (1966), 150.

107 Hannibal de. *TR*, 204–5.

107 Muster roll. SetG, 182; *S&G*, 188; CP, I, 260–1.

108 A Polignac. Albaret, 123.

109 Fashionable society. Daudet, *Autour*, 22.

109 His great. CdeG, 37; *WBG*, 41; *GW*, 49.

110 Throwing back. *TR*, 8–9.

111 There are. SetG, 475–6; *S&G*, 482; *Cities*, II, 325–6.

111 His relations. Princess Elizabeth Bibesco, 'Marcel Proust', *New Statesman*, 25 November 1922, 236.

112 This English. Clermont-Tonnerre, *Montesquiou et Proust*, 205.

112 People of. Corr., XIX, 486.

113 If there. Marcel Plantevignes, *Avec Marcel Proust* (1966), 515–6.

113 What strikes. Proust, *Contre Sainte-Beuve* (1954), translated in Sylvia Townsend Warner, *By Way of Sainte-Beuve* (1958), 282.

113 I followed. Albaret, 1, 16, 46.

114 Conformed to. Brooke, 'Proust and Joyce', 17.

114 Are you. Misia Sert, *Two or Three Muses*, 95–6; Corr., XXI, 651.

115 Never discriminated. *SetG*, 414; *S&G*, 420–1; *Cities*, II, 237.

115 A table. Jean Cocteau, 'Marcel's Nautilus' (translated by V. Schiff), *Adam*, 56.

116 I had. Mark DeWolfe Howe ed., *Holmes–Laski Letters* (1953), II, 834.

116 I avow. *TR*, 229.

116 Third-rate snob. *Holmes–Laski Letters*, I, 619.

117 Despite my. Corr., XIX, 93.

117 Aesthetic discovery. Corr., XV, 154–5.

118 Men spattered. Sir Harold Acton, *The Last Bourbons of Naples* (1961), 515.

119 Heroines of. 'Death of Queen of Two Sicilies', *The Times*, 20 January 1925, 11c.

119 She is. Alphonse Daudet, *Les Rois en exil* (1880), 33.

119 Soldier-queen. *LaP*, 235, 308–9; *Prisoner*, 226, 296–7; *Captive, II*, 56, 157.

120 One of. *TR*, 198.

120 Little clan. *DCCS*, 185; *WBS*, 191; *Swann*, I, 259.

121 The most. *LaP*, 314; P, 301–2; *Captive, II*, 165.

122 I have. Bibesco, 'Heartlessness', 427.

122 If Marcel. Lucien Daudet, *Autour*, 19.

123 Violent heartless. Daudet, *Autour*, 24–5.

123 Mania for. Clermont-Tonnerre, *Montesquiou et Proust*, 140.

123 Extraordinary being. Corr., XIII, 228.

123 Despite being. Corr., XIII, 245–6.

124 Like quatrefoils. *DCCS*, 70; *WBS*, 73; *Swann*, I, 93–4.

125 We were. *CG*, 13; *GW*, new, 17.

125 Throughout her. *CG*, 347; *GW*, new, 357.

126 Don't scold. Corr., I, 347.

126 Friendship is. Corr., II, 464.

126 Less because. Corr., III, 373.

127 I have. Corr., XIII, 119.

127 No one else. De Lauris, *Ami*, 43.

127 Savoir vivre. *TR*, 56.

127 Under an. *WBG*, ii, 287–8.

128 It didn't. Albaret, 233.

128 My duty. *TR*, 359–60.

128 Friendship according. Beckett, *Proust*, 46–7.

129 Falsehood is. *SCG*, 266–7.

129 Man is. *SCG*, 47.

129 To reach. Corr., XI, 292.

130 Proust's book. Corr. XII, 333.

130 Society people. Corr., VIII, 40.

130 Don't mention. Corr., XX, 158.

130 Sincerity obliges. Clermont-Tonnerre, *Montesquiou et Proust*, 161.

131 Most of. Louis Gautier-Vignal, *Proust connu et inconnu* (1976), 14.

132 I don't. Corr., XVIII, 490.

CHAPTER 5: HIDE THE CORPSE IN MY BEDROOM

134 Swann is. Hudson, 'À la Recherche', 210–11.
135 Not the. Corr., XVIII, 296.
135 Baron de. Albaret, 255.
135 Who was. OJFF, 317; SYGF, 330; WBG, II, 66–7.
135 I turned. OJFF, 318–9; SYGF, 332; WBG, II, 68–9.
136 Strange secret. SetG, 429; S&G, 435; Cities, II, 258.
136 I am. Corr., XIX, 695.
137 Pretty original. Corr., XI, 287.
137 Sturgess [sic]. Corr., XX, 578.
138 Such tastes. Corr., XXI, 444.
138 Those valleys. Corr., XXI, 436.
138 The richness. Corr., XXI, 416.
139 Coherence stunned. Emmanuel Berl, Sylvia (1952), 133–4.
140 Inversion. Jean-Martin Charcot and Valentin Magnan, 'Inversion du sens génital', Archives de Neurologie, 4 (1882), 53–7.
140 The beginning. Valentin Magnan, Des Anomalies (1885), 18.
140 I tried. Corr., XIII, 246.
140 Girlish air. SetG, 396; S&G, 402; Cities, II, 211.
140 Shy suppliant. Captive, II, 10.
141 It's horrible. La P, 203; P, 196; Captive, II, 10.
141 Like all. Corr., XIII, 246.
141 How conspicuously. Georges de Lauris, À un ami (1948), 9, 26.
141 Special taste. SetG, 20; S&G, 22; Cities, I, 25.
141 Convinced. Corr., XIII, 246.
142 I admire. Corr., I, 101–2.
142 Jaded and. Corr., I, 122–3.
143 A year. Corr., III, 87.
143 To have. Corr., II, 97.
144 The prettiest. Corr., VIII, 138.
144 I half-opened. LaP, 71; The P, 68; Captive, I, 98.
145 I recall. SetG, 231; S&G, 237; Cities, I, 130.
145 Marcel Proust. Lauris, Ami, 34.
146 Only one. Clermont-Tonnerre, III, 13.
147 Unassailable. Corr., VIII, 112.
147 The woman. CG, 375; GW, new, 385.
148 Old coquette. Corr., II, 464.
148 Salaism. Corr., II, 470.
148 His Blue. Corr., III, 134.
148 Marcel kept. Bibesco, Adam, 23.
148 Dreyfusard, anti-Dreyfusard. Corr., III, 43.
149 Friends without. Cities, I, 20–1.
149 Emotional abnormality. Bibesco, 'Heartlessness', 424.
150 Young telegraph. Corr., VIII, 76.

150 With Oriental. SetG, 239; S&G, 245; Cities, I, 341.

151 Loafer. H. Montgomery Hyde, The Trials of Oscar Wilde (1948), 138, 173.

152 Strange that. Norman Rich and M. H. Fisher eds., The Holstein Papers, IV (1963), 505.

153 Nothing shows. Rémy de Gourmont, 'L'amour à l'envers', Mercure de France, 1 December 1907, 476.

153 It's so. Corr., VIII, 111–2.

154 Poor Mama. Corr., VIII, 136–8.

154 Monsieur. Corr., VIII, 208.

155 The invert. LaP, 231; P, 222; Captive, II, 50.

155 For the. LaP, 194; P, 187; Captive, II, 1–2.

156 Hereditary malady. F, 651; SCG, 369.

156 One can. Le TR, 11; FTA, 11; TR, 10.

156 A jolly. TR, 278.

157 His nature. S&G, 428.

157 Morel being. LeTR, 11; FTA, 11; TR, 10.

157 Delicacy, gracefulness. SetG, 23; S&G, 25; Cities, I, 30.

157 Feminine charms. Julius Rivers, Proust and the Art of Love (1980), 229.

157 Always curious. Corr., XVI, 163.

157 The bed. Hudson, 'Céleste', 332.

158 An excitable. Théophile Gautier, Mademoiselle de Maupin, 108, 113–4.

158 Had vices. Emile Zola, La Curée (1879 edition), 99, 185, 319.

159 Androgynous abortion. Emile Zola, Paris (1898), 72–3, 130.

160 This exchange. Joris-Karl Huysman, À rebours, Baldick translation, 111.

160 Dirty slapper. LaP, 204; Prisoner, 196–7; Captive, II, 11–12.

161 Fearing that. Fugitive, 564.

161 After so. Corr., XXI, 444.

162 Love between. Charles Féré, L'instinct sexuel (1899), 157.

162 Mountain chain. SetG, 464–5; S&G, 471; Cities, II, 310.

162 Passion often. Féré, 157.

162 Not the. SetG, 11; S&G, 13; Cities, I, 13.

163 I believe. LaP, 232; P, 223; Captive, II, 51.

163 Sodomists form. SetG, 33; S&G, 35; Cities, I, 45.

163 Often manifest. Féré, 158.

164 Uranists are. Féré, 164.

164 A need. Féré, 166.

164 Whole art. TR, 251.

165 Sadists of. CCS, 162; WbyS, 165; Swann, I, 224–6.

165 Sinned against. Émile Laurent, Les bisexués (1894), 97, 182–3.

166 Have they. SetG, 435; S&G, 440–1; Cities, II, 266.

166 The kernel. Albaret, 255.

167 Entering the. Craft & Stravinsky, 74.

167 The mere. SetG, 306; S&G, 312; Cities, II, 84.

167 Violent scenes. LaP, 205; P, 197; Captive, II, 12, 33.

168 Flying louse. Albaret, 189.

168 Satisfyingly sacrilegious. Hayman, *Proust*, 375.

168 Avoid mentioning. Corr., XII, 249.

169 Lovers to. *SetG*, 17; *S&G*, 19; *Cities, I*, 21.

170 If he. Corr., XIII, 228.

170 He died. Corr., XIII, 245–6.

170 She represents. Sachs, *Sabbat*, 282.

170 I shan't. Albaret, 38.

171 The men. Clermont-Tonnerre, III, 36, 39.

172 When people. *Le TR*, 42; *FTA*, 42.

173 American Jewesses. *Le TR*, 67; *FTA*, 67.

173 Martial ardours. E. M. Forster, *Abinger Harvest* (1936), 95.

173 Whether the. *Le TR*, 141; *FTA*, 142–3.

174 Was surprised. Corr., X, 333.

174 Their Master. Corr., XIX, 696.

175 Someone showed. Sachs, 278–9.

175 A paved. Sachs, 280–1.

176 The neighbours. Corr. XVIII, 330–1; Tadie, 816–7.

176 This frightful. Jaloux, 93, 95–6, 100.

177 Precisely because. Albaret, 194, 197.

177 Frank imperative. *SetG*, 257; *S&G*, 262; *Cities, II*, 13.

178 Resembled an. *SetG*, 420; *S&G*, 426.

CHAPTER 6: THE PERMANENT POSSIBLITY OF DANGER

179 Long ago. 'The Development of M. Proust', *Times Literary Supplement*, 9 June 1921, 368.

179 A foolish. Violet Hunt, 'Proust's Way', Scott Moncrieff, *Proust Tribute*, iii–12.

181 High-brow private. Wyndham Lewis, *Apes of God*, 262.

181 London intellectual. Corr., XX, 388.

181 When Monsieur. Léon Pierre-Quint, *Marcel Proust* (1925), 90–1, 208.

182 Morphine aspirin. Corr., XX, 163.

182 The first. Corr., XX, 254.

182 Hellish existence. Corr., XX, 293-4.

182 Nothing but. André Gide, *Journals*, I (1996), 1124.

182 If without. Corr., XII, 238.

183 Highly-strung. Corr., XIX, 575.

183 Put these. Painter, II, 306.

184 I remind. Corr., XX, 80.

184 At times. Corr., XX, 212.

184 Scabrous. Clermont-Tonnerre, *Montesquiou et Proust*, 232.

184 Bit shocked. Corr., XX, 384–5.

184 I love. Corr., XXI, 69.

185 A conspiracy. Pierre-Quint, *Proust*, 209–10.

185 Loathsome monster. A. B. Walkley, 'The New Proust', *The Times*, 12 March 1924, 10b.

185 The writing. Charles Souday, 'Les Livres', *Le Temps*, 12 May 1921, 3.

186 Skirted round. Corr., XX, 259-60.

186 New lump. Ezra Pound, 'Paris Letter', *The Dial*, vol. 71 (1921), 209-10, 458-60.

187 The little. D. Paige ed., *The Letters of Ezra Pound 1907-1941* (1951), 332.

187 Adolescent boyhood. R. Ellis Roberts, 'French Gothic', *Observer*, 24 September 1922, 6a.

187 It seems. *TLS*, 9 June 1921, 368.

188 Moral diseases. Harvey Wickham, *The Impuritans* (1929), 189-90, 223.

188 Absurd. Corr., XX, 372.

188 Charlusiennement. Corr., XX, 413.

188 Nothing is. Corr., XX, 528.

189 Andrée and. SetG, 227; S&G, 233; *Cities*, I, 324.

190 Hypocrite lecteur. Marcel Proust, *Chroniques* (1927), 212, 222, 226, 228.

191 Beneath any. LaP, 73; P, 70; *Captive, I*, 101.

191 Don't get. Clermont-Tonnerre, I, 174.

191 Their honour. SetG, 17; S&G, 19; *Cities*, I, 21-22.

192 Fattish or. Gide, *Journals*, I, 1124.

192 Delicate situation. Corr., XII, 243.

192 Disgraceful promiscuity. LaP, 298; P, 286; *Captive, II*, 142.

193 If we. LeTR, 72; FTA, 73; TR, 1970, 90.

193 In Paris. Graham Robb, *Strangers* (2003), 60.

193 The congenital. Phyllis Grosskurth ed., *The Memoirs of John Addington Symonds* (1984), 177, 267.

193 Stable boy. David Felix, *Keynes* (1998), 108.

194 Fine lady. SetG, 369; S&G, 375; *Cities, II*, 173.

195 Generally this. Jacques Georges-Anquetil, *Satan conduit le bal* (1925), 229.

196 One is. Philip Mansel, *Prince of Europe* (2003), 36, 38, 51.

196 Freemasonry far. SetG, 18-19; S&G, 21; *Cities*, I, 23-4.

197 Melodrama. Wickham, *Impuritans*, 191, 193-4.

197 Their special. SetG, 20; S&G, 22-3.

198 Extremists who. SetG, 21; S&G, 23.

198 Anti-social types. Corr., XX, 310, 312.

198 Annoyed sodomites. Corr., XX, 577-8.

199 Right to. Corr., XX, 240.

199 Transposing. André Gide, *Journal*, I (1996), 1125, 1126, 1143.

200 Sodome et. Louis de Robert, *Lettres à Paul Faure* (1943), 174.

200 It's the. André Blanchet ed., *Correspondance de Paul Claudel – Francis Jammes – Gabriel Frizeau* (1952), 325.

200 Has started. Corr., XXI, 444.

200 Contradictory sentiments. Corr., XX, 269.

200 One feels. Corr., XXI, 166.

200 Vivid. Corr., XX, 391, 400.

200 God is. François Mauriac, *Du côté de chez Proust* (1947), 66-7; Mauriac, *Écrits Intimes*, 216; cf. François Mauriac, *Second Thoughts* (1961), 112.

201 The secret. Mauriac, *Écrits Intimes*, 219.

201 The publication. Sisley Huddleston, *Bohemian Literary and Social Life in Paris* (1928), 330.

201 Princesse Murat. Corr. XX, 262.

201 You accelerate. Corr., XX, 578.

201 Proust's influence. Clermont-Tonnerre, II, 247.

202 Not in. Corr., XX, 286.

202 The last. R. W. B. & N. Lewis eds., *The Letters of Edith Wharton* (1988), 441.

202 The great. Edith Wharton, *The Writing of Fiction* (1925), 159, 173–4.

202 The beginning. Corr., XX, 380-2; Claude Pichois and Roberte Forbin eds., *Colette: lettres à ses pairs* (1973), 42–3.

203 Overwhelmed by. Colette, *Oeuvres*, III (1991), 628.

203 Connoisseurs of. Clermont-Tonnerre, IV, 25.

204 This vice. Anquetil, *Satan conduit*, 226, 228.

204 Frank. A. B. Walkley, 'More Proust', *The Times*, 17 May 1922, 12a; A. B. Walkley, *More Prejudice* (1923), 37–8.

205 Psychological portrait. Arnold Bennett, 'The Last Word', Scott Moncrieff, *Tribute*, 147.

205 No Englishmen. Clive Bell, 'A Foot-Note', Scott Moncrieff, *Tribute*, 87–8.

206 Proust's method. E. E. Kellett, 'Marcel Proust', *New Statesman*, 9 March 1929, 700–1.

207 It makes. Vladimir Nabokov, *Ada* (1969), part I, chapter 27: Library of America edition (1996), 136.

207 His temperament. Charles Briand, *Le secret de Marcel Proust* (1950), 406, 422.

208 By trying. Wickham, 195, 209–10, 214.

208 Richly comic. Aldous Huxley, *Eyeless in Gaza* (1936), 8.

209 Proust was. *Adam*, 34.

209 Finding the. Richard Ollard ed., *The Diaries of A. L. Rowse* (2003), 168.

209 Unlike Gide. Pamela Hansford Johnson, 'The Novel of Marcel Proust', in George Painter ed., *Marcel Proust: Letters to his Mother* (1956), 13.

210 How amazingly. E. M. Forster, *Anonymity* (1925), 11.

210 For me. Brooke, 7.

210 The first. Francis Birrell, 'Marcel Proust: the Prophet of Despair', *The Dial*, 74 (1923), 472–3.

211 Special cult. *Adam*, 27.

211 Each generation. Sachs, *Sabbat*, 283–9.

212 Maurice Sachs. Paul Claudel, *Journal*, II (1969), 645.

213 Do not. Jean Cocteau, 'Marcel's Nautilus', *Adam*, 57.

CHAPTER 7: MY AWFUL CLAIRVOYANCE

214 I have. Corr., XXI, 121.

214 First there. Elizabeth Bibesco, 'Marcel Proust', *New Statesman*, 25 November 1922, 236.

215 His senses. Hudson, 'Céleste', 333.

215 The last. Joseph G. Jean-Aubry, *Joseph Conrad's Life and Letters*, II (1927), 291.

216 Temps perdu. Ellen FitzGerald, 'Marcel Proust', *The Nation* (USA), vol. 161, 7 December 1921, 674.

216 The last. Wyndham Lewis, *Apes of God*, 242.

216 The old. *Le TR*, 322; *FTA*, 326; *TR*, 429.

217 The meaning. *Le TR*, 238; *FTA*, 240; *TR*, 313.

218 Paris is. Clermont-Tonnerre, IV, 18.

219 Published every. *LaP*, 211; *The P*, 203; *Captive*, *II*, 19–20.

220 Fiction. Lewis, *Apes*, 264–6.

221 Fiacres. Sisley Huddleston, 'Paris Week by Week', *Observer*, 8 January 1922, 8c.

221 Paris is. Sisley Huddleston, 'Paris Week by Week', *Observer*, 30 April 1922, 8c.

222 Quiet wrath. Lord Derwent, *Return Ticket* (1940), 98–101.

223 Artistic spectacles. 'Paris Night Guides: Street Pests for the Unwary', *The Times*, 9 March 1922, 9e.

223 Post-war Paris. 'Chasing a Husband with a Revolver', *The Times*, 27 June 1921, 9d.

223 Her eyes. *Le TR*, 251; *FTA*, 253; *TR*, 328.

224 Moral ruin. Ambroise Got, 'Le Vice Organisé en Allemagne', *Mercure de France*, 161 (1 February 1923), 655.

225 Gliding swaying. Derwent, *Return Ticket*, 101–2.

225 Black pearl. Jean Hugo, *Regard de la mémoire* (1983), 201.

225 Choreographic demonstration. Corr., XXI, 58.

225 The last. Ellmann, *Joyce*, 523.

226 An entire. Richard Ellmann ed., *Letters of James Joyce*, III (1966), 27.

227 Modernism is. Percy Scholes, 'The Death of Modernism', *Observer*, 29 January 1922, 8b.

229 The rostrum. Clermont-Tonnerre, IV, 147.

230 The religious. *LaP*, 236; *The P*, 227–8; *Captive*, *II*, 57.

230 The art. Wyndham Lewis, *Time and Western Man* (1993; originally 1927), 30–2.

231 Awful treachery. Edith Sitwell to Sydney Schiff, 26 September 1930, Add. Ms. 52922, BL.

234 The supreme. Derwent, *Return Ticket*, 122–5.

235 The Duchess. Clermont-Tonnerre, II, 134.

235 This terrible. Hugo Vickers, *Gladys, Duchess of Marlborough* (1979), 160–1.

236 Adulatory kiss. Sir Harold Nicolson, *Peacemaking 1919* (1933), 261.

236 Ravishing Madame. Corr., XX, 344.

236 The vulgarity. Clermont-Tonnerre, I, 195.

236 Day by. 'M. Coué', *The Times*, 3 July 1926, 15c, 19f.

237 If one. Corr., XX, 343–4.

237 Imbecile. Corr., XXI, 389.

237 Dream. Corr., XX, 485.

237 We are. Vickers, *Gladys Marlborough*, 179.

237 Always imagined. Sir Martin Gilbert ed., *Winston S. Churchill Companion Volume V/2* (1981), 822.

238 When in. Winston Churchill, 'A Friend's Tribute', *The Times*, 2 July 1934, 10b.

238 Could not. Corr., XX, 396.

238 I only. Corr., XX, 435.

239 If I. Jacques Copeau, *Journal 1901-1948*, II (1991), 222.

239 Recommendation. Corr., XX, 450.

239 I could. Corr., XX, 565.

239 I find. Corr., XXI, 86.

239 That's not. Corr., XX, 481.

240 The psychologically. Corr., XX, 464.

240 All the. Corr., XX, 473.

240 The French. FitzGerald, 'Marcel Proust', 676.

240 Your compatriots. Corr., XX, 570.

241 Anecdotal, high-society. Corr., XXI, 29.

241 Enrich. Corr., XXI, 38.

241 He amuses. Albaret, 125.

241 From fear. Corr., XX, 601.

241 Look at. Hugo, *Regard de la mémoire*, 201.

242 This new. Corr., XXI, 23.

242 Infinite mental. Corr., XXI, 27.

242 Slept a. Corr., XXI, 88.

243 Everyone had. Denis Brian, *Einstein* (1996), 139.

244 The visit. 'Paris s'amuse', *The Times*, 21 April 1922, 15e.

244 Einstein. Wydham Lewis to Sydney Schiff, 1922, Add ms 52919, BL.

244 Your magnificent. Corr., XXI, 396.

244 How I. Corr., XX, 578.

245 Full of. Sisley Huddleston, 'Paris Week by Week', *Observer*, 15 October 1922, 8a.

245 Einstein created. Christa Kirsten and Hans-Jurgen Treder eds., *Albert Einstein in Berlin 1913–1933*, I (1979), 227–8.

245 A great. Albaret, 335–7.

246 Then suddenly. Stephen Hudson, 'Céleste', the *Criterion*, II (April 1924), 346.

CHAPTER 8: RICH AMATEURS

247 Quasi-confidential. Corr., XXI, 64.

247 The only. Albaret, 224.

247 They were. Hudson, 'Céleste', 342.

247 Weary. Corr., XXI, 342–3.

248 Tomato No 2. *SetG*, 248; *S&G*, 254; *CP*, II, 1.

249 Beloved friend. T. S. Eliot, 'Violet Schiff', *The Times*, 9 July 1962, 18e.

249 Mon très. Emilio Marinetti to Schiff, 25 November 1914, Add. 52923, BL.

249 Amica Carissima. Paolo Tosti to Violet Schiff, 19 August 1911, Add 52923, BL.

250 Dearest Sydney. Edith Sitwell to Sydney Schiff, 26 September 1930, Add. 52922, BL.

250 I love. Vincent O'Sullivan and Margaret Scott eds., *Letters of Katherine Mansfield*, IV (1996), 185.

250 I don't. Richard Aldington to Sydney Schiff, 17 March 1931, Add. Ms. 52916, BL.

250 Its sympathy. Sacheverell Sitwell to Sydney Schiff, 1 November 1926, Add ms 52922, BL.

250 Heartening letters. Edwin Muir to Schiff, 28 November 1924, Add ms 52920, BL.

250 There is. Vincent O'Sullivan and Margaret Scott, *Mansfield Letters*, IV, 351.

251 A gifted. Corr., XXI, 79.

251 Your letters. Corr., XX, 502.

251 Marvellously true. Corr., XXI, 80.

252 Generally considered. Hudson, *Richard Kurt*, 87–8; *True Story*, 232.

252 No one. Hudson, *Richard Kurt*, 15; *True Story*, 201.

252 Lord Furness. Hudson, *Tony*, 121.

254 Her courage. Hudson, *Richard, Myrtle and I*, 139, 167.

254 One great. *RMI*, 56.

254 A woman. Fane, 66.

254 Angel Violet. Corr., XXI, 239.

254 The most. Fane, 86.

255 Du côté. Hudson, *RMI*, 211–12, 215, 217–9.

256 Our kind. Hudson, 'Céleste', 340.

256 Idiot Walkley. Corr. XXI 305.

257 Beastly little. Hudson, 'First Meetings', 202.

257 Proust really. Stella Benson to Schiff, 26 March 1925, Add 52916, BL.

258 The complicated. Richard Aldington, 'The Approach to M. Marcel Proust', *The Dial*, vol. 69 (1921), 344, reprinted in Aldington, *Literary Studies* (1924), 176.

258 Elemental truthfulness. Stephen Hudson, 'À la Recherche du temps perdu', *Art and Letters*, vol. 2 (1919), 204.

258 He possessed. Hudson, 'Portrait', Scott Moncrieff, *Tribute*, 6.

259 He says. Diary of Stella Benson, 17 September 1925: Add 6792, CUL.

259 When we. Hudson, *Prince Hempseed*, 110–11.

260 Without doubt. Theophilus Boll and Violet Schiff eds., *Stephen Hudson: Richard, Myrtle and I* (1962), 18.

260 Their Gauguins. Vincent O'Sullivan and Margaret Scott eds., *Collected Letters of Katherine Mansfield*, III (1993), 274; Stephen Hudson, 'First Meetings with Katherine Mansfield', *Cornhill Magazine*, 170 (1958), 202-212; *Athenaeum*, 7 November 1919, 1153; J. Middleton Murry, *Novels and Novelists by Katherine Mansfield* (1930), 102–3.

260 You're such. O'Sullivan and Scott, *Mansfield Letters*, III, 281.

260 Mr Schiff. O'Sullivan and Scott, *Mansfield Letters*, III, 291.

261 We lived. O'Sullivan and Scott, *Mansfield Letters*, IV, 329–30.

261 Too tired. Valéry Larbaud, *Journal 1912–1935* (1955), 350–1.

262 Marvellously well. Corr., XVIII, 364.

262 Cher Monsieur. Corr., XIX, 434.

263 I should. Wyndham Lewis, *Apes of God*, 248.

263 Marcel Proust. Clermont-Tonnerre, *Montesquiou et Proust*, 134.

263 But no. Sir Harold Nicolson, *Peacemaking*, 275-6; Harold Nicolson, 'Marcel Proust et l'Angleterre', *Revue Hebdomadaire*, 6 June 1936, 12–13.

264 Was penetrated. Hudson, 'Portrait', Scott Moncrieff, *Tribute*, 8.

264 Must have. Diary of Stella Benson, 17 September 1925, Add 6792, CUL.

264 You tell. Corr., III, 109.

264 A young. Corr., XXI, 145.

265 I am. Corr., XVIII, 168.

265 Sorry about. Fane, 69.

265 Ali my. Corr., XXI, 158.

266 Feminine haunches. Lewis, *Apes of God*, 238.

266 The worst. 'Officer's Fight with Miner', *The Times*, 27 March 1919, 9c; 'Ex-Officer and

Village Girl: Acquittal of a Cornish Miner', *The Times*, 9 June 1919, 7a.

266 I knew. Hudson, *Tony*, 100.

267 Kitson has. Corr,. XXI, 294–5; Charles Quest-Ritson, *The English Garden Abroad* (1992), 91.

267 Kitson the. Corr., XXI, 305.

267 Tutoyer does. Corr., XXI, 392.

267 Recently I. Corr., XXI, 79–80.

268 There are. Corr., XXI, 141.

268 Enormous importance. Corr., XXI, 175.

268 Possibly our. Corr., XXI, 304.

269 This Eliot. Corr., XXI, 345.

269 Despite a. Corr., XXI, 116.

271 A Dreyfus. Corr., XXI, 158.

271 The contradiction. Fane, 76.

272 A bounder. Diary of Stella Benson, 24 May 1928, Add. 6796, CUL.

272 A peculiar. Fane, 87.

272 Magnificent powers. Corr., XXI, 141.

272 My sisters. Corr., XXI, 144–45.

274 Violet has. Corr., XXI, 158.

274 I am going. Corr., XXI, 158.

274 I don't. Corr., XXI, 162.

274 I love. Corr., XXI, 163.

275 Charming and. *Adam*, 260, 11.

275 My very. Corr., XXI, 175–76.

276 I have. Corr., XXI, 185.

276 As he. Hudson, 'A Portrait', 7.

276 Expressed violent. Pierre-Quint, *Proust*, 111.

276 Useless to. Corr., XXI, 195.

277 Once before. Corr., XXI, 238.

278 Will I. Corr., XXI, 234–5.

278 I can. Corr., XXI, 262.

278 I am suddenly. Corr., XXI, 266.

278 Marvellous that. Corr., XXI 294.

279 You have. Corr., XXI, 341–3.

280 Violet has. Corr., XXI, 295.

280 The letter. Corr., XXI, 347.

281 For a. Corr., XXI, 390.

281 No-one here. Corr., XXI, 303–4.

282 I believe. Violet Schiff, 'A Night With Proust', *London Magazine*, 3 (1956), 20.

283 A sad. Philip Ziegler, *Osbert Sitwell* (1998), 141.

283 Virulent enemy. Osbert Sitwell, 'A Few Days in an Author's Life', in *All at Sea* (1927), 21–9. See also G. Orioli, *Adventures of a Bookseller*, 1937.

283 Sir Philip. Peter Stansky, *Sassoon* (2003), 110.

283 Intelligent but. Corr., XXI, 449.

283 I refuse. Corr., XXI, 475–7.

284 Really very. Corr., XXI, 534–5.

284 Happy Few. Violet Schiff to Sylvia Townsend Warner, 13 May 1958, Add ms 52922, BL; Violet Schiff, 'A Night with Proust', 22.

284 Can with. Hudson, 'À la Recherche', Art and Letters, 200.

284 The principal. Jaloux, 70–1.

285 A sentence. E. M. Forster, Abinger Harvest (1936), 94.

286 Intoxicated. Cyril Connolly, The Evening Colonnade (1973), 232.

286 Great as. TR, 96.

287 The worse. Sir John Rothenstein, Summer's Lease (1965), 185.

287 Dear Madame. Corr., XXI, 373.

287 My dear. Corr., XXI, 392.

287 Your delicious. Corr., XXI, 389.

287 Your letters. Corr., XXI, 449.

287 I've been. Corr., XXI, 469.

288 Whatever the. Corr., XXI, 473–5.

288 It's hard. Corr., XXI, 534–5.

CHAPTER 9: 18 NOVEMBER 1922

290 Dear close. Corr., XXI, 301.

290 Whom I. LaP, 189; The P, 182; Captive, I, 269–70.

291 Royal. Edmond Jaloux, Avec Marcel Proust (1953), 12–13.

291 You're going. Léon Pierre-Quint, Proust, 87.

291 Unspeakable pimps. Corr., XXI, 351.

292 Blind drunk. Léon Pierre-Quint ed., Quelques lettres de Marcel Proust (1928), 34.

292 An opportunity. Corr., XXI, 352, 358.

292 A thousand. Corr., XXI, 411.

292 Think with. Corr., XXI, 385–6.

293 One thinks. Corr., XXI, 409.

293 At every. Corr., XXI, 476.

293 Once again. Corr., XXI, 461.

293 The acrid. Corr., XXI, 503–4.

294 Of all. Hudson, 'Céleste', 339, 345.

295 Slack like. SetG, 240, 244; S&G, 245, 249; Cities, I, 342, 347.

295 He was. Albaret, 343, 348, 351.

296 Send for. Painter, II, 359.

296 When I. René Gimpel, Diary of an Art Dealer (1966), 195.

296 At first. Albaret, 352.

296 Is that. Albaret, 358.

297 At thirteen. Gimpel, Diary, 195.

298 If one. LaP, 188; The P, 181; Captive, I, 269.

298 Every death. TR, 351.

299 Here are. Anon., 'Marcel Proust', Saturday Review, 9 December 1922, 868.

299 Faced with. E. G. Twitchett, 'The English Proust', *London Mercury*, XXII (July 1930), 227.

299 Proust est. John Peale Bishop, *New Directions: Number Seven*, 462.

299 When they. Clermont-Tonnerre, *Montesquiou et Proust*, 247–8.

300 A call. Duc de Gramont, 'Proust as I knew him', *London Magazine*, II (November 1955), 30.

300 The death. Ford Madox Ford, *It was the Nightingale* (1934), 177, 179.

300 He had. Pierre-Quint, *Quelques lettres*, 41.

300 So powerful. Jaloux, 32–3.

300 Same God. Misia Sert, *Two or Three Muses* (1953), 97.

301 November 19th. 'Marcel Proust', *Saturday Review*, 9 December 1922, 868.

301 It seems. Ford, *Nightingale*, 178.

301 Camille you. Camille Wixler, 'Proust au Ritz: souvenirs d'un maître d'hôtel', *Adam*, 394 (1976), 21.

302 Each month. Fernand Vandérem, 'Les Lettres et la vie', *La Revue de France*, III (15 June 1922), 858; Corr., XXI, 298–9.

302 The Ancien. Lucy Moorehead ed., *Freya Stark Letters*, VI (1981), 58.

302 Sordidly furnished/ only when. François Mauriac, *Écrits Intimes* (1953), 184.

303 What will-power. Gabriel de la Rochefoucauld, 'Souvenirs et Aperçus', *Nouvelle Revue Française*, XX (1923), 72.

303 A type. Paul Claudel, *Mémoires improvisées* (1954), 335.

303 His hands. Mauriac, *Écrits Intimes*, 216.

303 The last. Jaloux, 27–8.

304 I crossed. Maurice Martin du Gard, *Les Mémorables*, I (1957), 263.

304 I saw. *Cahiers André Gide*, IX (1979), 382.

304 Oh it. Gimpel, *Diary*, 195.

305 Laid out. Mauriac, *Écrits Intimes*, 116.

305 We must. Mauriac, *Écrits Intimes*, 213–4.

307 Proust wrote. François Mauriac, *Mémoires intérieures* (1959): 1960 trans. 106–7.

307 They say. Malcolm Cowley, 'A Monument to Proust', *The Dial*, 74 (1923), 240.

307 J'ai plusieurs. Bell, *Proust*, 34.

307 His brother. Wickham, *Impuritans*, 188.

307 Just before. Princesse Marthe Bibesco, *La vie d'une amitié*, I (1951), 85.

308 One morning. Jean Hugo, *Le Regard de la Mémoire* (1983), 209.

308 Ah! Proust. *Cahiers André Gide*, IX, 384.

308 Paralysed by. Roger Martin du Gard, *Correspondance générale*, III (1986), 193.

308 Proust's death. Richard Ludwig ed., *Letters of Ford Madox Ford* (1965), 147.

308 It seemed. Elizabeth Bibesco, 'Marcel Proust', *New Statesman*, 25 November 1922, 235.

309 To judge. A. B. Walkley, 'Many books in one', *The Times*, 29 November 1922, 10a; Walkley, *More Prejudice*, 42.

309 His death. Ralph Wright, 'A Sensitive Petronius', *Nineteenth Century*, 93 (March 1923), 378.

309 The French. Philip Carr, 'Marcel Proust', *Observer*, 26 November 1922, 6c.

309 The great. Hudson, 'A Portrait', Scott Moncrieff Tribute, 8.

310 It is. Stephen Hudson, 'Témoignage d'un romancier', *Nouvelle Revue Française*, XX (January 1923), 256.

310 Ten years. Richard Ellmann ed., *Letters of James Joyce*, III (1966), 69.

310 I didn't. Jaloux, 38.

310 A little. *LaP*, 176–7; *Prisoner*, 169–70; *Captive, I*, 249–50.

313 I don't. G. Jean-Aubry, *Joseph Conrad's Life and Letters*, II (1927), 292.

313 The nineteenth. Cowley, 'Monument to Proust', 239.

313 Inventor. José Ortega y Gasset, 'Le temps, la distance et la forme chez Proust', *NRF*, XX (January 1923), 268.

313 A new. Robert-Ernst Curtius, 'Marcel Proust', *NRF*, XX (January 1923), 265.

313 Fruitfully. Emilio Cecchi, 'Marcel Proust et le roman Italien', *NRF*, XX (1923), 283.

314 Is he. John Middleton Murry, 'Proust and the Modern Consciousness', *Times Literary Supplement*, 4 January 1923, 9c.

314 The most. Philip Guedalla, *A Gallery* (1924), 271.

315 Dukes princes. Martin du Gard, *Mémorables*, I, 265.

315 A tremendous. Ludwig, *Madox Ford Letters*, 147.

316 The Marcel. Albert Flament, 'Tableaux de Paris', *Revue de Paris*, 15 December 1922, 871.

316 Avec un. Gabriel Astruc, *Le Pavillon des fantômes* (1929), 81.

316 I always. Martin du Gard, *Mémorables*, I, 263–4.

316 Was astonished. Mauriac, *Écrits Intimes*, 193.

316 The only. Albert Thibaudet, 'Marcel Proust et la tradition française', *NRF*, XX (January 1923), 138–9.

317 I do. *SetG*, 35; *S&G*, 40; *CP, I*, 49.

319 The idea. *LaP*, 177; *P*, 170; *Captive, I*, 251.

Index